£2·75

G

A Publication distributed by Heron Books

POLITICS

THE
ATHENIAN
CONSTITUTION

ARISTOTLE
384-322 BC

ARISTOTLE

POLITICS

THE ATHENIAN CONSTITUTION

Edited, translated and with an introduction by
JOHN WARRINGTON

Distributed by
HERON BOOKS

ARISTOTLE

Born at Stagira in 384 B.C. Studied at Plato's
Academy 367–348, and spent the next three
years at the court of Hermias in Assos. He
then moved to Mitylene in Lesbos and
taught there until 343, when he became
tutor to Alexander. After the latter's accession to the throne of Macedonia in 336,
Aristotle returned to Athens and founded
the Lyceum. He fled to Chalcis in Euboea
following Alexander's death in 323, and
died there in 322.

Published by arrangement with
J. M. Dent & Sons Ltd.

To WILFRID

———

ἡ γὰρ ἐξουσία τοῦ πράττειν. ὅ τι ἂν ἐθέλῃ τις οὐ
δύναται φυλάττειν τὸ ἐν ἑκάστῳ τῶν ἀνθρώπων φαῦλον.

CONTENTS

THE ATHENIAN CONSTITUTION

PART I: CONSTITUTIONAL HISTORY TO 403 B.C.

PART II: THE CONSTITUTION OF ATHENS, *circa* 325 B.C.

INTRODUCTION

IT was during his first Athenian residence, as a student of the Academy (367–347 B.C.), to which he had come from his home in Stagira at the age of seventeen, that Aristotle made his first acquaintance with political theory, through Plato's *Republic*, *Statesman*, and *Laws*. All three of these works are criticized, not always with perfect fairness to their author, in Books II and III of the *Politics*.

Soon after his master's death Aristotle left Athens and joined a small Platonic circle at Assos, in the Troad, where he enjoyed close relations with Hermias, ruler of the neighbouring city of Atarneus, whose niece and adopted daughter he ultimately married. Here he remained until 344 B.C., and doubtless learned much of the more practical side of politics, especially in the sphere of foreign relations and economics, in which his friend Hermias was deeply involved. The lessons of this period are reflected in parts of Books II, IV, and VII of the *Politics*.

The next two years were spent in the island of Lesbos, where Aristotle devoted himself almost exclusively to biological studies. Then, in 342 B.C., he was summoned to the Macedonian court to act as tutor to Philip's son Alexander, and in that position he resided until 336 B.C. at Pella, which was then on the way to becoming, if it was not already, the political centre of the Greek world.

By this time Aristotle had already published four political dialogues and the *Protreptikos*. Only fragments have survived, though some authorities have detected traces of their teaching in the *Politics*, notably in Books VII and VIII. To a date very soon after Alexander's accession we must probably assign two lost pamphlets addressed to the new monarch, perhaps at his request: 'On Kingship' and 'On Colonies.'

I. THE POLITICS

So much for the Stagirite's early political training and accomplishment. The most fruitful period of his life, in this as in most other fields, were the years 335–322 B.C., the years of his second Athenian residence, as head of his own school, the Lyceum. Scholars are divided as to the dates at which the several parts of the *Politics* were written; but an exhaustive study of the evidence provides strong reason for believing that, despite variations of form and style, all belong to this last and most mature stage of Aristotle's career.

The eight books of the *Politics*, it must be noted, are not a single work, but an unrevised and in some places unskilful conflation of distinct (and mostly unfinished) treatises made partly by Aristotle himself and partly by one of his subsequent editors. The subject-matter of these treatises represents the second part of a course on what we should now call social science, the first part consisting of the *Nicomachean Ethics* to which Aristotle often refers in the following pages.

The influence of the *Politics* upon subsequent theory has been very considerable. From it and from Plato's *Statesman* Europe received the first notion of constitutionalism; and Aristotle's thought descended through St Thomas Aquinas to Hooker, and from Hooker, through Locke, to Burke. The fourth book, moreover, as Sir David Ross has pointed out, is the parent of Machiavelli's *Principe*.

The initial problem confronting me in the preparation of an English rendering of the *Politics* for Everyman's Library was to decide the best order in which to present the several books. There has long been much disagreement among scholars on this point. W. L. Newman, upon whose edition and commentary (4 vols., 1887–1902) this translation is based, prints Books VII and VIII immediately after Book III; and some editors have also transposed Books V and VI. But there is, as Sir David Ross has made abundantly clear, the most compelling internal evidence that the traditional order, which dates at least from the first century and which I have followed here, is the order in which Aristotle himself intended that the eight books should be read.

Next it was clear that no reader who was not a classical scholar could hope to thread his way through the often complicated argument of the *Politics* without some guidance.   Space prohibited anything in the nature of a commentary; and it therefore seemed best to present the eight books under a number of headings and subheadings, and to break down these in turn into lettered and numbered sections.   The scheme is, I think, made clear in the table of contents (pages vii–ix), which should be studied before the text.   I have ignored the conventional chapter numbers, since they do not always represent a logical division of the matter under discussion; but Bekker numbers are inserted within square brackets in the text.

Two other problems had to be solved in the interests of clarity. Passages of various lengths frequently occur to interrupt or at any rate to complicate arguments and expositions that will already tax the reader's powers of concentration to their utmost. I feel confident that Aristotle would have placed these passages as footnotes, had the contrivance been known to him, and I have dealt with them accordingly.   They are followed by the letter 'A' within brackets.   All other footnotes are mine.   Finally, I have placed six passages in an appendix.   Nos. I and II are most probably interpolated fragments.   No. III has all the appearance of a later editorial insertion, since the words are repeated at the beginning of Book VII.   No. IV is another editorial addition, originally no doubt an isolated fragment representing an alternative treatment of the preceding subject. No. V is regarded by most modern commentators as an interpolation.   No. VI is most probably a fragment written by Aristotle but inserted here by one of his editors.

II. THE ATHENIAN CONSTITUTION

The second part of this volume contains *The Athenian Constitution*, the manuscript of which was discovered in Egypt as recently as 1890. The beginning has been lost, but it has been possible to reconstruct almost the whole of the badly mutilated ending from previously known fragments.

Three great political compilations were made under Aristotle's supervision by research students at the Lyceum. The first was an account of the constitutions of 158 Greek states (metropolitan and colonial), known as *Politeiai*. It formed the basis of the latter part of Book II and of Books IV to VI of the *Politics*. The second and third were respectively an account of the institutions of non-Greek states and a collection of what may be described as cases in international law. Of these last two only fragments survive. *The Athenian Constitution* is all that remains of the *Politeiai*. It is generally admitted to have been written by Aristotle himself about 330 B.C. and perhaps revised by him some five years later.

My translation is based upon the edition of Sir J. E. Sandys (1912). Though dividing the work into two, I have followed his chapter numbers throughout. I have, however, as in the *Politics*, made use of headings and subheadings, lettered and numbered sections, as indicated in the list of contents (pages ix–x). I have also used the same system of footnotes as explained above, and have placed one passage—an undoubted interpolation—as an appendix.

Pascal declared the *Politics* to have been written 'for fun' and 'as if to regulate a madhouse'! There is no grain of truth in this celebrated witticism, but the idea seems to have resulted from an all too common error against which it is necessary to warn those readers who may approach the *Politics* without adequate understanding of ancient Greek institutions and ideals.

Many terms employed by Aristotle can be translated only by words that are likely to create in the modern mind notions far removed from what the author intended.   This is particularly true of the three terms *polis*, *politeia*, and *arche*, which have been rendered here, for want of better English equivalents as 'state,' 'constitution' or 'form of government,' and 'government' or 'administration.'   The Greek city-state was very different both in size and quality from the massive entity denoted by our word 'state' to-day.   Its constitution was rather a way of life or social ethic than a body of rigid laws acting within a strictly limited sphere of official organization.   Its ideal government as conceived by Aristotle should imply leadership and guidance towards an ever higher standard of welfare within the framework of the city-state rather than the heavy-handed and ubiquitous control of an impersonal bureaucracy and the self-seeking rule of party cliques.   These facts show that Aristotle's work is for the most part irrelevant to twentieth-century conditions. To apply its standards and criticisms to the present-day political scene is to involve oneself in a fatal misunderstanding and to lose sight of its immense value in the study of ancient history and social development.

If this volume has any merits they are due, as in the *Metaphysics*,[1] to the learning and counsel of Sir David Ross.   Its shortcomings, whether of translation, of style, or of arrangement, are all mine.

1959   JOHN WARRINGTON.

POLITICS

Book I

THE HOUSEHOLD

A. DEFINITION AND STRUCTURE
OF THE STATE

[1252ª] Experience teaches us that every state is an association, and that every association is formed with some good end in view, for an apparent good is the spring of all human activity.   Consequently, the state or political association, which is supreme and all-embracing, must aim at the sovereign good.   It is therefore erroneous to maintain, as some do,[1] that a statesman, a king, a household manager, and a master of slaves are the same. According to this theory, they differ not in kind but in the number of their subjects.   In other words, the ruler over few is called a master of slaves; over more, a household manager; over more again, a statesman or monarch.   Such a view implies that there is no difference between a large household and a small state.   King and statesman are alleged to differ from one another as an absolute governor from one who governs according to the rules of statesmanship, every citizen taking his turn first as ruler then as ruled.

Now all this is quite wrong, as will be clear to anyone who studies the question according to our usual method.   In politics, as in other branches of science, the compound must be resolved into its simple elements, which are the smallest parts of the whole.   We must therefore ask what are the elements of which a state is composed.   In that way we shall learn how they differ, and whether it is possible to draw any scientific distinction between the several forms of government.

If you consider the state—or anything else, for that matter— in relation to the origins from which it springs, you will arrive at the clearest understanding of its nature.   First, there must necessarily be a union of those who are indispensable to one another, i.e. of male and female for the sake of procreation; and this union arises not from an arbitrary decision, but because human beings, like other animals and the plants, have a natural urge to leave behind them a reproduction of themselves. Necessity likewise demands a union of natural ruler and natural subject for their mutual preservation.   One who possesses the

[1] Cf. Plato, *Politicus*, 258 E–259 D.

5

deliberative faculty is intended by nature to be lord and master, while he who can do no more than give effect with his body to what the other has designed is a subject, and by nature a slave. Hence master and slave have a common interest.

[1252b] By nature, then, the female is marked off from the slave. Nature is no skinflint, like a smith who fashions Delphic knives; [1] she makes each thing for a separate use, because every instrument is most perfect when devised for one rather than for many purposes. Among barbarians, it is true, females and slaves rank together. But this is simply because barbarians lack the ruling element; a marriage among them is one of slaves, male and female. Wherefore the poets [2] declare: 'Right it is that Hellenes rule barbarians,' as if recognizing that a barbarian and a slave are one in nature.

From these two relationships—husband and wife, master and slave—the household takes its rise. Hesiod [3] aptly says: 'First a house, then a wife, then an ox [the poor man's servant] for the plough.' The household, therefore, is an association established by nature for the supply of men's everyday needs. Its members are called by Charondas [4] 'associates of the bread-bin,' and by Epimenides the Cretan [5] 'associates of the manger.'

The union of several households, for the purpose of supplying something more than everyday wants, results first in the village; and the most natural form of a village appears to be that of a family colony consisting of children and grandchildren, whom some describe as 'milk-fellows.' This is the reason why Greek states were originally governed by kings, as the barbarians still are. They were made up of persons who, since every household is subject to its eldest member, were accustomed to individual rule, and they retained that form of government because of their consanguinity. As Homer says: [6] 'Each one is absolute ruler of his children and his wives'; for they lived in scattered groups, according to the fashion of ancient times. Indeed, the fact that men are, or were at first, governed by kings has led to a universal belief that the gods are ruled likewise. For we

[1] These were intended for all sorts of purposes.
[2] Euripides, *Iphigenia in Aulis*, 1400.
[3] *Works and Days*, 405.
[4] Legislator of Catana and other cities, fl. *c.* 500 B.C.
[5] Semi-legendary poet of the sixth century B.C. According to Diogenes Laertius he was also credited with a prose treatise on the Cretan constitution.
[6] *Odyssey*, ix. 114. He is speaking of the Cyclopes. Aristotle, and Plato before him, appear to have considered Homer's account of them as a mythical picture of primitive society.

imagine not only the forms of the gods, but also their way of life, as resembling our own.

When several villages unite so as to form a single association large enough to be almost if not wholly self-sufficient, that association has reached the level of a state. Though it owed its origin to the bare necessities of life, it continues to exist for the sake of a *good* life. Hence, if the earlier forms of society are natural, so too is the state, which is their end. For a thing's nature is its end: what a thing is when fully developed we call its nature, whether we are referring to a man, a horse, or a household. [1253ª] Again, the final cause or end of a thing is the best, and self-sufficiency [1] is therefore the best.

I have now made it clear that the state is a creation of nature, and that man is by nature a political animal. He who is stateless by nature and not just by chance is either subhuman or superhuman, like the man reviled by Homer as 'classless, lawless, heartless'; [2] for being naturally without a state, he is a lover of war and may be compared to an unprotected piece in a game of draughts.

Now why is man more of a political animal than any bee or other gregarious creature? The reason is obvious: nature, as the saying goes, does nothing in vain, and man is the only animal endowed with speech. Mere sound is indicative of pleasure or pain, and therefore belongs also to the rest of the animal world; [3] but the power of speech is intended to express what is advantageous and what harmful, what is just and what unjust. It is precisely in this that man differs from other animals: he alone has any notion of good and evil, of justice and injustice; and an association of living beings possessed of this gift makes a household and a state.

The state is prior in nature to the household and the individual, because a whole is necessarily prior to its part. For instance, if the entire body be annihilated, there will be no hand or foot, except in the ambiguous sense in which we speak of a stone hand. [4] All things are defined with reference to their function or potency, so that when they are no longer fit to exercise that function we cannot say they *are* such and such—only that they *have the same name*. That the state is a creation of

[1] Which is the aim of the state.
[2] *Iliad*, ix. 63.
[3] Their nature is capable of no more than the experience of pleasure and pain, and the indication thereof to one another.—(A.)
[4] A hand that has perished is no more a hand than is one of stone.—(A.)

nature and prior to the individual is clear from the fact that an individual, when isolated, is not self-sufficient and is thus the equivalent of a part in relation to the whole. A man who cannot live in society, or who has no need to do so because he is self-sufficient, is either a beast or a god; he is no part of a state.

All human beings, then, are endowed by nature with the social instinct. But he who first constructed a state was the greatest of benefactors; for just as man when brought to perfection is the noblest of living things, so when cut off from law and justice he is the most degraded of them all. Armed injustice is a frightful menace, and man is equipped from birth with weapons intended for the use of intellectual and moral virtue but which he can employ in a very different service. Without virtue, therefore, he will be the most abandoned and most savage creature imaginable. Justice, on the contrary, is bound up with the state; its administration, which consists in determining what is just, is the principle of order in political society.

B. HOUSEHOLD MANAGEMENT

1. PARTS OF THE HOUSEHOLD

HAVING discovered that every state is made up of households, we must consider household management before turning to the state. [1253^b] The departments into which it falls correspond to the parts of which a complete household consists, i.e. freemen and slaves. Now we should always begin the study of a thing by examining it in its simplest elements; and the primary or simplest elements of a household are master and slave, husband and wife, father and children, giving rise to three relationships—despotic, marital, and paternal.[1] We must inquire what each of these is and what it ought to be. But there is still another department of household management, viz. the art of acquisition, which some think is the whole, others the most important part of it. This too will engage our attention; but first let us discuss master and slave, looking to the needs of practical life and trying to obtain some better theory of their relations than is afforded by current beliefs.

2. SLAVERY

There are some who maintain that the exercise of authority over slaves is a kind of science. They believe, as I remarked at the outset, that there is no fundamental difference between it and household management, the rule of a statesman, or monarchical government. Others regard the control of slaves as contrary to nature; they hold that the distinction between a slave and a freeman is due to mere convention, that since it is founded upon force it is unjust.

Now without necessaries men cannot live at all, let alone live well; hence property is essential to the household, and the science of acquiring it is part of household management. Again, arts which have a definite end in view require suitable instruments for the attainment of that end, and the same holds good in household management. Finally, some instruments are

[1] I use the words 'marital' and 'paternal,' although neither is adequate to the relations they describe.—(A.)

inanimate, others animate; e.g. the pilot of a ship has an inanimate instrument in the rudder, and an animate one in the lookout man, for in every art a servant is a kind of instrument.

It follows, therefore, (1) that an article of property is an instrument for maintaining life, (2) that property is an aggregate of such instruments, (3) that a slave is an animate article of property. It also follows (4) that the class of assistants as a whole is an instrument presupposed by all other instruments. For if every instrument could fulfil its task, obeying or anticipating its employer's will,[1] like the famous statues of Daedalus,[2] or the tripods of Hephaestus which the poet describes[3] as entering the assembly of the gods of their own accord; if, likewise, the shuttle wove and the plectrum played the lyre without a hand to guide them; then no builder would need assistants, and no master slaves.

[1254ª] Do not forget, on the other hand, that the instruments commonly so called are instruments of production, whereas a household article is one of action. The shuttle, for example, is not only of use, but it *produces something else*; a garment or bed can only be *used*. Further, since production and action differ in kind, their respective instruments must differ in the same way. Now life is action and not production, so that the slave is an auxiliary of action. Again, we speak of an article of property as of a part. This is because a part is not *only* a part of something else, but belongs to it entirely; the same applies to an article of property. Hence, while a master is only master of his slave without belonging to him, the slave is not only the slave of his master but belongs to him absolutely. We have thus discovered the nature and capacity of a slave: (1) he who, though remaining a human being, is by nature not *sui juris* but belongs to another, is by nature a slave; (2) he is said to belong to another who, though remaining a human being, is also an article of property; (3) an article of property is an instrument of action and separable from its possessor.

We must now ask the question whether there *actually is* anyone thus intended by nature as a slave, anyone for whom that condition is advantageous and right; or is all slavery a violation of nature? The answer is not difficult, on grounds either of

[1] Cf. Athenaeus, *Deipnosophistae*, 267 e.
[2] Cf. *De Anima*, 406 b8; Plato, *Meno*, 97 D; *Euthyphro*, 11 B.
[3] Homer, *Iliad*, xviii. 376.

reason or of plain fact. For that some should rule and others be subject is not only necessary but expedient; some are marked out from birth for subjection, others are born to rule.

There are many kinds of ruler and of ruled; [1] for wherever you have a composite whole made up of parts, whether continuous or discrete, there you will find a ruling and a subject element. This duality is inherent in living creatures from the very nature of the universe; but there is some such principle, e.g. the rules of harmony, even among things devoid of life. The inanimate world, however, is somewhat beyond the scope of our inquiry.

Every living thing is composed, in the first place, of soul and body; the former is by nature the ruling element, to which the other is in subjection. But we must limit our inquiry regarding nature's purpose to those things which are true specimens of their kind, excluding those which are corrupt. Hence we must study a man who is in perfect condition of both body and soul. In him we shall see the true relation of the two elements; whereas in natures that are more or less permanently corrupt [1254b] the body may often appear to rule over the soul, because they are in an evil and unnatural state.

At all events, it is in living creatures that we can first observe a form of rule akin to that wielded by a master over his slaves, and another similar to that exercised by a statesman over fellow citizens. The soul rules the body in the first of these ways; intellect governs the appetites as a statesman or a king. Now the soul's dominion over the body, and that of the intellect or rational element over the passionate, are evidently natural and expedient, whereas the equality of the two or a reversal of their roles is always harmful. The same holds good of men in relation to animals. Tame animals have a better nature than wild ones; and all of them are better off when ruled by man, because their safety is then guaranteed. Again, the male is by nature superior and the female inferior; one rules and the other is ruled —a principle which necessarily extends to all mankind.

Those, therefore, who are as much inferior to others as are the body to the soul and beasts to men,[2] are by nature slaves, and benefit, like all inferiors, from living under the rule of a master.

---

[1] The excellence of a rule is always proportionate to that of its subjects. It is better, for example, to rule men than wild beasts; for the effect of one ruling and another being ruled may be fairly described as a 'work,' and we know that the better the workmen the better the work they produce.—(A.)

[2] Such is the case with those whose sole function is the use of their bodies and who can do no more than that.—(A.)

He, therefore, is by nature a slave who can (and therefore does) belong to another, and who shares in reason to the extent of apprehending without possessing it. Brute beasts, on the other hand, cannot apprehend reason; they merely obey their instincts. But the use made of slaves differs little from that made of tame animals: the physical energy of both helps to supply their master's needs.

It is also nature's intention to distinguish even the bodies of freemen and slaves: the latter are usually endowed with strength to suit their employment, while the upright carriage of the former renders them unfit for servile work but adapts them to social life whether as soldiers or civilians. But the very opposite frequently occurs: slaves may have the bodies or the souls of freemen. Yet who can deny that if there were invariably as much difference between the bodies of freemen and slaves as there is between the statues of the gods and the average human form, all would acknowledge that the inferior class should be slaves of the superior? And if this is true in the case of the body, with much more justice it may be said in that of a difference in the soul; though it is not so easy to detect the beauty of the soul as it is of the body. [1255ª] Clearly, then, some individuals are by nature free, others by nature slaves; and for these latter slavery is both expedient and right.

It is easy to see that those who take an opposite view are not wholly unreasonable. 'Slave' and 'slavery' are words capable of a twofold application, for a man may be a slave by law as well as by nature. The law I have in mind may be described rather as a convention, according to which everything taken in war is held to belong to the conquerors. But there are many jurists who impeach this pretended right as they would an orator who put forward an unconstitutional measure. They consider it outrageous that the victim of force should be the slave and subject of another merely because that other can do him violence by virtue of his superior strength. Some argue one way, some another, and there are highly intelligent people on both sides.

Now what is the origin of this dispute, and why do the conflicting views overlap? Well, there is a sense in which goodness, when possessed of the necessary means, has the greatest power of wielding force; and conversely, superior power is found only in conjunction with some kind of superior excellence. The result is that *power seems to imply goodness*; and the dispute is seen to turn simply upon the question of justice, which some identify with mutual goodwill, others with the *de facto* rule of the stronger. If the two views are opposed separately to one another,[1] neither line of argument[2] has any plausibility, let alone cogency, against the view that the superior *in goodness* should rule, or be master.

Others, however, imagine they can justify slavery arising from war on the broad ground that it is authorized by law and that what is legal is *ipso facto* just. But they contradict themselves; for suppose the cause of the war is unjust—what then? Furthermore, no one would venture to say that he is really a slave who is undeserving of that fate; otherwise, men of the highest rank will be slaves, or children of slaves, if they or their parents have had the ill luck to be taken prisoner and sold. The Greeks accordingly reject the term 'slave' as applicable to Greeks, and confine it to barbarians. But this is merely harking back to the natural slave of whom we spoke at the outset; it is in fact an admission that some men are slaves under any circumstances and others under no circumstances. The same distinction is made in regard to nobility. For Greeks consider themselves noble everywhere, even beyond their own frontiers, but recognize the barbarian as noble only in his own country—assuming thereby that there are two kinds of nobility and freedom, one absolute and the other relative. Theodectes[3] makes Helen say: 'Who dares reproach me with the name of servant when I have divine ancestors on both sides?' People who talk like that are in effect distinguishing slave and free, noble and ignoble, on the basis of good and evil. [1255[b]] They think that, as men and beasts beget offspring of their own species, so a good man will spring from good stock. But this is what nature, though she may intend it, often fails to accomplish.

Clearly, then, there is some foundation for this difference of view, and all are not *by nature* either slaves or freemen. Clearly, too, there is in some cases a hard line of demarcation between the two classes, making it both expedient and right that one should consist of slaves, the other of masters—that one should render obedience while the other exercises the dominion which nature intended it to have. But any abuse of this authority is

---

[1] i.e. removed from their common ground.
[2] Viz. on the one hand that the stronger has *always* the right to rule, and on the other that he *never* has.
[3] *Helena*, Frag. 3, Nauck[3].

harmful to both; for the part and the whole, like the body and the soul, share a common interest, and the slave is part of his master—a living though separate part of his master's body. Therefore, when the relation of master and slave is founded in nature they are friends with a common interest, but when it is based upon nothing but law and force the opposite is true.[1]

A master is so called, not because of any knowledge he may have but because he has a definite character; and the same holds good of slaves and freemen. I am not, of course, denying that there is a science appropriate to the master and another appropriate to the slave. · There was a man at Syracuse, for example, who made a living by teaching slaves their routine duties; and instruction of this kind might well be extended to include cooking and other such menial work, for some tasks are more honourable, some more necessary, than others. As the proverb says, 'there are slaves and slaves, masters and masters'; but these branches of knowledge are all alike servile.

The master may similarly learn how to employ his slaves; for he is master by virtue not of *acquiring* but of *using* them. On the other hand, there is nothing whatever important or dignified about such knowledge, because the master need only be able to order what the slave should know how to fulfil. Hence masters whose position is such that they are not obliged to toil keep a steward and devote themselves to philosophy or politics. But the art of acquiring slaves—acquiring them justly, I mean— differs from that of a master as well as from that of a slave; it is a species of hunting or warfare.[2] So much, then, for the distinction of master and slave.

[1] The foregoing remarks are sufficient to prove that the rule of a master is not that of a statesman, and that all the various kinds of rule are not (as some maintain they are) the same as one another; for the subjects of one are by nature free, of another by nature slaves. Household management is monarchical, because every house is subject to one head, whereas the rule of a statesman is the government of freemen and equals.—(A.)

[2] According to Aristotle, the just and natural way of acquiring slaves is by raids upon those who are by nature slaves.

3. The Art of Acquisition

[1256ª] We have already shown that a slave is an article of property; let us, therefore, follow our usual method [1] and consider property in general, together with the art of acquiring it. The first question is, whether this art is identical with that of household management, or part of it, or whether it is auxiliary thereto; and if the last, whether it is so in the same way that the art of making shuttles is auxiliary to that of weaving, or as the art of casting bronze is to that of statuary.[2]

It is perfectly clear that the art or science of household management is not *identical with* that of acquisition; for one (clearly the former) uses material (household goods) furnished by the other. There is some disagreement, however, as to the art of acquisition itself. Since (1) he who would engage in acquisition must needs consider from what sources goods and property may be procured; and since (2) property and riches are of many kinds; then the question arises whether farming, and indeed the care and provision of food in general, is part of the art of acquisition, or quite distinct therefrom. Moreover, there are many kinds of food as well as of property, and therefore many varieties of life among both animals and men. None of these can live without food, and differences of food have given rise to differences in their ways of life.

Some beasts are gregarious and others are solitary, whichever is most suitable for their nourishment, i.e. according to whether they are carnivorous, herbivorous, or omnivorous. Nature, you see, has determined their several modes of living in such a way that they can quite easily obtain the food which they prefer; and since the various species of carnivorous and herbivorous animals have different tastes, one naturally liking one thing and another another, their ways of life also differ. A similarly wide variety is found within the human race. The laziest of all mankind are pastoral nomads, who lead a leisured life and obtain their sustenance, without any trouble, from domestic animals; since their flocks and herds must move from place to place in search

[1] i.e. by examining the whole in the light of its parts.
[2] These are not instrumental in the same way: one provides tools and the other material. By 'material' I mean the substratum out of which any work is fashioned; e.g. wool is the material of the weaver, bronze of the statuary. —(A.)

of pasture, they themselves are obliged to follow, cultivating, as it were, a living farm. Others live by some form of the chase: some, for example, are brigands or pirates; some, i.e. those who dwell near lakes or marshes or rivers or a sea in which there are fish, are fishermen; while some are fowlers or hunters. But the majority derive their living from the cultivated fruits of the earth.

Such, roughly speaking, are the modes of subsistence found among those—[1256^b] be they pastoral nomads, farmers, brigands, fishermen, or hunters—who obtain their food by direct means, without recourse to exchange and retail trade. Some, however, lead a comfortable existence by combining two or more of these pursuits and supplying the deficiencies of one with the produce of another. One man, for example, may live as both shepherd and brigand, another as both farmer and hunter, and so forth as need requires.

Property, therefore, in the sense of what is absolutely necessary to support life, appears to be given by nature herself to all, from birth into maturity. Vermiparous or oviparous animals bring forth, together with their offspring, sufficient food to last until the newly born can provide for itself; whereas viviparous animals contain within them during a certain period a supply of nutriment called milk, on which to feed their young. Similarly, we may conclude that, when this stage is passed, plants exist for the sake of animals, and brute beasts for the sake of man— domestic animals for his use and food, wild ones (or at any rate most of them) for food and other accessories of life, such as clothing and various tools.

Since nature makes nothing purposeless or in vain, it is undeniably true that she has made all animals for the sake of man. In one respect, therefore, the art of war is a natural subdivision of the art of acquisition, because the latter includes the chase, a form of warfare which is naturally just because it is intended to be waged against wild beasts and against those men who, though they are meant by nature to be ruled by others, will not voluntarily submit.

And so there is one form of the art of acquisition which is by nature part of household management, in so far as the latter must either find ready to hand, or itself provide, the storeable necessaries of life which are useful to the family or political community. These 'storeable necessaries,' of course, are the elements of true wealth; and a good life requires no unlimited amount of property, despite Solon's remark in one of his poems that 'no bound to riches has been fixed for man.' [1] There is indeed a boundary fixed, as there is in the other arts also; for no art has unlimited instruments, whether as regards number or size, and riches are a collection of instruments for use in the household or in the state. We see, then, *that* there is, and also *why* there is, a natural art of acquisition which is practised both by managers of households and by statesmen.

There is another way of obtaining property, which is particularly and with good reason known as the art of acquisition [1257ª], and which has given rise to the belief that there are no limits to property or riches. Being closely allied to that of which we have just been speaking, it is not seldom identified therewith. True, there is no great difference between them, but they are definitely not the same. The first is natural whereas the one with which we have now to deal is the fruit of a special kind of experience and skill. Let us, therefore, begin with the following remarks.

Every article of property has two possible uses. Both apply to the thing as such, but not in the same way; for one is the primary, the other the secondary use of it. Take a shoe: it may be worn or it may be exchanged for something else; but both are uses of that shoe. If you pass it on to someone else who needs it, in return for money or food, you are certainly making use of the shoe as such, but not in accordance with its primary purpose, for it was not made as an object of exchange. And the same holds good of all possessions. Exchange is possible in every case: it is of natural origin, arising from the fact that some men have too much and others too little for their needs. From this we may safely conclude that retail trade is not naturally a part of the art of acquisition, otherwise men would have discontinued the practice of exchange as soon as their wants were satisfied. In the most elementary association, i.e. in the family, there can be no occasion for it; but its advantages become apparent when the association is enlarged. The members of the family once held all their goods in common; but later, when the family split up, the several villages had at their disposal many different things which they had to barter for what they needed. This kind of exchange is still in use among barbarous races who exchange with one another the necessaries of life, but nothing

---

[1] Bergk, *Poetae Lyrici Graeci*, Solon, 13, 71.

8·15–10m

more, giving and receiving wine, for instance, in return for corn and other such commodities.

Now exchange on such a basis is not contrary to nature, nor any part of the art of acquisition, for it helps to satisfy men's natural requirements. But, as we might expect, it did result in another form of exchange. When countries began to rely more and more upon foreign sources for their needs, importing what they lacked and exporting their own surpluses, money inevitably came into use. The necessaries of life are not all easy to transport; and so men agreed to employ among themselves, for the purposes of mutual exchange, something of intrinsic use and easily applicable to everyday requirements, such as iron, silver, or some other metal. The value of this material was at first determined simply by weight or size, but in course of time it was stamped to save the trouble of weighing and to indicate the amount it represented.

[1257^b] Once the use of coin had been introduced, there emerged from the barter of essential commodities the other form of the art of acquisition, viz. retail trade. This was, in all likelihood, at first a simple affair, but it afterwards developed a more complicated structure, as soon as men learned by experience where and how the greatest profits might be made. The emergence of retail trade from the use of coin has led many to suppose that the art of acquisition is principally concerned with money-making, and that its function is to discover from what sources money may be best accumulated. Wealth, in fact, is often imagined to consist in large quantities of coin, because one form of the art of acquisition, viz. retail trade, is concerned with money. Some, however, maintain that coinage is a sham—unnatural, a mere convention—on the grounds (1) that those who use it have only to substitute another form of currency and it immediately becomes worthless, and (2) that it is of no use as an alternative to any of the necessaries of life, since he who has plenty of coin may often lack necessary food. It is indeed paradoxical to call a man wealthy who, in spite of his great possessions, is doomed to starvation—like Midas in the legend, whose insatiable prayer caused everything set before him to turn into gold.

For such reasons they look for a different notion of riches and of the art of acquisition, different, that is, from the mere accumulation of currency. Quite right, too; for the natural art of acquiring wealth in the shape of natural riches, which is a part of household management, *is* a different thing from retail trade. The latter is the art of producing wealth by the sole means of exchange; and it is associated with the amassing of coin, because coin is the unit and measure of exchange. Furthermore, there is no limit to the riches derived from retail trade. For as in the art of medicine there is no limit to the pursuit of health, or in the other arts to that of their respective ends,[1] so too in retail trade the end, i.e. the acquisition of spurious riches, has no bounds. But there *is* a limit, on the other hand, to that form of the art of acquisition which consists in household management; the indefinite accumulation of riches is not its aim. From this point of view, therefore, it might be said that all wealth must have a limit; but experience shows the opposite to be true, for those engaged in acquisition increase their hoard of currency indefinitely.

The reason why the two modes of acquisition are confused is the close connection between them: the instrument is identical in each case, although differently used, and so they overlap. For each is a use of property, but not for the same purpose: the end in the one case is accumulation, but in the other it is something altogether different. Some people, therefore, imagine that to acquire wealth is the object of household management, and their one idea in life is either to grow increasingly rich, or at any rate sit tight on what money they have. This attitude results from their being so intent upon living rather than upon living *well*: [1258ᵃ] they are anxious to possess unlimited means for the gratification of their unlimited desires. Those who do aspire after a good life seek the means to bodily pleasures; and since these appear to depend on acquisition, their whole concern is to make money. Hence the other form [2] of the art of acquisition. Since their enjoyment depends on having more than is necessary, they look to the art which yields that superfluity; and if they cannot obtain it through the art of acquisition, they have recourse to other means and make unnatural use of every gift. I say 'unnatural use,' because courage, for example, is not intended to produce wealth, but to inspire confidence; neither is wealth the goal of the military or of the medical art, the former of which aims at success in warfare and the latter at good health; and yet some men direct all their faculties to the acquisition

[1] The horizons of medicine and other arts are unbounded. But since the end is itself a limit, there is a limit to the *means* employed.—(A.)
[2] Money-making as distinct from exchange.

of wealth, as if money-making were the end to which all else must be subservient.

We have now discussed (1) the *unnecessary* form of the art of acquisition, explaining why men think they need it, and (2) the *necessary* form our study of which has shown (*a*) that it is different from the other, and (*b*) that it is a natural part of household management, intended to provide subsistence, and therefore (unlike the other form) limited in scope.

We have thus found an answer to our original question: [1] Is the art of acquisition the business of the household manager and the statesman, or is property something they can take for granted? Well, nature supplies political science with the raw material of humanity independent of any effort on the part of that science; and she may therefore be expected to provide the sustenance of earth, sea, etc., leaving the household manager to use her gifts.[2] Otherwise there is no apparent reason why medicine as well as the art of acquisition should not be part of household management.[3] Here, then, is the answer to our question. Just as from one point of view the household manager and the ruler of a state should take precautions for their subjects' health, whereas from another point of view that duty falls rather on the doctor, so also the acquisition of property is in one sense the concern of household management, but in another sense that of a subsidiary art. Generally speaking, however, as I remarked above, it is for nature to furnish the means of life in advance. She must provide sustenance for whatever is born into the world, as appears from the fact that new-born animals are nourished in every case upon the residuum of the matter from which they derive their origin. Hence the natural form of the art of acquisition is always acquisition from fruits and animals.

As I have said, the art of acquisition is twofold: one form is a part of household management, the other is retail trade. The first of these is both necessary and commendable; but the other, which is a mode of exchange, is rightly censured as being [1258^b] an unnatural procedure whereby men profit at one another's expense. Usury is detested above all, and for the best of

---

[1] Page 15, lines 3–8.
[2] Thus it is not a weaver's business to *make* but to *use* wool, and to be able to distinguish good serviceable wool from inferior kinds.—(A.)
[3] After all, the members of a household require health as much as life or any other necessary.—(A.)

reasons. It makes profit out of money itself, not from money's natural object,[1] and therefore it is the most unnatural means of acquiring wealth.

Farming, Exchange,[2] Mining, etc.

We have said enough about the art of acquisition from the theoretical standpoint, and must now consider its practical side. One can philosophize indefinitely about matters of this kind, but in practice one is limited by circumstance as follows. The fundamental divisions of this art in (I) its purest form are: (1) *Knowledge of live-stock.* It is important to know which kinds are most profitable, where, and how; a man who breeds or purchases, e.g., horses, oxen, sheep, or other animals, should learn which of these pay better than others, and which give the best return in particular places, for locality has a bearing on their respective values. (2) *Cultivation*, which includes (a) tillage and planting, (b) bee-keeping, (c) poultry-farming and the care of fish-ponds. (II) Exchange embraces: (1) *Commerce*, the first and principal division, which includes (a) the provision of a ship, (b) carriage of goods, (c) exposure for sale; and these differ again according as they are safer or more profitable than others. (2) *Usury.* (3) *Service for hire*, either (a) in the mechanical arts, or (b) in unskilled bodily labour.

(III) There is yet another form of the art of acquisition: it is intermediate between (I) and (II), because, while it is partly natural, it is concerned likewise with exchange. This form has to do with things won from the earth, and from those things which grow from the earth and are useful despite the fact they bear no fruit. Such are the cutting of timber, and mining in all its various branches.

I have spoken here in general terms about the several forms of acquisition; a detailed discussion of each might be useful in practice, but it would be tedious to dwell upon them at greater length now.[3] A number of authors have written on these and

---

[1] Money was intended as a means of exchange, not to increase at interest. This term 'interest' [Gk τόκος=offspring], which means the birth of money from money, is applied to usury because the offspring resembles the parent. —(A.)

[2] Note that the following section classifies the art of acquisition differently from above.

[3] Those occupations are most truly arts in which there is the least element of chance; those are the meanest which most deprave the body; those are most servile in which most physical energy is expended; and those are the most illiberal which have the least need of excellence.—(A.)

kindred subjects,[1] and their works may be consulted by those who are interested. Still, it is worth while assembling from scattered sources a number of accounts which show how certain individuals have managed to grow rich. They are all helpful to those who set store upon the art of acquisition. There is the story about Thales of Miletus and his financial ruse, which, though it involves a principle which is universally applicable in commercial dealings, is told particularly of him on account of his reputation as a sage. Thales was reproached for his poverty, which was taken as proof that philosophy is useless. However, so the story goes, he knew from his observation of the stars, while it was yet winter, that the following year would produce an enormous crop of olives; so, having a little money available, he paid deposits for the use of every olive-press in Miletus and Chios, which he was able to hire at small cost because no one bid against him. Now when harvest-time came round, and many presses were required all at once and quite suddenly, he let them out upon what terms he pleased, thereby making a handsome profit. In this way he demonstrated that philosophers can easily become rich if they care to do so, but that this is not their ambition. Thales is supposed to have provided a brilliant illustration of his wisdom; but, as I was saying, his stratagem is of universal application, and is merely the creation of a personal monopoly. It is a scheme to which whole states have been known to have recourse when in need of money, by creating a monopoly, e.g. in provisions.

There was also a man in Sicily, who had been entrusted with a sum of money, and used it to buy up all the iron from the smelting works. Later, when the merchants came from various market-towns to buy, he was the only seller, and without greatly increasing the normal price he made a profit of 200 per cent. When this came to the ears of Dionysius, he allowed the man to take his earnings, but would not permit him to remain in Sicily, fearing that he had discovered a way of making money which would be detrimental to the tyrant's own interests. This man's discovery was identical with that of Thales: each had managed to create a personal monopoly. It is as well for statesmen also to understand these things. For a state is often in as much need of money and of such means of raising it, if not more so, than a household; and this is why some politicians devote themselves entirely to finance.

[1] e.g. Charetides of Paros and Apollodorus of Lemnos on tillage and planting.—(A.)

4. MARITAL AND PATERNAL AUTHORITY

There are, as I have explained,[1] three divisions of household management: the master's rule over his slaves (which has already been discussed), that of the father over his children, and that of the husband over his wife. The husband and father, we said, rules over his wife and children as over free beings in each case; but the form of rule differs [1259^b]. He rules his children as does a king his subjects; towards his wife he is in the position of a statesman governing fellow citizens. The male is naturally more fitted to command than the female (except where there is a miscarriage of nature), the elder and full-grown than the younger and less mature. In the majority of cases where there is government by a statesman the citizens rule and are ruled by turn, an arrangement which implies that they are equal in nature and differ in no way whatsoever. On the other hand, the ruler for the time being seeks to create a difference in respect of outward forms, modes of address, and titles, as witness the remark of Amasis about his foot-pan; [2] and it is in this relation that the male stands to the female *at all times*, not merely for a term.

The rule of a father over his children is monarchical; for it is based upon love and seniority in years, which is the specific nature of kingly rule. Wherefore Homer has aptly called Zeus 'father of gods and men,' because he is king of them all. A king should be the natural superior of his subjects, though one with them in race; and this is the relation between elder and younger, between father and child.

5. VIRTUE IN RULERS AND RULED

It is clear, then, that household management is concerned more with men than with inanimate things; with human excellence than with the excellence of property, which we call wealth; and with the virtue of freemen than with that of slaves. To begin with, it might even be asked whether slaves have any virtue at all, apart from and above merely instrumental and ministerial excellence. Can they, I mean, have temperance, fortitude, justice, etc.; or is their capacity limited to physical qualities at another's beck and call? Whichever alternative we adopt, there are difficulties in the way. If slaves have virtue, how will they

[1] Page 9, lines 6–9.   [2] See Herodotus, ii. 172.

differ from freemen? And yet, seeing that they are human beings and have a share in reason, it is surely out of the question to maintain that they are incapable of virtue. A similar problem arises in the case of women and children, whether they too have virtues: should a woman be temperate, brave, and just; and is a child to be deemed temperate and intemperate, or not?

Let us put the question in its most comprehensive form, and ask whether or not the virtue of a natural ruler is the same as that of a natural subject. If both are expected to possess a noble nature, why should one of them invariably govern and the other invariably obey? [1] On the other hand, it is paradoxical to suppose that the one ought while the other ought not to have virtue; for unless ruler and ruled alike are temperate and just, how can they respectively rule and obey well? He who is licentious and cowardly will never do his duty.

[1260ª] It is evident, therefore, that while both parties must have a share of virtue, there are different kinds of virtue as there are differences between natural subjects. In this matter we have been guided by the nature of the soul. The soul has naturally two elements, a ruling and a ruled; and each of these has a different virtue, one belonging to the rational and ruling element, the other to the irrational and subject element. Now this same principle obviously applies to the household and to the state; whence we may infer a general law requiring naturally ruling and naturally ruled elements. But the kinds of rule differ: the freeman rules the slave in one way, the male the female in another, the man the child in yet another. True, the parts of the soul [2] are present in all these, but they are present differently in each. For the slave has absolutely no deliberative faculty; the woman has, but its authority is imperfect; so has the child, but in this case it is immature. The same must necessarily be supposed true in respect of the moral virtues: slaves, women, and children all have a share in them, but only to such an extent as fits each for the performance of his or her duty.

The ruler should accordingly possess moral virtue in its complete rational form, because any function taken absolutely demands a master-craftsman, and reason is such a craftsman. His subjects, on the other hand, require it only in the degree

---

[1] The situation cannot arise from a difference in degree; for the difference of ruling and being ruled is a difference in kind, which is certainly not true of the difference between more and less.—(A.)

[2] i.e. rational and irrational elements.

proper to each. Clearly, then, moral virtue is common to them all. But temperance, fortitude, and justice are not, as Socrates believed,[1] the same in a man as in a woman; a man's fortitude is shown in ruling, a woman's in obeying. This holds good of all other virtues, as will be more apparent if we examine them in detail. It is mere self-deception to say generally that virtue consists in 'a good disposition of soul,' or in 'doing what is right,' or in anything of the kind. Far better than such definitions is the method adopted by those who follow Gorgias [2] and enumerate the virtues.

Women, children, and slaves, therefore, must be considered as having their peculiar qualities. As the poet says of women, 'Silence is a woman's glory'; [3] but it is not equally the glory of a man. Since the child is imperfect, his virtue is obviously not relative to himself but to the fully developed human being and to the latter's guiding authority. The virtue of a slave is likewise relative to his master. Now we decided [4] that a slave is useful to the satisfaction of his master's needs, so that he will obviously require no more than the minimum of virtue which will prevent him failing in his duty through cowardice or lack of self-discipline. It may be asked whether, if what I am now saying is true, virtue is not likewise necessary for artisans, since they often fall short of what is required of them owing to intemperance. But surely there is a great difference between the two cases. Whereas the slave shares his master's life, the artisan is less closely connected with a master; he requires virtue only in proportion as his status for the time being approximates to that of a slave. The meaner sort of artisan is a slave, not for all purposes, but for a definite servile task. Again, while [1260[b]] the slave exists as such by nature, this is not so of the shoemaker or other artisan. Manifestly, then, it is from the master *qua* master [5] that the slave must derive the kind of moral virtue which he ought to possess. They are mistaken, therefore, who would not have us reason with a slave, but only command him; for slaves are in more need of instruction than are children.

But enough of this subject for the present. The relations of husband and wife, father and child, as well as the virtues of each,

---

[1] Plato, *Meno*, 72 A.–73 C.
[2] Ibid., 71 E, 72 A.
[3] Sophocles, *Ajax*, 293.
[4] Page 12, lines 5–7.
[5] And not from the master *as possessing the art of mastership*, which teaches the slave his duties.—(A.)

what is good and what bad in their mutual intercourse, and how the good is to be pursued and the bad avoided—all these questions must be considered when we come to discuss the various forms of government.[1]   Every household is part of a state; the said relationships are part of the household; and the goodness of the part must be considered with reference to that of the whole.   Assuming, therefore, that the virtues of women and children contribute to the excellence of a state,[2] we must postpone the subject of their training until we have decided how the state is to be governed.

This being so, we may consider our present inquiry as complete, and start anew by examining the several theories of ideal government.

[1] Aristotle does not fulfil this promise.
[2] That they do so contribute is plain from the fact that women are half the free population, while children are the citizens of to-morrow.—(A.)

Book II

PROPOSED IDEAL CONSTITUTIONS

A. THEORETICAL SYSTEMS OF GOVERNMENT

1. PLATO'S 'REPUBLIC'

[1260ᵇ27] I propose to consider what form of political association is best of all for those who have it in their power to live exactly as they please. But before offering constructive views of my own [1] I must investigate (*a*) some theoretical systems which are commonly admired, and (*b*) a number of forms now obtaining in states that are admittedly well governed. In this way we shall bring to light whatever is good and useful. Nor must it be thought that in seeking to improve upon them I am anxious at any cost to show off my superior wisdom; I have undertaken this inquiry for the sole reason that all existing constitutions are defective.

Let us begin at the point which naturally presents itself first to our consideration. The members of a state must either have (1) all things in common, or (2) some things in common and some not, or (3) nothing in common. It is manifestly impossible that they should have *nothing* in common, because the state is a community, and must have at least a common place of residence.

[1261ᵃ] Fellow citizens are those who share in one state, and one state means one place of residence. We are therefore left with the question, whether a state is more likely to be well conducted if its members hold *everything possible* in common, or if some things are excepted from common ownership.

In Plato's *Republic*,[2] Socrates advocates a community of (A) wives and children, and (B) property.[3] There is nothing to prevent such an arrangement; but is it an improvement on the present order of things?

(A) *Wives and Children*

Community of wives involves more than one difficulty. First, it is quite clear that the end for which Plato urges the

[1] Books VII and VIII.
[2] 423 E, 457 C, 462 B.
[3] In point of fact Plato recommends community of wives and children only in the guardian and warrior classes.

necessity of such an institution is not borne out by his argument. Second, as a means to the end which he has in view for the state, his scheme, taken literally, is impracticable; but he nowhere explains how it should be interpreted.

(I) The premiss from which Plato argues is that 'the highest unity of a state is its highest good.' But (1) it cannot be denied that there is a degree of unity beyond which the state will cease to be a state. Plurality is of the very nature of a state, which, as it progresses towards unity, is gradually transformed into a family and thence into an individual.[1] Hence, even if this end were attainable, it were best avoided as condemning the state to ultimate annihilation.

(2) The state consists not only of a number of men, but also of men of different kinds; similars cannot form a state. It is not the same as a military league organized for mutual defence. The usefulness of such an alliance is dependent on its quantity, even though the members are one in kind; it is like a weight which depresses the scales more heavily in the balance.[2] But the elements from which a unity is formed differ in kind; and therefore, as I remarked in the *Ethics*,[3] every state is dependent for its well-being on the principle of reciprocation, even among freemen and equals. These cannot all rule at once, but must hold office for a year or some other term, or at any rate succeed one another according to some regular plan. In this way all take their turn of government, just as if shoemakers and carpenters were to exchange occupations instead of pursuing their respective trades without intermission. It would be best if this last arrangement held good in politics as well, i.e. that the same persons remained constantly in power, wherever possible. But where such a system is impracticable, [1261^b] owing to the natural equality of the citizens (all of whom have a right to share in the government, whether to govern be good or bad), the next best thing is that equals should in turn retire from office and, having done so, be treated all alike. Thus one party rules and the other is ruled alternately, as if they were no longer the same persons. And even those who are rulers for the time being hold

---

[1] The family may be described as more of a unity than the state, and the individual than the family.—(A.)

[2] A state differs likewise from a tribe, except when the latter is no mere agglomeration of villages, but is united in a confederacy like that of Arcadia. —(A.)

[3] *Nichomachean Ethics*, 1132ᵃ32.

a variety of offices. The above considerations go to prove (a) that a state is not by nature a unit in the sense in which some say it is; and (b) that whereas a thing's highest good is that which preserves it in being, Plato's 'highest good of the state' is in reality its destruction.

(3) From another point of view also it is wrong to attempt this extreme unification of the state. A household is more self-sufficing than an individual, a state than a household; but a state comes into existence only when the community is large enough to be self-sufficing. Therefore, if self-sufficiency is desirable, the lesser degree of unity is preferable to the greater.

(II) Even supposing that the utmost degree of unity were a correct ideal for the state, (1) it will surely not be achieved by 'all men saying "mine" and "not mine" at the same time.'[1] The word 'all' is ambiguous. If it be taken to mean each and every individual, then perhaps the state of affairs envisaged by Plato may be to some extent realized; each man will call the same individual his own son or his own wife, and so of his property and whatever else falls to his lot. Such, however, will not be the meaning of those who have wives and children in common; they will speak not severally but collectively, and will refer to their property likewise. Clearly, then, there is a fallacy in the term 'all'; like 'both,' 'odd,' and 'even,' it is ambiguous, and gives rise to logical puzzles even in abstract argument. That all persons should call a thing 'mine' in the sense that *each* does so is impracticable, however fine it may sound; and if the words are understood in their *collective* sense, the unity implied is by no means conducive to harmony.

(2) The formula has this additional drawback, that what is common to the greatest number is cared for least. Men think principally of what is their own, and if they have the common interest at heart it is only to the extent that they are personally concerned therein. Apart from anything else, we are all inclined to neglect a duty which we expect another to fulfil, just as in families many servants are often less useful than a few. Each citizen will have a thousand sons, *but not as an individual*; any and every boy will be equally the son of any and every father, and on that account will be neglected by all alike.

(3) [1262ª] Each person will be connected with any given

[1] Such, according to Plato [*Republic*, 462 C], is the sign of a state's perfect unity.—(A.)

member of the whole citizen body by a mere fractional relationship varying with the size of the population,[1] and will feel only a
fractional joy or sorrow at that member's prosperity or adver-
sity.   Nor will he feel even this without some uncertainty; for
he will not know whether he ever had a child, much less whether
it has survived.   Which, then, is better—that each should call
X 'mine' in such a way as makes X the same relation to two
thousand or ten thousand citizens, or to use the word 'mine' in
the sense now familiar in Greek states?   As things are, one man
describes as 'my son' an individual whom another calls 'my
brother,' 'my cousin,' 'my relative' (by consanguinity or
affinity), or again 'my fellow clansman,' 'my fellow tribesman.'
How much better it is to be a real cousin than a Platonic son!

(4) It will be impossible to prevent brothers recognizing one
another, or children their parents and vice versa; for children
resemble their parents, and they will inevitably conclude their
relationships from that resemblance.   Some geographers provide us with concrete examples of this truth: they say, for
instance,[2] that in parts of Upper Libya, where wives are common
property, the children are assigned to their respective fathers
because of their likeness to them.   There are also females of
other animal species, e.g. mares and cows, which have a strong
tendency to produce offspring resembling their male parent, as
was the case, for instance, with the Pharsalian mare Faithful.[3]

(5) Other disadvantages, which the author of such a community will find it hard to prevent, are assaults, involuntary and
even voluntary homicides, quarrels, and slanders.   All these are
most unholy acts when perpetrated against one's parents or near
relations, though not to the same degree where there is no kin-
ship.   Besides, they are far more likely to occur if the relationship is unknown, and then, when they do occur, the customary
expiation is impossible.

(6) It is strange that Plato, who would make the children
common, forbids direct intercourse between men but allows
other practices of the kind between father and son or brother
and brother, than which nothing is more unseemly, considering
that love of this kind is shameful enough without overt expres-
sion.   It is equally curious that he forbids such intercourse on

[1] i.e. he will say 'X is my son,' or 'He is So-and-so's,' naming in this way
each of a thousand or more fathers who are comprised in the state.—(A.)
[2] Cf. Herodotus, iv. 180, to which Aristotle is probably referring.
[3] So called because she faithfully gave back what she had received from the
stallion.   Cf. Historia Animalium, 586ª12.

no other grounds but the violence of the pleasure, as if the relationship of father and son or of brothers made no difference at all.[1]

(7) Community of wives and children seems better suited to the farmers than to the guardians: [1262^b] if the former have wives and children in common they will be less closely united in the bonds of affection, as a subject class should be if they are to remain obedient and not rebel. Broadly speaking, the results of the system proposed by Plato will be opposite to those which one expects of sound legislation, opposite indeed to the very goal which he has in view. The fraternal spirit is commonly recognized as the greatest good of states,[2] preserving them from sedition; and Plato himself praises nothing so highly as the unity of the state, which he and mankind in general take to be the result of that spirit. But the sort of unity which he commends will be like that of the lovers in the *Symposium*,[3] who, as Aristophanes says, long to grow together in the excess of their affection and be merged into a single entity—in which case one or both would inevitably perish. But in a state having wives and children in common, the fraternal spirit will wear thin; no father will readily say 'my son,' nor any son 'my father.' As the sweetness of a little wine mingled with a great deal of water is imperceptible after the mixture, so, in a community such as that recommended by Plato, the very idea of relationship implied by these names will vanish; there will be no reason why a father should care about his so-called son, or vice versa, or a brother about his brother. The two factors which principally inspire concern and affection—that a thing is one's own, and that it is the keystone of one's hopes and fears—cannot exist in this sort of community.

(8) As for transferring new-born children from the artisan and farming class to that of the guardians, or vice versa,[4] how is this to be effected? Moreover, those who give up and transfer their children are bound to know whom they are so transferring, and to whom.[5] Again, the evils mentioned in (5) and (6) above are more likely to occur among those who are transferred to the lower orders or who are promoted to the guardian class; for they

[1] See *Republic*, 403 A–C.
[2] Cf. *Nic. Eth.* 1152^{a}22.
[3] Plato, *Symposium*, 191 A, 192 C.
[4] *Republic*, iii. 415 B.
[5] And hence a child cannot be entirely separated from the class to which it originally belonged.

will no longer refer to members of the class which they have left
as 'brother,' 'son,' 'father,' or 'mother,' and will therefore not
be hindered from crime by the thought of their consanguinity.
So much, then, for a community of wives and children.

(B) *Property*

Next we must consider the disposition of property: should the
citizens of a perfectly organized state hold it in common, or not?
This question may be treated separately from the legislation [1]
affecting women and children. [1263ᵃ] Even supposing the
latter continue, as at present in all Greek states, to belong to
individuals, may there not be some advantage in the common
ownership and/or use of property?   For example, (1) land may
be privately owned, but the produce stored for common con-
sumption,[2] as is the practice of some nations.   Or (2) there may
be common ownership and cultivation of the land, while its
produce is shared among individuals for their private use, as is
said to be the custom among certain barbarians.   Or (3) the land
and its produce may be alike common.

With regard to (2) and (3): (*a*) when the farmers are not the
owners, the situation will be different and more easily handled;
but when they labour for their own benefit the question of ownership will give rise to endless disputes.   If there is a disproportion
between toil and reward, those who work hard in return for
little will inevitably bear a grudge against those who receive or
consume a great deal but do little by way of compensation.

(*b*) It is a universal truth that men find difficulty in living
together, i.e. in sharing all human relations, especially when it
comes to holding property in common.   Examples of this may
be found in the behaviour of fellow travellers (who almost
invariably disagree over commonplace matters and quarrel
about mere trifles), as well as in the fact that we are most easily
annoyed by those of our servants with whom the daily round
brings us into most frequent contact.

(*c*) These are only some of the drawbacks arising from the

----

[1] i.e. the legislation proposed in Plato's *Republic*.

[2] This is the scheme which Aristotle prefers.   Sir David Ross (*Aristotle*,
pp. 245-6) sums up Aristotle's view on this subject as follows.   'In so far as
socialism means a better organization of industry by the state, Aristotle would
be in sympathy with it. . . .   But in so far as it means the taking away from
private industry of its rewards, the attempt to create an equality of possessions
which the natural inequality of capacity and industry will constantly upset,
he is an individualist, and no one has better expressed the common sense of
individualism.'

common ownership of property. Our present system—amended, of course, by good customs and the control of wise legislation—will prove far better; for it will have the advantages of both schemes, i.e. of common and of private property. In one respect only [1] is it desirable that property be held in common; as a general rule the opposite arrangement is to be preferred. For when everyone has a separate interest,[2] one main source of disagreement will be removed, and work will prosper all the more because each man will be occupied about his own business. Moreover, moral virtue will ensure that, as the proverb says, 'friends have all things in common.'[3] Even to-day there are traces of such a scheme, reminding us that it is not impracticable; it exists already to some extent in certain well-regulated states and may be carried further. In these states every man has his own property, but he places part of it at the disposal of his friends and shares the use of another part with all his fellow citizens. The Spartans, for instance, use one another's slaves and horses and dogs as if these were their own; and when they lack provisions on a journey they take what they find in the surrounding countryside. It is evidently better, therefore, that property should be subject to private ownership, but its use common; and it is the special business of the legislator to make the necessary arrangements to that end.

(d) How vastly more pleasant it is to be able to regard something as one's very own! Surely [1263b] regard for self is a natural feeling and no mere random urge. Self-love in the sense of selfishness (like love of money in the sense of avarice) is rightly deplored; but some partiality for such things as oneself, property, etc., is almost universal.

(e) To lend a helping hand, or to do a kindness, to one's friends or guests or companions is a source of infinite satisfaction; but it is possible only when one has private property. Such advantages are precluded by extreme unification of the state. Besides, the evidence of two additional virtues is openly destroyed under a system of this kind. I mean temperance in respect of women [4] and liberality in the matter of property.[5]

---

[1] i.e. the use of produce.
[2] Cf. *Republic*, ii. 374.
[3] Ibid., iv. 424 A.
[4] It is the sign of an honourable character to abstain through temperance from interfering with another man's wife.—(A.)
[5] Where men have everything in common, no one will any longer show himself open-handed in any shape or form, since liberality is manifested in the use of private property.—(A.)

(*f*) The legislation recommended in Plato's *Republic* may wear the handsome mask of benevolence. Its proposal is welcomed on the grounds that everybody will thereby, in some miraculous way, become everybody's friend—especially since the author denounces [1] present evils, such as actions for breach of contract, convictions for perjury, flattery of the rich, and so forth as the fruits of private ownership. In point of fact these abuses are due to a very different cause; they proceed from the wickedness of human nature. We find, as a matter of fact, that quarrelling is most frequent among those who possess and enjoy all things in common. It may *seem* that few men disagree in consequence of owning common property, but that is simply because there are not nearly so many of them as there are private owners.

(*g*) We must take account not only of the disadvantages from which those who hold property in common will be saved, but also of the benefits they will lose. Their life will be absolutely impossible. Plato's fallacy must be attributed to the wrong notion of unity from which his argument derives. True, the state, like the family, must have some degree of unity, but *only* some degree: if it moves beyond a certain point in that direction, it will no longer be a state; and even without going so far, it may deteriorate, just as a harmony is spoiled if reduced to unison, or rhythm to a single beat. The state, as I have said,[2] is a plurality; it should be formed into a social unit by means of education. How curious, then, that the author of an educational system which he believes will render the state virtuous should hope to improve his citizens by the measures which we have described rather than by customs, laws, and methods of intellectual training, like those in force at Sparta and in Crete, where the legislator has made property common to the extent of supplying common meals. [1264ᵃ] We cannot afford to disregard the experience of ages; you may be sure that if the methods advocated in Plato's *Republic* were sound, they would not have gone unrecognized by so many generations. Much of the information at man's disposal has not been organized into a scientific whole, much of it is never used at all; but there is very little that has not been brought to light at one time or another. We should learn a good deal about the soundness or otherwise of Plato's methods, were we able to watch such a form of government as he advocates in process of construction. No legislator could hope to build a

---

[1] *Republic*, 464, 465.   [2] Page 30, line 8.

state unless he distributed and divided its constituent parts into associations for common meals on the one hand, and on the other into clans and tribes; and it is therefore obvious that Plato's suggested legislation does nothing more original than forbid the guardians to cultivate the soil, a practice which the Spartans already try to avoid.[1]

(h) Plato does not tell us, and it is difficult to guess, what the general form of his proposed state will be. The citizens who are not guardians are in a majority, and yet he lays down no rules with regard to them. Are the farmers, for example, to hold their property in common, or is each individual to have his own? And are their wives and children to be individual or common?

(i) If, like the guardians, they are to have all in common, how will they differ from them; or again, what will they gain by submitting to them? What motive, indeed, will they have to submit at all, unless the ruling class adopts the clever policy of the Cretans, who grant their slaves the same institutions as their own, but forbid them physical training and the possession of arms?

(ii) If, on the other hand, they are to follow the practice of other states with regard to these matters, what sort of community will there be? Surely, two cities in one,[2] each hostile to the other, with the guardians a mere garrison of occupation, and the farmers, craftsmen, etc., ordinary citizens. This, however, will mean that all the litigation, squabbling, and similar abuses for which he blames other states [3] will be rife among his own lower classes. Admittedly, he says that, having so good an education, they will not require many regulations for the policing of the city, control of the markets, and so forth; [4] but then he confines his education to the guardians. Further, he allows the farmers to hold property only upon condition of their paying tribute; [5] but this is calculated to render them far more unmanageable and conceited than the helots, penestae, and slave populations in general. Plato nowhere determines whether or not community of wives, children, and property is necessary for

---

[1] Aristotle here, as so often, is unfair to Plato. There is no strict parallel between the Spartan peers, who owned the land, and Plato's guardians, who did not; nor between the helots and Plato's owner-farmers.

[2] Cf. *Republic*, iv. 422 E.

[3] Ibid., v. 464, 465.

[4] Ibid., iv. 425 D.

[5] Ibid., v. 464 C. The 'tribute' was a quota of their produce payable to the guardians.

the lower equally with the upper classes; nor has he anything definite to say about such kindred questions as the education, form of government, and laws applicable to the lower classes. It is by no means easy to supply an answer, and yet the character of these latter classes is far from unimportant if the common life of the guardians is to be maintained.

[1264ᵇ] Moreover (iii), if Plato establishes a community of wives but retains private property, who will see to the house while the men look after the fields? Who indeed will do so in case (i) above, where the farmers have their wives as well as their property in common? Then again, it is ridiculous to conclude from the analogy of brute beasts [1] that men and women should pursue the same occupations; for a brute beast has no household duties.

The principles of government, too, as outlined by Plato, are risky inasmuch as he would establish a permanent ruling class, which cannot but cause unrest even among the lower classes, but more especially among the high-spirited fighting men. And yet one cannot escape the fact that those whom he would have as rulers must always belong to the same class; for the gold which God mingles in the souls of men [2] is not bestowed now upon one sort and now upon another, but always upon the same. Further, Plato deprives the guardians even of happiness, arguing that a legislator's business is to make the state happy *as a whole*.[3] But the whole cannot be happy unless all, or most, or at least some, of its parts are so. Happiness, you see, is not like the even principle in numbers: this latter may exist in the whole but in neither of its parts; not so happiness. Well, then, if the guardians are not happy, who will be? Certainly not the artisans or the masses in general.

[1] Ibid., v. 451 D.
[2] Plato says [*Republic*, iii. 415 A] that God mingles gold in some, and silver in others, from their very birth; but brass and iron in those who are destined for the rôles of artisans and husbandmen.—(A.)
[3] *Republic*, iv. 419, 420.

2. PLATO'S 'LAWS'

The foregoing are only some of the grave disadvantages attaching to the political scheme developed by Plato in the *Republic*. More or less the same weaknesses are found in his later work, the *Laws*, and it is therefore advisable to glance at the constitution therein described. In the *Republic* Plato dealt fully with just a few points: the community of women and children, the community of property, and the distribution of political power. The citizen body is divided into two classes— one of farmers, the other of fighting men;[1] and from this last is recruited a third class of counsellors and rulers of the state.[2] But Plato fails to tell us whether or not the farmers and artisans are to have any share in government, and whether or not they too are to possess arms and be liable for military service. True, he maintains[3] that women should enjoy the same education as the guardians and take part in military service; but the remainder of the dialogue is padded out with digressions remote from the main subject, and with discussions upon the education of the guardians.

[1265ᵃ] The greater part of the *Laws* consists of detailed enactments; little is said about the constitution of the state, which, though originally intended as a practical type, is gradually developed into an ideal pattern. For, excepting the community of women and property, he draws the same picture here as he has done in the *Republic*: there is the same form of education in both; the citizens of both are exempt from servile occupations; and both make provision for common meals. Notice, however, that in the *Laws* he extends these common meals to women; and the fighting men number 5,000,[4] whereas in the *Republic* there are only 1,000 of them.[5]

(1) The discourses of Socrates[6] are always of outstanding quality; they have grace and originality, and they show a keen spirit of inquiry. Shortcomings, however, are almost unavoidable. One cannot, for instance, help commenting on the figure 5,000; a territory as large as Babylon or some equally enormous site will be required to support that number of people in idleness,

---

[1] Ibid., ii. 373 E.
[2] Ibid., iii. 412 D.
[3] Ibid., v. 451 E.
[4] *Laws*, v. 737 E, where the actual number given is 5,040.
[5] *Republic*, iv. 423 A.
[6] Aristotle identifies the Athenian Stranger of the *Laws* with Socrates.

not to mention a crowd of women and attendants many times
as great.   One is never justified in making an assumption that
lies outside the bounds of possibility.

(2) According to Plato,[1] a legislator should go to work with
his eye on two points—the territory and its inhabitants.   But
(a) he will also do well to keep neighbouring countries in view,
firstly because his state is to have a political as opposed to an
isolated existence.   A state must employ such arms as are
adapted to foreign service [2] and not merely of use at home.
Even supposing that a life of active service is not the best, either
for individuals or for states, the fact remains that a state should
be formidable to its enemies, whether they are invading or in
retreat.   (b) We must also inquire whether the amount of
property should not be defined differently, i.e. more clearly,
than in the *Laws*, where Plato says [3] that a man should have so
much property as will 'enable him to live temperately,' which is
the equivalent of 'to live well.'   This is too vague a conception;
besides, a man may live temperately and yet miserably.   A
better formula would be, that a man should have that amount of
property which will enable him to live temperately but liberally,[4]
if only because temperance and liberality are the only praiseworthy habits attaching to the use of property.[5]   (c) It is inconsistent to equalize landed property unless at the same time one
controls the birth-rate.   Plato, on the other hand, would set no
limit to the population; [6] he thinks, in accord with present
experience, that it will even itself out in consequence of a certain
number of marriages proving infertile, however many children
are born to others.   [1265^b] But in a state like that described in
the *Laws* it will be necessary to regulate the population more
stringently than is done to-day.   At present, no matter how
large the citizen body, property is so distributed that no one is
destitute; but if it is made indivisible, as in the *Laws*, the surplus
population, however large or small, will get nothing.   One

[1] Cf. *Laws*, iv. 704–9 and v. 747 D.
[2] Ibid., i. 625 C seqq.
[3] Ibid., v. 737 D.
[4] If you separate the two, liberality will degenerate into luxury and
temperance into hardship.—(A.)
[5] It is impossible, for instance, to use property *mildly* or *courageously*; but
one can do so with temperance and liberality, which are therefore inseparably
bound up with property.—(A.)
[6] See, however, *Laws*, v. 740 B–741 A.   Aristotle cannot have overlooked
this passage; he would probably have justified his criticism here by remarking
that Plato, whatever he intended, proposes no effective means to achieve his
purpose.

would indeed have thought it even more necessary to limit reproductive intercourse than to limit property. In that case the permitted birth-rate should allow for the probable figures of infant mortality and of barrenness or sterility in married persons. To leave the birth-rate unrestricted, as is done in the majority of states, is a sure cause of poverty, which in turn begets revolution and crime. Pheidon of Corinth, in fact, one of the earliest legislators, thought that the number of family allotments and the number of citizens should be kept equal to one another, even though the allotments were originally of different sizes; but in the *Laws* the opposite is recommended. We shall have to explain later on what we think is the better arrangement.[1]

(3) The *Laws* fail likewise to determine how the rulers will differ from the ruled; Plato says merely that they are related as the warp to the woof, which are made of different wools.[2]   (4) He allows a man's whole property to increase fivefold;[3] why then should not his plot of land also increase to a certain extent? Again (5), will his distribution of farmhouses contribute to good household management? He assigns to each citizen two separate houses in different parts of the allotment,[4] but it is difficult to run two houses.

(6) Plato's entire system of government falls somehow between the two stools of democracy and oligarchy; it is what is known as a polity, with the citizens drawn exclusively from those who bear arms.[5] Now, if he intended to frame a constitution suitable to the majority of states, he was no doubt right, but not if he meant it as next best after his ideal constitution as described in the *Republic*: many would prefer the Spartan form [6] of government, or some other system more aristocratic than that represented by the *Laws*. Some, in fact, hold that the best constitution is a mixture of all existing schemes. This is why they admire the Spartan regime. It is a compound, they say, of oligarchy, monarchy, and democracy; the kings form the monarchical, the council of elders the oligarchical element, while democracy is represented by the ephors, who are chosen

---

[1] See pages 199, 205, and 217–18 for a partial but inadequate fulfilment of this promise.
[2] *Laws*, v. 734 E, 735 A.
[3] Ibid., v. 744 E.   Plato says 'fourfold,' but we may infer from thecontext that he meant four times the value of the allotment *plus* the allotment itself.
[4] Ibid., v. 745 C.
[5] Cf. page 78, line 15.
[6] But in Book IV he treats the Spartan constitution as an example of polity.

from among the people.[1] [1266[a]] But according to the *Laws*,[2] the best constitution should be a compound of democracy and tyranny, which either cannot be called constitutions at all, or which are, at best, the worst of all. One is nearer the truth in attempting to combine more than two forms, because the excellence of a constitution is proportionate to the number of its elements. That proposed in the *Laws* seems devoid of any monarchical strain; it is a cross between oligarchy and democracy, with the former predominating. This is apparent from the mode of appointing magistrates.[3] Their choice by lot from a prepared list of candidates combines both elements; but to compel the rich by law to attend the assembly [4] and vote for magistrates, or to discharge other political duties, while the rest may please themselves, is an oligarchical feature. So is the attempt [5] to make sure that a majority of these magistrates shall be chosen from the rich and the most important officers from the highest income group. The same kind of feature characterizes the election of the council.[6] All are obliged to vote in the choice of candidates to represent the first and second property classes; the same number of candidates as in each of these latter cases is chosen to represent the third property class, although here the obligation extends only to voters of the first three classes. Selection of candidates to represent the fourth property class is compulsory on the first and second only. Then, says Plato, an equal number representing each property class is to be chosen from the candidates thus selected. The result, of course, will be a preponderance of members drawn from the higher income groups, because many of the lower classes will not vote at all since they are not compelled to do so. These considerations, and others which we shall notice when the time comes to discuss the best constitution, prove that it should not be a compound of democracy and monarchy. There is also danger in the election of magistrates from a body of candidates which has itself been elected; [7] for a mere handful of people have but to combine, and the elections will always go as they desire. So much for the *Laws* and the constitution it proposes.

---

[1] Others maintain that the ephoralty is tyrannical, and that the democratic element is to be found in the system of common meals and the general pattern of everyday life.—(A.)

[2] iii 693 D, 701 E; iv. 710; vi. 756 E, which Aristotle here misinterprets.

[3] Ibid., vi. 756, 763 E, 765.   [4] Ibid., vi. 764 A.

[5] Ibid., vi. 763 D, E.   [6] Ibid., vi. 756 B–E.

[7] Ibid., vi. 753 D.

3. PHALEAS OF CHALCEDON

Other constitutional schemes—some of them drawn up by amateurs, others by philosophers and statesmen—come nearer to systems now in force than do either of Plato's. No one else, for example, has proposed such innovations as community of wives and children or common meals for women; most legislators begin with what is fundamental. Some hold that the regulation of property is the most important item in any such programme, because it is always the pivot of revolutionary movements.

Phaleas of Chalcedon, recognizing this fact, was the first to propose equal distribution of landed property among all the citizens of a state. [1266^b] He believed that an arrangement of this kind could be made without much difficulty in a new colony, but not so easily in a long-established community. Here, he thought, the quickest means of accomplishing reform would be for the rich to give but not receive dowries, and for the poor to receive but not to give them.

Plato, in the *Laws*,[1] held that accumulation should be allowed up to a certain point; but, as I have noted,[2] he would allow no citizen to accumulate more than five times the amount owned by any other citizen.

Now (1), those who make such laws should remember something that is too often forgotten, viz. that if you are going to fix the amount of a man's property you must also fix the number of his children. For if the children become too many for the property, the law [3] will have to be abrogated; quite apart from which, it is undesirable that many should descend from wealth to poverty, because such people are almost certain to foster revolution. Some of the old lawgivers recognized that political society is affected by the equalization of property. Solon and others, for example, introduced laws restricting the amount of land which an individual might possess. Other laws forbid the sale of property; no Locrian,[4] for instance, may sell his property unless he can show beyond all shadow of doubt that he has suffered some grave misfortune. Again, there have been laws providing that original allotments of land must be kept intact;

---

[1] v. 744 E.
[2] Page 41. Phaleas, a contemporary of Plato, dealt with landed property; Plato was concerned with a man's entire property.
[3] i.e. the law imposing equality of property.
[4] The reference is probably to the Italian Locrians.

and the abrogation of such a law at Leucas made the constitution too democratic by admitting men to office on the strength of less than the prescribed qualification.   Property, however, may be equally distributed in such a way that the amount is either too large or too small, in which case the owner will live either in luxury or in penury.   Clearly, then, it is not enough for the legislator to equalize property; he must aim also at moderation in the unit upon which equality is based.   Even so, he will not do much good by prescribing this amount for all alike; it is not so much the *property* as the *desires* of men that need equalizing, and that cannot be done unless the laws provide a satisfactory education.   Phaleas would no doubt reply that this is exactly what he has in mind when he says that every state should have equality both of property and of education.   Still, he should have told us what *kind* of education he proposes; there is no use in having one and the same education for all if that 'one and the same' tends to breed avarice or ambition, or both.   Again, civil discord arises not only from inequality of property, but also from inequality of the offices which may be held.   Note, however, that distribution of property works in the opposite way from distribution of office.   The common people are driven to rebellion by *inequality* in the distribution of property; educated men become restive when office is *equally* distributed—'office and honour,' as Homer says, 'are one and the same for both good and bad.' [1]

(2) Men take to crime not only (*a*) for the necessaries of life,[2] but also (*b*) for mere pleasure: they wish to gratify a longing which goes beyond the bare necessities of life, and even (*c*) to fulfil a craving for superfluities with a view to painless delights.[3] How are these three disorders to be cured?   The first by a modest estate and some kind of occupation; the second by temperate habits.   As for the third, those who desire to be independent of others for their enjoyment must look to philosophy and nowhere else for a remedy, because all other pleasures presuppose the assistance of our fellow men.   As a matter of fact, the greatest crimes are due to excess rather than to want. Men do not, for example, play the tyrant in order to keep out the cold; and hence great honour is bestowed not so much upon a man who kills a thief as upon one who slays a tyrant.

[1] *Iliad*, ix. 319.
[2] Phaleas expects to find a remedy for such crimes in the equalization of property, which will prevent a man turning to highway robbery through cold or hunger.—(A.)
[3] See *Nic. Eth.* 1176[b]18.

The constitution of Phaleas, accordingly, will do no more than prevent petty misdemeanours. Besides, (3) it is designed chiefly to promote the state's internal welfare, whereas a legislator should also have regard to his immediate neighbours and to the outside world at large. The government must be organized with a view to military strength, about which Phaleas says nothing; so too must property, which should be adequate not only to supply home requirements, but also to meet danger from without. The property of the state should not be so large as to invite the envy of more powerful neighbours while the owners are powerless to resist invasion, nor yet so small that the state cannot wage war even against others of equal power and similar institutions. Phaleas says nothing definite on this point; but it should be borne in mind that *some* degree of wealth is an advantage. Exactly how much? Well, I suggest it ought not to be so excessive as to encourage a stronger neighbour to attack more readily than he would do were it less. There is a story that when Autophradates was preparing to besiege Atarneus, Eubulus bade him consider how long it would take to reduce that stronghold, and then to reckon up the cost entailed thereby. He was willing, he said, in return for a smaller sum than that, to evacuate Atarneus at once. His words impressed Autophradates who forthwith abandoned the siege.[1]

(4) (*a*) It is all very well to claim that equal distribution of property is one of those things that help to deter the citizens from quarrelling among themselves. Even so, the upper classes will be dissatisfied, believing themselves worthy of more than an equal share of honours; and this fact is not seldom at the root of sedition and revolution. (*b*) [1267^{b}] Man's greed is unbounded. There was a time when he was satisfied with an allowance of two obols,[2] but now that this has become traditional there is an unending demand for more and more. Most men live for the gratification of desire, which is of its very nature insatiable. Hence the first step towards reform is not so much to equalize property as to train conscientious people not to *desire* more, and to prevent the baser sort from *getting* more.

[1] Eubulus was a Bithynian money-changer who had got possession of Atarneus and Assos at a time when the Persian empire was breaking up. He was succeeded, about 352 B.C., by Hermias, who was Aristotle's host when he left Athens following Plato's death. The episode to which Aristotle refers occurred probably about 359 B.C. when the Persians under Autophradates were operating in this region against the revolted satrap Artabazus.

[2] Each Athenian citizen was granted this sum in the fifth century B.C. to pay for his seat in the theatre during dramatic festivals.

These latter must be kept down, though not by unjust means. (c) Phaleas sets about equalizing property in the wrong way. His measures affect only the land, whereas it is possible to be rich in slaves, cattle, and money, as well as in abundance of what are commonly called movables. So one must either attempt to equalize the distribution of all or none of these things, or else some moderate maximum must be imposed. It is also evident from the legislation of Phaleas that he has quite a small state in mind, if, as he supposes, all the artisans are to be public slaves and not to form a supplementary part of the citizen body. But any such law should apply only to those engaged on public works, as at Epidamnus, or on the plan once devised for Athens by Diophantus.

From these observations you may judge the value or otherwise of the constitutional scheme proposed by Phaleas.

4. HIPPODAMUS OF MILETUS

Hippodamus,[1] son of Euryphon, was a native of Miletus. Not only did he aspire to learning in the field of natural science, but he was the first person not a statesman who set himself to inquire into the best form of government. (1) The city which he had in mind was to consist of 10,000 souls divided into three classes—one of artisans, one of farmers, and a third of professional soldiers for defence. (2) He divided the land similarly into three parts—sacred, public, and private. The first of these was to maintain the established worship of the gods, the second to support the military, while the third was to be the property of the agricultural class. (3) He favoured only a threefold division of the laws, corresponding to the three subjects of legal action which he distinguished, viz. assault, damage, and homicide. He likewise proposed a single court of supreme jurisdiction, to which all cases of appeal against decisions of the lower courts might be referred, and this tribunal was to consist of elders chosen for the purpose. Moreover [1268ᵃ] he considered that judgment should not be given by means of a voting-pebble, but that each member of the court should hand in a

[1] Hippodamus was the first town-planner, and it was he who laid out the Peiraeus. Apart from his architectural innovations, he was a man who loved the limelight, which led him into eccentric habits. The result was that some looked upon him as a crank, with his flowing hair and those expensive ornaments worn with cheap but warm clothing which he affected both in summer and winter.—(A.)

tablet inscribed with the formula of simple condemnation, left blank to indicate simple acquittal, or suitably marked to distinguish partial condemnation and partial acquittal.[1] Hippodamus objected to the existing procedure on the grounds that it might compel a juror to perjure himself whichever way he voted. He proposed (4) that anyone who invented something beneficial to the state should be rewarded, and (5) that the children of those killed in action should be supported out of public funds.[2] (6) He would have all magistrates elected by the people, i.e. by the three classes mentioned in (1) above; and those so elected were to watch over the interests of the public, of aliens, and of orphans.

Beyond these points there is little else worthy of remark in the constitution of Hippodamus; but the following objections may be raised. With regard to (1), all three classes (artisans, farmers, and soldiers) have political rights;[3] but the farmers have no arms, and the artisans neither arms nor land, so that they become in effect slaves of the military class. It is consequently impossible for them to share in all the offices; for generals, police officials, and most of the principal magistrates must be drawn from among those who carry arms. But how can those who have no direct share in the government be loyal citizens? It may be argued that those who possess arms should be superior to both the other classes; but this is unlikely unless they are numerous. And if they *are* superior, why should the others enjoy political rights to the extent of having power to elect magistrates? In any case, of what use are farmers to the state? Artisans there must certainly be; every state needs them, and they can make a living by their several crafts, no matter what the constitution. The farmers too might justify their existence as part of the citizen body if they provided the military class with food; but Hippodamus assigns them land of their own, which they cultivate for their personal benefit. With regard to (2), a question as to the public land from which the military are to be supported. If these latter cultivate it themselves, they will be indistinguishable from the farmers whom Hippodamus recognizes as a separate class. If, on the other hand, there is to be a body of farmers distinct both from those who cultivate their own land and from the military, it will form a fourth class

---

[1] This last provision was intended to overcome the objection next mentioned.
[2] He believed this to be something quite new; but such a law has long been in force at Athens [cf. Thucydides, ii. 46] and elsewhere.—(A.)
[3] i.e. in so far as they elect to magistracies.

which will have no share in anything and will be alien to the constitution. Now if anyone suggests that the same individuals will cultivate both their own *and* the public lands, I reply that it will be a difficult matter for them to produce enough for the maintenance of two households; [1] and why, [1268^b] in this case, should there be any distinction between public and private land, when they might obtain food for themselves and supply the military from the land as a whole, cultivated as a number of separate allotments? Surely all this is most confused.

Passing to (3), his method of securing a judicial decision is equally disappointing. (*a*) To allow a qualified verdict even when the issue is perfectly straightforward, is to convert the juror into an arbitrator. A qualified verdict is possible in a court of arbitration, even where there are several arbitrators, for they can confer with one another as to their decision. But this is not so in a court of law; on the contrary, most legislators are careful to prevent the members holding any communication with one another. Besides, imagine the confusion that will result if a juror assesses damages at less than the plaintiff asks! Suppose the claim is for twenty minae, and one juror allows, say, ten,[2] another five, and a third four minae. In this way they will continue to split up the damages: at one end of the scale some will grant the whole amount, and others at the opposite end nothing at all; how is the matter to be decided? (*b*) There is no question of perjury on the part of a juror who votes for simple acquittal or condemnation, provided the indictment has been laid in an unqualified form; after all, the juror who acquits in such a case is not deciding that the defendant owes nothing, but merely that he does not owe the twenty minae. Perjury arises only when a juror believes the claim unjustified but votes against the defendant.

As to (4), there is a fine ring in the proposal to reward those who discover anything beneficial to the state. But it is dangerous to lend such a scheme the authority of law: it will certainly encourage informers, and may even result in political upheavals. This question involves another and somewhat different problem. Some have doubted the expediency of making any change in the time-honoured laws of a state, even if they are capable of improvement; and if such a change is always inexpedient, we

---

[1] A farmer's own and that of a soldier.
[2] Or the claim may be for a larger sum, and one juror will allow something less.—(A.)

cannot easily accept the scheme put forward by Hippodamus: it would facilitate the introduction of measures which, though disguised as public benefits, are calculated to destroy the laws or the constitution. While on this subject it will be as well to examine it in a little more detail; for, as I was saying, there is some difference of opinion, and it may sometimes appear wise to make a change. Elsewhere in the field of knowledge change has proved an unquestionable advantage. Medicine, for instance, and physical training, along with many other arts and crafts, have departed from tradition; and therefore if politics be considered an art, it must surely benefit likewise. That it has actually done so is proved by the fact that ancient usages were extremely simple and uncivilized: the early Greeks, for example, went about armed [1] and bought their brides of one another.[2] Moreover, the few survivals of ancient law are altogether ridiculous: [1269ᵃ] at Cyme,[3] for example, there is a law that in cases of homicide the accused may be tried for murder if the prosecutor brings forward a certain number of witnesses from among his own kinsfolk. The common run of men desire what is good and not merely what is traditional; and it is reasonable to suppose that the first human beings (whether they were earth-born or had survived some cataclysm) were similar to ordinary or even weak-minded people nowadays.[4] It would therefore be absurd to rest contented with their ideas. Even written laws should not be exempt from alteration. For in politics, as in other arts, it is impossible to write down every rule with absolute precision; legal enactments must be general in scope, but actions are concerned with particulars.[5] Hence it is clear that sometimes and in some cases the law should be changed. But if we look at the matter from another angle, there would seem to be need of the utmost caution. It is bad policy to get into the way of abrogating laws without careful consideration, and when the advantage to be gained is likely to be small it is manifestly better to overlook some mistakes both in legislation and in government. The state will benefit less by effecting a change than it will lose by continually flouting the authority of law. The analogy drawn from the arts is

---

[1] Thucydides, i. 5, 6.
[2] Cf. Herodotus, v. 6.
[3] It is not known to which city of this name Aristotle refers.
[4] So, at any rate, tradition says [cf. Plato, *Laws*, iii. 677 B; *Timaeus*, 22 D] concerning the earth-born men.—(A.)
[5] Cf. Plato, *Politicus*, 295 A.

misleading; for to alter a law is not the same thing as changing an art. Law has no power to secure obedience other than that of habit. But habit can only develop over a period of time, so that undue readiness to change from existing laws to new ones is to weaken the force of law. Even if it is permissible to make such a change, it may fairly be asked whether this is true of all laws and under every form of government. Again, are they to be changed by anyone at random or only by certain persons? There is a great difference between these alternatives, so let us postpone their discussion to a more suitable time.[1]

[1] He does not resume the subject.

B. EXISTING FORMS OF GOVERNMENT

1. SPARTA

Two questions arise concerning the social and political organization of Sparta and Crete, as indeed of most other systems of government: first, whether a particular law is good or bad when judged by the norm of an *ideal* regime; and secondly, whether such a law is or is not in harmony with the principles and character of the constitution *as actually established* by the legislator.

(1) It is agreed that leisure is an essential of every well-ordered state: the citizens must be free from the necessity of supplying their own day-to-day requirements. But it is difficult to see how this can be arranged. The penestae in Thessaly [1] have often risen against their masters, as have the helots against the Spartans, for whose misfortunes they continually lie in wait. Nothing like this has ever happened in Crete, [1269ᵇ] for the probable reason that here the neighbouring cities, even when at war with one another, never ally themselves with disaffected serfs, because they themselves have dependent populations and it does them no good to countenance rebellion. But when the helots first revolted, all Sparta's neighbours (Argives, Messenians, Arcadians) were her enemies; and the original revolt of the serfs in Thessaly was due to that country being still at war with the neighbouring Achaeans, Perrhaebians, and Magnesians. Besides, the management of slaves is likely to prove difficult at the best of times. Unless kept in hand, they become insolent and consider themselves as good as their masters; if harshly treated they are embittered and conspire against them. Now results of this kind go to show that a state has yet to learn the right method of handling its subject population.

(2) The licence permitted women defeats the aim of the Spartan constitution and is harmful to the welfare of that state. For as husband and wife are constituent elements of a household, we may regard the state as about equally divided into men and women; so that, in a state where the women are disorderly, half

[1] The penestae were serfs, corresponding more or less to the Spartan helots.

of it may be considered as without the rule of law. And this is what has happened in Sparta. Her lawgiver [1] wished to make the whole civic body tough and self-disciplined, and no one can deny the men are so; but he overlooked the women, who give free rein to every form of intemperance and luxury. In such a state it is inevitable that wealth is too highly prized, especially if the men are dominated by their womenfolk, as is so with most militaristic and warlike races, except the Celts and a few others [2] who openly favour homosexual intercourse. It was apparently not without good reason that the old mythologer paired off Ares with Aphrodite, for indeed all martial races seem prone to passionate devotion to members of their own or of the opposite sex. The latter prevailed at Sparta, and in the days of her hegemony women had their fingers in many a pie. But what is the difference between women ruling and the rulers being ruled by women? The result is the same. Spartan women have exercised a most pernicious influence even in the matter of physical courage, which is of no use in daily life but only for purposes of war.

There was an example of this during the Theban invasions,[3] when, unlike the women of other states, they were utterly useless and caused more confusion than the enemy. Female licence at Sparta dates from the earliest times, and this is not altogether surprising. [1270ᵃ] For during a long series of wars against the Argives, Arcadians, and Messenians the men were constantly from home on active service; and having been trained to discipline by army life (which has many good points), they placed themselves in the legislator's hands when peace returned, ready enough to accept whatever he laid down. But according to tradition, when Lycurgus tried to subject the women to his laws, they stubbornly refused, and he gave up the attempt. Such, then, are the causes [4] not only of particular events, but of this flaw in the constitution. We are not, however, asking what is or is not to be excused, but what is right or wrong; and female licence, as I have suggested, tends somehow to foster avarice, as well as spoiling the harmony of the constitution in itself.

(3) My last remark inspires a further criticism, directed this

---

[1] Lycurgus. He is now regarded as a legendary figure—an old Arcadian deity whose cult was taken over by Sparta.

[2] e.g. (in the Greek world) Thebans, Cretans, and Chalcidians.

[3] 369–362 B.C.

[4] The causes to which Aristotle here refers are the absence of the men on active service, and lack of preparatory discipline in the women.

time at the unequal distribution of property. It so happens that some of the Spartans have very large estates, others quite small ones; and so a small minority has gained possession of the land. This has been badly handled by legislation; for while the law-giver would rightly have us despise those who sell or purchase their land, he empowers anyone who pleases to give or bequeath it. Both practices, of course, have the same result. In point of fact, about two-fifths of the whole country belong to women, thanks to the number of heiresses and the practice of giving large dowries. It would surely have been better to have prohibited dowries altogether, or to have fixed them at a moderate, if not quite small, amount. As things are, a man may give his heiress in marriage to anyone he chooses, and, if he dies without having disposed of her by will, his heir male may do so. Hence, although the country would have supported 1,500 cavalry and 30,000 heavy infantry, the total number had fallen [1] below 1,000. History shows how inadequate were Sparta's property laws. She was overwhelmed by a single defeat; lack of men was her ruin. It is said that her early kings used to extend the rights of citizenship to aliens, and that therefore, despite their long-drawn-out wars, they suffered no shortage of manpower. We are told, in fact, that at one time Sparta had no fewer than 10,000 citizens. Whether or not this is true, it would have been better for her to have maintained her numbers by an equal dis-tribution of property. But the law relating to the procreation of children is the opposite of helpful in this last respect. The legislator, wishing [1270ᵇ] the Spartans to be as numerous as possible, encouraged his citizens to produce as many children as they could.[2] Yet it is obvious that, granted a high increase in the birth-rate, a proportionate distribution of land will force many such children into poverty.

We come now (4) to a criticism of the Spartan ephoralty, a board of magistrates which enjoys supreme authority in matters of the highest importance. Its members are chosen from the whole people, with the result that very poor men often find themselves elected to an office where their indigence lays them open to bribery. The annals of Sparta contain many such instances, including the recent affair at Andros [3] when some of

---

[1] Before the Theban invasions.
[2] His encouragement took the form of a law exempting the father of three sons from military service, and the father of four from all state-imposed obligations.—(A.)
[3] It is not certain to what episode Aristotle refers.

the ephors were bribed and did their best to ruin the state. Their power, indeed, is so great, amounting almost to tyranny, that even the kings have been obliged to seek their favour. And in this way, too, not only the royal office, but the constitution as a whole has deteriorated; democracy has superseded aristocracy. It is true, of course, that the ephoralty does hold the state together; their right to share in the highest office keeps the people contented, and this result, whether intended by the legislator or merely accidental, has proved beneficial. If a constitution is to be permanent, all sections of the community must desire its continuance, as is the case at Sparta. The kings do so because it upholds their dignity; the nobles because they are represented in the senate;[1] and the people because all have a chance of election to the ephoralty. It is perfectly right that all citizens should be eligible; but (a) the method of their election is altogether wrong—childish beyond words;[2] and (b) since the ephors have jurisdiction in important cases[3] (although they are quite ordinary men), their decisions should be based not on private judgment, but on written rules drawn up in legal form. Moreover (c), their way of life is inconsistent with the spirit of the constitution. They have far too much licence, whereas the rest of the citizens are subject to a discipline so stern that they find it intolerable and escape from the law into the secret indulgence of sensual delights.

(5) The senate is not what it might be. (a) You may say that its members are good men, well trained in manly virtue, and that therefore they are an asset to the state. But it is open to dispute whether the judges of so high a court[4] should hold office for life; after all, there is such a thing as mental as well as physical senility. [1271ª] Besides, (b) there is real danger when men have been educated in such a manner that the legislator himself cannot trust them; and we know for certain that many of those holding this office have taken bribes and been guilty of favouritism in public affairs. It would be better if they were answerable for their conduct, which at present they are not. You may reply that all Spartan magistrates are responsible to the ephors; but I maintain that this confers too great a prerogative on the

---

[1] The office of senator is a reward of virtue.—(A.)

[2] The exact method is uncertain. Plato (*Laws*, 692 A) describes the ephorate as 'an office as good as filled by lot'; from which Susemihl and others conclude that the procedure involved some form of taking auspices.

[3] Scrutiny of accounts, private contracts, and constitutional issues.

[4] The senate tried cases of homicide.

ephoralty, and that control should not be exercised in this way. Further, (c) the Spartan method of electing senators is absolutely puerile.[1] Nor is it desirable that men should offer themselves for election; the worthiest should be obliged to take office whether they like it or not. But in this matter the legislator clearly reveals the same intention as appears elsewhere in his constitution: he was trying to form a body of citizens eager for distinction, and therefore adopted this procedure[2] in the election of senators; for no one would seek office unless he were ambitious. Yet of all human cravings, ambition and avarice are, I should say, the most powerful motives of crime.

(6) Whether or not kings are an advantage to states, we shall consider at another time.[3] In any case they should be chosen, not as at present in Sparta,[4] but on the basis of their personal life and conduct. It is clear that the legislator himself entertained small hope of fashioning them into models of mankind; at all events, he shows considerable mistrust of their virtue. This is why the Spartans, when dispatching their kings on embassy, used to have them accompanied by other envoys with whom they were at variance; and quarrels between the kings themselves were looked upon as a political advantage.

(7) Whoever originated the common meals known as *phiditia* deserves little credit for his regulations. These gatherings should be chargeable to public funds, as in Crete; but at Sparta each person is expected to contribute his share, though some are extremely poor and cannot afford to do so. The result is to frustrate the legislator's intention. He devised common meals as a popular institution, but their present organization is quite the opposite: the very poor find it difficult to take part in them, though ancient custom ordains that failure to contribute entails the loss of citizen rights.

(8) The Spartan admiralty law has been rightly criticized as a root of dissension; to appoint an admiral as a check upon the kings, who are permanent commanders-in-chief, is to set up yet another king.

(9) The aim [1271^b] of Spartan legislation is exactly such as

---

[1] Plutarch (*Lycurgus*, 26) tells us that senators were chosen by the comparative loudness of the shouts of approval which greeted the appearance of each candidate in the assembly.
[2] i.e. of offering oneself for election.
[3] Book III, pages 92–100.
[4] The two Spartan kings held office jointly and represented the two Heraclid families of the Eurypontidae and Agidae.

Plato rightly criticizes in the *Laws*.[1]   That legislation is directed
to a single aspect of virtue—the military virtue, which is a source
of power.   So long as the Spartans were at war they continued
to flourish; but as soon as they had won an empire they collapsed,
for they knew not how to employ their leisure, having never
engaged in any employment higher than war.   They are guilty,
besides, of a no less disastrous error in recognizing that the goods
for which men strive are obtained by virtue rather than by vice,
and yet at the same time imagining that these goods are preferable to the virtue whereby they have been acquired.

(10) The Spartans mismanage their public revenues; for
while they are obliged to fight large-scale wars, the treasury is
empty and they begrudge the payment of taxes.[2]   Most of the
land is owned by the citizens,[3] who accordingly turn a blind eye
to one another's contributions.   The legislator has engendered
a situation the opposite of beneficial, by making the state poor
and the citizens avaricious.

Enough, then, with regard to the Spartan constitution of
which these are the principal defects.

2. CRETE

The constitution of Crete [4] bears a close resemblance to that
of Sparta; in some points it is quite as good, though for the most
part less neatly devised.   Most of the older constitutions are
less elaborate than later ones, and it has been aptly remarked [5]
that the Spartan is virtually an imitation of the Cretan.   According
to tradition, Lycurgus,[6] on laying down the guardianship of King
Charillus, went abroad and spent most of his time in Crete,
where the city of Lyctus forms a bond between the two
countries.[7]

---

[1] i. 625 E, 630.
[2] Cf. Thucydides, i. 80, 4.
[3] i.e. the Spartan 'peers,' as distinct from the perioeci and helots.
[4] Since Crete never formed a single state, these words must refer to the
constitution which prevailed in all or most of the Cretan cities.
[5] By Herodotus, i. 65.
[6] The supposed legislator of Sparta.   See page 52, footnote 1.
[7] The Lyctians were a colony of Sparta, who, on their arrival in Crete,
took over the legal system then in use among the inhabitants.   Even to-day
the perioeci are governed by the original code supposed to have been drawn
up by Minos.   Moreover, the island is so situated that nature seems to have
intended it for sovereignty in the Greek world: it dominates the whole sea
around which most of the Hellenes are settled—one end no great distance

The Cretan institutions are analogous to the Spartan. (1) The helots cultivate the lands of Sparta, the perioeci [1272ᵃ] those of Crete; and both Cretans and Spartans have a system of common meals. These were anciently called by the Spartans not *phiditia* but *andria*, and the Cretan use of this latter word shows that common meals originated in Crete. (2) The two constitutions are likewise analogous: (*a*) the ephors have the same functions as the so-called cosmoi in Crete, the only difference being that there are five ephors as against ten cosmoi; (*b*) the kingly office once existed in Crete, but was later abolished, and the cosmoi are now commanders-in-chief of the armed forces; (*c*) all classes have a voice in the assembly, which, however, can do no more than ratify the decrees of the elders and the cosmoi.

(1) Common meals are better organized in Crete than in Sparta, where the law obliges every man to contribute so much per head, or else, as I have already noted, to forfeit the rights of citizenship. (*a*) The Cretan system is on a more popular footing: one portion of all agricultural produce and live-stock raised on public land, as well as of the rent in kind paid by the perioeci, is devoted to state worship and public services; the other is reserved for common meals, so that men, women, and children [1] are provided for out of public funds. (*b*) The lawgiver has devised many ingenious ways of (i) securing moderation at table (in the advantages of which he is a firm believer), and (ii) segregating women from men in order to control the birth-rate.[2] All these facts go to show that common meals are better managed in Crete than in Sparta.

(2) The cosmoi, however, are an institution inferior even to the ephoralty, the defects of which they share without any of its good points. Like the ephors, they have no special qualifications, but in Crete this drawback is not offset by any constitutional advantage. At Sparta the ephoralty is open to all alike; and since the entire citizen body has thus a share in the highest

---

from the Peloponnese, the other reaching almost as far as Asian Triopium and Rhodes. From Crete Minos established a thalassocracy, subduing some of the islands and colonizing others, until at last he invaded Sicily, and died there near Camicus.—(A.)

[1] It is clear from Plato (*Laws*, 780 E) that the women and children were not actually present at the common tables.

[2] He sanctions intimacy between males, the morality of which I shall have an opportunity of discussing at another time.—(A.) [The undertaking is nowhere fulfilled.]

office, they are interested likewise in the permanence of their constitution. In Crete, however, the cosmoi are chosen not from the whole people, but from certain families.[1] And it is no use arguing in favour of the institution that the people are content to be excluded; for the office, unlike the ephoralty, is not one of profit. Besides, the cosmoi function in an island and are therefore removed from corrupting influences.[2]

The remedy employed to counteract the effects of this ill-conceived arrangement is quite inappropriate, suited rather to a close oligarchy than to a constitutional state. The cosmoi are often driven from office by a conspiracy of their own colleagues, or of private individuals; and they are also permitted to resign before their term has expired. No, all such matters are better regulated by law than by current whims, which are an unsafe guide. Worst of all is the practice of suspending the office of the cosmoi, a device which the nobles frequently employ in order to impede the course of justice. This goes to show that the Cretan form of government, though to some extent constitutional, is to all intents and purposes a close oligarchy.

Another habit of the Cretan nobles is to create factions among the common people and their own friends; to erect, on that basis, as many monarchies; and then to quarrel and fight among themselves. What is this but the temporary abolition of the state and dissolution of the body politic? A state in this condition is in mortal danger, for her enemies can then attack her at will. However, as I have remarked, Crete is saved by her geographical situation; distance has produced the same effect as the Spartan law excluding strangers, and she has no foreign possessions. This is why the perioeci remain quiet, whereas the Spartan helots are perpetually in revolt. But when invaders from overseas lately found their way into the island,[3] the weakness of its constitution stood revealed. So much for the Cretan form of government.

---

[1] The Cretan elders are elected from among those who have served as cosmoi, and the same criticism is applicable to them as to their Spartan counterparts: their irresponsibility and the fact that they hold office for life is a privilege out of all proportion to their merits, while their discretionary powers, unchecked by written law, are positively dangerous.—(A.)

[2] Aristotle may have in mind the Persian empire or the Greek cities of the mainland. Cf. Herodotus, v. 51.

[3] The reference is most probably to the operations of Phalaecus and his mercenaries in 345 B.C.

3. CARTHAGE

The Carthaginian constitution is universally admired as superior in many ways to those of other states, although in some particulars it bears a strong resemblance to that of Sparta. All three forms of government, in fact—Cretan, Spartan, and Carthaginian—are closely allied, but differ widely from others. Carthage has many fine institutions. The excellence of her governmental system is apparent from the fact that it retains the loyalty of the masses. She has never experienced anything worth calling revolution, and has never been subject to a tyrant.[1]

Points of resemblance between the Carthaginian and Spartan constitutions are as follows. (1) The common meals of the clubs correspond to the Spartan *phiditia*; (2) the Hundred and Four are a body of magistrates similar to the ephors, though whereas the latter are chosen from all and sundry, the former are elected on ground of merit—a distinct improvement. There is also (3) a similarity between the Carthaginian suffetes and elders and the kings and senate at Sparta. But here again the Carthaginian organization is superior. The suffetes are not necessarily drawn from one and the same family irrespective of its virtues; they are chosen from some distinguished house, and that by election rather than in order of seniority. The office confers extensive powers, [1273ª] and if those appointed to it fall below standard they can do much harm—as the kings have already done at Sparta.

Most of the defects, or deviations from the ideal state, for which the Carthaginian constitution may be criticized are common to all the forms of government mentioned above. Some of the deviations from aristocracy and from polity incline rather to (*a*) democracy, others to (*b*) oligarchy.

(*a*) The suffetes and elders, if unanimous, may decide whether to submit or to withhold a measure from the popular assembly; otherwise that decision lies with the people themselves. Whatever the suffetes and elders *do* lay before the assembly is not only heard but also determined there, and anyone who cares to do so may oppose it—a proceeding which is never allowed in Sparta or Crete.

(*b*) Oligarchical features are: (i) that members of the pentarchies,[2] who have jurisdiction in some important matters, are

[1] Aristotle is no doubt referring exclusively to the period when Carthage was an aristocracy. Cf. page 170, *infra*.
[2] Boards of five magistrates of whom nothing more is known.

chosen by co-optation; (ii) that the pentarchies elect the supreme council of One Hundred; [1] and (iii) that they hold office for longer than any other magistrates. [2] That these boards are unpaid and not chosen by lot is characteristic of an aristocracy; so too are such practices as the trial of all suits by magistrates with universal jurisdiction, as against the Spartan system whereby each class of magistrates has its own exclusive field of jurisdiction.

The Carthaginian constitution, however, deviates from aristocracy towards oligarchy chiefly in a way (iv) that commends itself to popular opinion. It is generally considered that magistrates should be chosen not only for their merit but also for their wealth, because no one can rule satisfactorily without the leisure derived from easy circumstances. If, therefore, election on account of wealth and election on account of merit be respectively characteristic of oligarchy and aristocracy, there must be a third form of government, including, among others, that of Carthage; for the Carthaginians choose their officials (especially the highest, viz. the suffetes and generals) with an eye both to merit *and* to wealth. We must, however, acknowledge this deviation from aristocracy as an error on the legislator's part. His most important duty from the outset is to make sure that the highest class, both in and out of office, shall enjoy leisure and not demean themselves in any way. Even though one must have regard to wealth for the sake of leisure, it is a bad thing that the greatest offices, such as those of the suffetes and generals, should be purchasable. The Carthaginian law as it stands sets a higher value upon wealth than upon virtue, and makes the whole citizen body avaricious. For whenever their masters deem anything honourable, the rest of the population inevitably follow their example; and where virtue is not [1273[b]] respected above all else, aristocracy cannot be firmly established. Those who have been to the expense of purchasing their places will make a habit of repaying themselves; for no one can suppose that while a poor but honest man will desire to profit, the baser sort, having incurred great expense, will not. Therefore they should rule who can rule best; and even if the legislator neglects to provide the good with adequate means, he should at least secure them leisure while in office.

[1] Probably to be identified with the Hundred and Four.
[2] They are virtual rulers both before and after their period of office.—(A.)

Again, it seems to me very bad policy to allow an individual to hold several offices, as the Carthaginians do. 'One man, one job' is a maxim every legislator should bear in mind; nobody should be expected to mend shoes as well as play the flute. Hence, where you have a large state, it is more in accordance with the principles of polity and democracy that a proportionately large number of persons should exercise the several functions of government. For, as we have seen,[1] this arrangement is fairer to all, and any task made familiar by repetition is better and more speedily performed. This advantage of distributing authority is proved by the organization of the army and navy, in both of which almost everyone has to command and to obey.

Although the Carthaginians have a constitution which is in effect oligarchical, they manage to avoid the perils of oligarchy by encouraging the spread of wealth. Every now and again they plant a section of the populace among their dependent cities, thereby healing the defects of their constitution and assuring the stability of the state. But here we may detect the hand of chance, whereas a legislator should himself take measures to forestall dissension. Under present conditions, if by some misfortune a majority of the subjects revolted, there would be no way of restoring order by legal means.

Such is the character of the Spartan, Cretan, and Carthaginian constitutions, which are rightly admired.

4. NOTES ON SOLON AND OTHER LEGISLATORS

Some political theorists have spent their lives without taking any part whatsoever in public affairs; about most of them I have already said all there is to say. Others have served as legislators, either in their own or in foreign states; and of these, some have only framed laws while others have drafted constitutions. Lycurgus (whose constitution for Sparta we have already discussed) and Solon did both.

(1) Solon is often thought to have been an excellent legislator, who put an end to the exclusiveness of the oligarchy, emancipated the common people, established the ancient Athenian democracy, and harmonized the different elements of the state. According to this view the council of Areopagus was oligarchic, the elected magistracy aristocratic, and the courts of law democratic. It would seem, [1274a] however, that the first two of

[1] Page 30, line 27.

these institutions existed before Solon and were taken over by him, but that he created the democracy by giving all citizens a right to sit in the courts. For this he is sometimes blamed, on the grounds that in conferring supreme power on the courts, members of which are chosen by lot, he destroyed the non-democratic elements. As the courts grew more powerful, the people began to dominate the scene; and in order to curry favour with them, the old constitution was transformed into our present democracy. Ephialtes and Pericles curtailed the power of Areopagus; Pericles also introduced the payment of juries, and in this way one demagogue after another added to the strength of the democracy until it became what we see to-day. True enough, but this result appears not to have been intended by Solon; it was due rather to unforeseen circumstances. The people had helped to lay the foundations of Athenian sea-power during the Persian war; they became swollen-headed in consequence, and followed the advice of worthless demagogues, notwithstanding protests from the better class. Solon himself probably gave the people no more power than was absolutely necessary: without the right of electing magistrates and calling them to account, they would have been virtually slaves and hostile to the government. On the other hand, he provided that all offices should be filled by the more reputable and well-to-do section of the community, i.e. by members of the pentecosiomedimni,[1] or of the zeugitae,[2] or again of the so-called knights.[3] The fourth class, consisting of labourers,[4] were ineligible.

Mere lawgivers were Zaleucus,[5] who legislated for the Epizephyrian Locrians, and Charondas of Catana, who did the same for his own city and for other Chalcidian foundations in Italy and Sicily. Philolaus of Corinth was another who legislated for a city not his own, viz. Thebes. A member of the Bacchiad family, he fell in love with Diocles, the Olympian victor; and when the latter fled from Corinth, disgusted at the incestuous love of his mother, Halcyone, Philolaus accompanied

---

[1] Landowners with an income of 500 measures of produce.
[2] With an income of 200 measures.
[3] With an income of 300 measures.
[4] With an income of less than 200 measures.
[5] Some people try to make out that Onomacritus was the first professional lawgiver, and that he, although a Locrian, was trained in Crete, where he lived by the exercise of his prophetic skill; that Thales of Crete [c. 680 B.C.] was his companion; and that Lycurgus and Zaleucus [c. 660 B.C.] were disciples of Thales. But all this rests on a chronological error.—(A.)

him to Thebes, where they both spent the remainder of their days and where their tombs are still pointed out.   These are in full view of one another, though one is visible from Corinthian territory [1] and the other not.   The story goes that the two men themselves appointed the sites—Diocles through horror at his misfortunes, so that the land of Corinth should not be visible from his tomb, and Philolaus that his might be.   [1274[b]] Such was the cause of their settling among the Thebans, whose legislator Philolaus afterwards became.   Among other enactments, he gave them laws regulating the procreation of children, which are known at Thebes as the Laws of Adoption.   This statute is peculiar to Philolaus, and was intended to preserve the original number of land allotments.

There is nothing remarkable in the legislation of Charondas, excepting the prosecution of false witnesses.   He was the first to introduce denunciation for perjury.   His laws are more exact and more carefully drafted than those even of modern legislators.[2]

Some of Draco's [3] laws have survived; but he legislated within the framework of an existing constitution, and there is no peculiarity about them deserving of mention, except their severity which took the form of heavy punishments.

Pittacus also was only a lawgiver, as distinct from the author of a constitution.   One statute peculiar to himself enacted that anyone who committed a crime whilst under the influence of drink should be more severely punished than if he had been sober.   Since men are more prone to violence in drink than when sober, he disregarded the excuse that might be urged in favour of a drunkard, and considered expediency alone.

Andromadas of Rhegium legislated for the Chalcidians in Thrace.   Some of his laws deal with homicide and heiresses, but nothing in them could be described as original.

So much, then, for our inquiry into constitutions which are actually in force, or which various writers have proposed.

---

[1] A distance of about forty miles.
[2] The next passage (1274[b]9–15) is almost certainly an interpolation.   See Appendix I, page 237.
[3] See page 308.

Book III

STATE AND CITIZEN

A. CITIZENSHIP

1. What is a Citizen?

[1274ᵇ32] It is impossible to understand the essence and attributes of any particular form of government until we have answered this question: What is the state? For (1) there is some difference of opinion—you often hear it said that the state has done so and so, while others attribute it rather to the oligarchy or the tyrant [1] as the case may be; and (2) the whole concern of a statesman or legislator is with the state, because (3) a constitution is simply an arrangement of those who inhabit a state, that is to say, of the citizens who compose it in the same way as do the several parts of any other whole. Clearly, therefore, we must begin by asking: [1275ᵃ] Who is a citizen, and what does that word connote? Here again is a moot point; no one will be universally recognized as a true citizen, for he who is so in a democracy will often be otherwise under an oligarchy.

Ignoring those upon whom citizenship has been expressly conferred, or who have obtained it through some other accidental means, we may say (1) that residence in a particular place does not make a man a citizen, for in this respect alien residents and slaves are on a level with him. Nor (2) is he a citizen who has merely the right of suing and of being sued in the courts, for this privilege may be secured to resident aliens by treaty. As a matter of fact, in many places resident aliens do not enjoy even *this* right to the full, but are obliged to choose a legal patron; so that they share only imperfectly in the common enjoyment of the right, and we call them citizens only in a qualified sense, in the same way as we do children, who are too young for the register, and old men who have been excused from civic duties.[2] No, we are looking for a citizen in the strictest sense, one who labours under no such deficiency. His special characteristic is that he has a share both in the administration of justice and in the holding of office. Now offices are of two kinds: some are

[1] Cf. Thucydides, iii, 62, 4 sqq.
[2] We do not refer to children and old men as 'citizens' without qualification, but add that they are respectively below and above the requisite age, or something of that kind. The exact words we may employ do not matter, since our meaning is clear enough. The status of disqualified citizens and exiles raises similar questions and answers.—(A.)

discontinuous, i.e. the same person may not hold them twice, or may do so only after a fixed interval; others, e.g. membership of the courts and of the popular assembly, have no time limit.   It may perhaps be urged that jurors and members of the assembly are not office-holders, that their duties give them no share in the government.   But it is surely ridiculous to maintain that those who have supreme power do not govern. ·In any case the dispute is a mere quibble, arising from the fact that we have no single word covering both the juror and the member of the assembly.   For the sake of accurate analysis, then, let us coin the phrase 'office held for an indefinite period' and designate the citizen as one who shares in the holding of office as defined. This is the most comprehensive definition of a citizen, and best suits all those who are so called.

It must not, however, be forgotten that when the underlying principles of any class of things differ in kind—one of them standing first, another second, and so on—the things belonging to that class, *considered as so belonging*, have little or nothing in common.   Now constitutions manifestly differ in kind; some are superior to others and [1275ᵇ] those which are perversions or deviation forms [1] are necessarily inferior to those which are perfect.   Hence the meaning of 'citizen' must differ according to the form of government.   The definition given above is particularly well suited to the citizen of a democracy, but not necessarily to those living under other constitutions.   There are states, for example, with no popular element, no popular assembly,[2] and in which the hearing of lawsuits is distributed among various boards of magistrates.[3]   All the same, we need not abandon our definition; it only requires modification to include citizens of non-democratic states.   In these latter, members of the assembly and jurors do not hold office for an indefinite period.   They do so for a fixed term; and the functions of deliberating upon and deciding all (or some) matters is assigned to all (or some) of those who enjoy such tenure.   The picture of a citizen now begins to emerge more clearly: (*a*) he who has the right to take part in the deliberative or judicial administration of a particular state is said to be a citizen of that

---

[1] I shall explain presently what I mean by 'deviation forms.'—(A.)

[2] i.e. no *regular* assembly, but only extraordinary convocation.—(A.)

[3] At Sparta, for instance, the ephors (sitting individually) try cases of contract, the senate those of homicide, and so on.   Much the same arrangement is in force at Carthage, where there are certain magistrates with universal jurisdiction.—(A.)

state; (*b*) a group of such persons large enough to be self-sufficing constitutes, broadly speaking, a state.

However, (3) a citizen is commonly defined as one whose parents are or were citizens; *both* parents, that is to say, and not merely the father *or* the mother. Others go still farther back and require as many as two or three or even more generations of citizen forbears. But this rough and ready definition has led others to ask how the grandparents or great-grandparents came to be citizens. Gorgias of Leontini, partly in irony and partly no doubt because he could find nothing else to say, once remarked that just as mortars are things made by mortar-makers, so too the citizens of Larissa are those who have been made by the 'craftsmen' whose trade it is to 'make Larisseans.' But the matter is really quite simple: if they possessed constitutional rights as defined above, then they were citizens. This is a more satisfactory answer to the question, because it is impossible for the test of descent from a citizen-father or mother to apply in the case of the first inhabitants or founders of a state.

There is, I grant, more difficulty as regards those who have obtained citizen rights in consequence of a revolution; e.g. the numerous foreigners and resident aliens of the slave class whom Cleisthenes enrolled in the Athenian tribes after the expulsion of the Thirty Tyrants. The doubt in such cases is, not who *is*, but whether or not he who is actually a citizen *ought to be* one; and then again, [1276ª] whether one who *ought not* to be a citizen *is* one at all, for what ought not to be is equivalent to what is unreal. Well, there certainly are men holding office who have no right to be doing so; but we still describe them as office-holders irrespective of their title. Now the citizen has been defined by his holding some kind of office (deliberative and judicial), and therefore the people in question must still be described as citizens.

2. WHAT IS THE STATE?

Whether those whom we recognize as citizens ought to be so or not is a question closely linked with our previous inquiry. I refer to the problem [1] whether or not a particular act is to be regarded as an act of the state when, for instance, there is a change-over from oligarchy or tyranny to democracy. On such occasions some decline to fulfil their treaty obligations and other

[1] See page 67, lines 3–6.

duties of the kind, on the grounds that these were contracted by, say, the tyrant and not by the state; they hold that some constitutions rest on force and are not established for the common good. But democracies may likewise be founded on violence, in which case we shall have to admit that the acts of a democracy are neither more nor less acts of the state in question than are those of an oligarchy or a tyranny. And this leads us naturally to inquire: Upon what principle are we to say that a state is or is not the same as it was before? To consider only the site and the inhabitants is a superficial approach; for both these may be divided, and some of the inhabitants may dwell in one place and some in another. The difficulty, however, should not be taken too seriously; for the word 'polis' [1] is ambiguous, and the problem is easily solved if that is borne in mind.

Similarly, it may be asked: In cases where men occupy one and the same site, upon what conditions are we entitled to think of the state as one? Surely not by virtue of its being enclosed within walls; for you might surround the whole of Peloponnesus with a wall. Babylon, we may say, is one example of a state whose compass is rather that of a nation than a city; it is supposed to have been captured three days before some of the inhabitants became aware of the fact.[2] True, the statesman must consider the size of the state, and whether or not it should consist of more than one racial element; but these questions may be usefully postponed to another occasion.[3]

Again, are we to say that so long as the race of inhabitants and their place of abode remain the same, the state retains its identity (although the citizens are continually dying and others being born), just as we say that rivers and springs retain *their* identity, even though the water is always flowing away and new supplies taking its place? No, we should rather hold that the state may change, notwithstanding the permanence of its racial stock. Remember, the state is an association, an association of citizens within the framework of a constitution; and therefore when the form of government changes and becomes something different, the state inevitably loses its identity. A tragic chorus, for instance, differs from a comic chorus, even though the members of both may be identical. Likewise we call any combination

---

[1] *Polis* means both 'state' and 'city.'

[2] Cf. Herodotus, i. 191; but he does not mention a period of three days.

[3] Aristotle discusses the size of the state at pages 197–200, and refers in passing to the number of racial elements on pages 143–4.

or compound different when the scheme of its composition
alters. Thus, for example, a harmony containing the same
notes is said to be different according as it is in the Dorian or
Phrygian mode. Now if this is true, it follows that we must
judge the identity of the state mainly with reference to its
constitution; and on this basis we can decide to call it the same
or not the same, without regard to continuity of stock. Whether
or not a state ought to fulfil its obligations once the form of
government has changed is another question.

3. Civic Virtue

Closely allied with the preceding topic is the question whether
or not civic virtue is the same as moral virtue;[1] but before we
embark on this discussion we must, of course, obtain some
general notion of what civic virtue is.

The citizen, like the sailor, is a member of an association.
Sailors have various duties to perform: one is a rower, another a
pilot, another a look-out man, and so on; but it is clear that
while the precise definition of each one's virtue will apply
exclusively to him, there is also a common definition applicable
to them all. All, you see, have a common end in view—the
safety of navigation. Now one citizen differs from another in
the same sort of way, and the safe working of their association,
viz. the constitution, is their common purpose. Civic virtue,
therefore, must be relative to the constitution; and whereas our
test of a good *man* is his possession of one single virtue, which is
virtue in the absolute sense, the fact that there are many forms
of government shows that we cannot say the same of the good
citizen. Hence a good citizen need not possess the virtue which
makes a good man.

We may approach the same question from another angle—
from that of the best or ideal constitution. Although each member of a state is expected to discharge his function properly, and
requires virtue in order to do so, the state cannot consist entirely
of good men. Therefore, since all the citizens cannot be alike,
civic and moral virtue cannot be identical. [1277ᵃ] All must
have civic virtue, for only so can the state be perfect; but all cannot possibly have moral virtue, unless we assume that in the
good state all the citizens must necessarily be good.

Again, the state is composed of dissimilar elements: just as a

[1] Cf. *Nic. Eth.* 1130ᵇ28.

living creature is made up of soul and body, the soul of rational principle and appetite, the family of husband and wife, property of master and slave, so too the state consists of all these and other disparate elements. Therefore the virtue of all the citizens cannot possibly be the same, any more than the excellence of a chorus leader is on a level with that of the performer who stands on either side of him.

The foregoing remarks are sufficient to make clear why the two kinds of virtue are not absolutely and always the same; but does that mean to say that civic and moral virtue will never be the same in individual cases? To this we reply that a good ruler is a good and prudent man, and that a would-be statesman should be prudent. Indeed, some hold that the very education of a ruler differs from that of a subject; and we do in fact see that the sons of kings are taught riding and the art of war. As Euripides says: 'No subtle arts for me,· but what the state requires,' [1] implying that a ruler needs a special kind of education. The virtue of a good ruler is therefore the same as moral virtue. Bearing in mind, however, that subjects as well as rulers are citizens, we must recognize that civic virtue and moral virtue cannot *always* be the same, although *in some cases* they may. The virtue of a ruler differs from that of an ordinary citizen; and this is perhaps the reason why Jason [2] said that he felt hungry when he was not a tyrant, meaning that he did not know how to live as a private person. On the other hand, of course, it may be urged that we admire a man for knowing how to obey as well as how to rule, and that we call him a fine citizen who is able to do both. Now if we agree that moral virtue is a ruling force,[3] and that civic virtue includes ruling and obeying, we cannot maintain that they are equally praiseworthy. Since, then, it is occasionally held (*a*) that the ruler and the subject should have *different kinds* of knowledge, and (*b*) that the citizen should have both kinds of knowledge, and share in both, the inference is immediately clear. (1) There is the rule of a master, by which I mean the kind of rule which is concerned with menial tasks. These the master need not know how to perform, but only how to employ others to discharge them. The former kind of knowledge—i.e. the ability to *perform* menial duties—is degrading. Such duties vary a good deal, and are executed by various classes of slaves, e.g. by manual workers (including

Aeolus, Frag. 16, Nauck².   [2] Tyrant of Pherae in Thessaly.
[3] i.e. it controls the appetites.

mechanics), who, as their name implies, live by the labour of their hands. This is why [1277ᵇ] in some ancient states the working classes were excluded from office, and continued to be so until the advent of extreme democracy. The good man, therefore, the statesman, and the good citizen certainly should not learn the crafts of their inferiors, except occasionally and for their own advantage; otherwise there will cease to be any distinction between master and slave.

But (2) we are not concerned with this kind of rule; there is another sort which men exercise over those who are their equals by birth and free. I refer to 'political' rule,[1] which the ruler must learn by obeying, as he would learn the duties of a cavalry or infantry general by serving under one, and by holding the rank first of a captain, then of a colonel. It has been aptly said,[2] that he who has not learned to obey cannot be a good commander. Ruling and obeying are two different things, but the good citizen ought to be capable of both; civic virtue consists in knowing how to govern like a freeman and how to obey like a freeman.

Returning now to the relation between moral and civic virtue: a good man, like a good citizen, must know how to rule and how to obey. Therefore, considering that the temperance and justice of a ruler are distinct from those of a subject, the virtue (e.g. the justice) of a good man cannot be one sort of virtue, but will include different sorts—one qualifying him to rule, the other to obey—differing as do the temperance and courage of a man and woman. A man would be looked on as a coward if his courage were no more than that of a brave woman, and a woman would seem forward if she were no more modest than a good man; indeed their respective functions in household management are different, for the man's duty is to acquire, and the woman's to look after what he has obtained. Prudence, i.e. directive wisdom, alone belongs exclusively to the ruler; all other virtues appear necessarily common to both ruler and subject. The virtue peculiar to the subject is definitely not prudence in this sense, but only right opinion; for the subject may be compared to a flute-maker, whereas the ruler is like a flute-player who uses what the flute-maker makes.[3]

---

[1] Aristotle means here the rule of a statesman over his fellow citizens in a free state.
[2] Cf. Solon (*apud* Diog. Laert., i. 60).
[3] Cf. Plato, *Republic*, x, 601 D, E.

The above considerations enable us to answer the question whether and to what extent moral virtue is the same as civic virtue.

4. QUALIFICATIONS FOR CITIZENSHIP

There still remains one question about citizenship: Shall we confine it to those who have a right to share in office, or is it to cover mechanics also? If mechanics, who may not hold office, are to be included, there will be citizens who can never attain that virtue of ruling and obeying, which is proper to a good citizen. On the other hand, if mechanics are *not* citizens, what is their status? They are certainly neither resident aliens nor foreigners. Surely we may reply [1278ª] that, as far as this objection goes, it is no more absurd to exclude them than to exclude slaves and freedmen from the above classes. It must be admitted that we cannot reckon as citizens all those without whom the state would cease to exist. Even children are not citizens in the same sense as adult men: the latter are citizens in an absolute sense, but children can be called citizens only if we add the qualification 'underdeveloped.' In ancient times there were some states in which all mechanics were slaves or foreigners, and this accounts for many of them being so to-day. The ideal state will not recognize a mechanic as a citizen; but where he *is* recognized as such our definition of civic virtue will not apply to every citizen, nor indeed to all who are merely free men, but only to those who are exempt from menial duties. Those who perform menial tasks are either slaves who minister to the wants of an individual, or mechanics and labourers who are public servants. Starting at this point and carrying our investigations a little further, we shall understand the position of mechanics and labourers; and indeed what has been said already is of itself, when properly grasped, sufficient explanation.

Since there are many forms of government, there must also be many kinds of citizen, especially of those who are subjects. Hence the mechanic and labourer will be citizens under one constitution, but not, for example, under an aristocracy or so-called rule of the best, in which offices are distributed according to virtue and merit; for the life of a mechanic or labourer is incompatible with the practice of virtue. In oligarchies, where the property qualification for office is high, no labourer can be a citizen; but a mechanic may, for craftsmen are often rich men.

At Thebes, however, there was a law that no tradesman could hold office who had not retired from business for at least ten years. In many states the law goes so far as to admit some foreigners to citizenship. In certain democracies, for example, a man is a citizen by virtue of his mother's citizenship, although his father is an alien. And a similar principle often holds good in the case of illegitimate children; the law confers citizenship upon them when there is a dearth of population. But as the birth-rate increases, first the children of a male or female slave are disqualified; then those of a citizen mother and an alien father; and ultimately the privilege is confined to those whose fathers and mothers are both citizens.

We see then that there are several kinds of citizen, and that he is called a citizen in the highest sense who shares in the offices and honours of the state. Compare, for example, Homer's words 'like some alien without honour'; [1] he implies that one who may not share in the offices and honours of the state is no better than a resident alien. But [2] where persons are excluded from office by underhand means, the privileged classes are out to deceive their fellow men.

[1278^b] As to the question whether moral virtue is identical with civic virtue, what I have said goes to prove that in some states a good man and a good citizen are the same, but in others different. Even when they are the same it is not every citizen who is a good man, but only the statesman and those who have or may have, singly or jointly with others, the conduct of public affairs.

[1] *Iliad*, ix. 648; xvi. 59. Achilles complains that he is so treated by Agamemnon.
[2] *Sc.* although exclusion from office may sometimes be justified.

B. CLASSIFICATION OF CONSTITUTIONS

HAVING answered these questions,[1] we must next consider whether there is one form of government or many,[2] and if many, what they are and how many, and what are the differences between them.

A constitution is the organization of a state with regard to its offices, especially to that which is supreme in all matters.[3] The civic body is everywhere sovereign in the state, and the civic body is in fact the constitution. In democracies, for example, the people are supreme, but in oligarchies the few; therefore we say that these two forms of government differ from one another, and so in other cases.

We must first ascertain (1) the end for which the state exists, and (2) by how many forms of government human society is regulated.

(1) As I explained in Book I,[4] when discussing household management and the control of slaves, man is by nature a political animal. Thus men feel a natural urge to live together, even when they do not require one another's help. But a common interest also brings them together as each one attains some degree of the good life, which is indeed the principal end, both of individuals and of states. Again, men coalesce and strive to maintain the political society for the sake of *mere* life, in which, I think you will agree, there is a noble element, so long as the evils of existence do not outweigh the good. We see men clinging to life even at the cost of great suffering, which goes to show that they find in life a natural sweetness and happiness.

(2) It is easy to distinguish the forms of rule commonly recognized; they have been often defined in works not peculiar to this school. Although the natural slave and the natural master have in fact a common interest, the master's rule is exercised chiefly for his own benefit, and only incidentally for that of the slave, whose extinction terminates the rule itself. But the

---

[1] What is the essence of a citizen, and what are the qualifications for citizenship?
[2] Aristotle has already assumed that there are many, and he does not in fact discuss the question.
[3] Cf. page 104, lines 22–5.
[4] Page 7.

rule over a wife and children, and over the household generally, which we call household management, is exercised mainly for the benefit of the ruled or for the benefit of ruler and ruled alike. Essentially it is exercised for that of the ruled, as we see to be the case with other arts, e.g. medicine and [1279a] gymnastic, although an art may be concerned incidentally with the good of the artist himself.[1]   As illustrations of this last point take a physical-training instructor and a ship's helmsman: there is no reason why the former should not occasionally join in the exercises of his class, and the latter is invariably a member of the crew. The instructor, like the helmsman, aims primarily at the welfare of those subject to his authority; but when he himself becomes one of them for the time being he shares incidentally in the benefit which they derive, without losing his identity as an instructor any more than the helmsman loses his as a helmsman though counted as a member of the crew. The same applies in politics: when the constitution rests on a basis of equality and likeness as between the citizens, the latter agree to hold office by turns. There was a time when they followed the natural course, each man accepting his period of duty and then giving place to someone else who would look after his interests as he had served others. But nowadays the profits to be gained from holding office and administering public property make men long to be permanently in authority; so much so that you might think the rulers were prone to sickness and could only maintain their health by continuing in office, so eagerly do they go place-hunting. The inference is clear. Those forms of government which have regard to the common good are right constitutions, judged by the norm of absolute justice. But those which take account only of the rulers' interest are all perversions, all deviation forms; they are despotic, whereas the state is a society of freemen.

The foregoing discussion leads us to consider next the number and nature of the various constitutions. In the first place we must ask what are the *right* forms; once they are recognized the deviations from them will be apparent. The terms 'constitution' and 'the government' mean the same thing; and the government, which is the supreme authority in every state, must be in the hands of one, or of the few, or of the many. Therefore, the right forms of government must be those in

[1] Cf. Plato, *Republic*, 341 D.

which (*a*) an individual, (*b*) a minority, or (*c*) a majority govern
for the common benefit of all; but governments which rule with
an eye to the private interest either of (*a*), (*b*), or (*c*) above are
deviation forms, for the members of a state, if they are to be
called true citizens, must share in its advantages.   The rule of
an individual, when it looks to the common good, is known as
kingship; the rule of a few, when it fulfils the same condition, is
called aristocracy; [1] but when the citizens as a whole govern the
state for the common benefit of all alike, we describe this form
of government by the generic name 'polity.'   There is good
reason for using the generic term.   One man or a few may excel
in virtue, but as the number increases it becomes proportionately difficult for them to attain perfection in every virtue,
though they may do so in military virtue, [1279^b] which is by no
means rare among the masses.   Hence in a polity the fighting
men have supreme power, and those who possess arms are the
citizens.

The deviation forms of the above are as follows: of kingship,
tyranny; of aristocracy, oligarchy; of polity, democracy.   For
tyranny is the rule of a monarch who has only his own interest
at heart; oligarchy has in view the interest of the well-to-do;
democracy, of the have-nots.   None of them looks to the
common good of all.

These forms of government give rise to a number of problems,
and it is therefore necessary to dwell a little longer on their
respective natures.   When one intends making a philosophical
study of any science, with an eye to something more than
practical considerations, one ought not to overlook or omit the
slightest detail—one must uncover the whole truth.

Now tyranny, as I have said, is monarchy ruling a political
association in the way that a master rules his slaves.   There is
oligarchy where the reins of government are held by men of
property, and conversely there is democracy, where power is in
the hands of the poorer classes rather than of the well-to-do.
Our first problem, then, concerns the distinction between democracy and oligarchy.   You have democracy when the many are
supreme; but what if those many are rich?   Likewise, you have
oligarchy when the few are in power; but what if the poor,
though *fewer* than the rich, control the state because they are

---

[1] So called either because the best men rule, or because they do so in the
best interests of the state and its citizens.—(A.)

stronger? In such cases our distinction between these forms of government would appear to be unsatisfactory.

Suppose, then, we associate wealth with the few and poverty with the many, and name the two constitutions accordingly— defining an oligarchy as that in which the wealthy few, and a democracy as that in which the many poor, are supreme. But here again there is a difficulty. If there are no forms of oligarchy and democracy other than those just defined, how describe the forms imagined above, in which there is a majority of rich men and a minority of poor, and each is supreme in its respective state?

The argument seems to demonstrate that the small number of the sovereign body in an oligarchy, or its large number in a democracy, is an accident due to the fact that the rich are generally few, and the poor generally numerous. But if that is so, the causes underlying the differences between oligarchy and democracy have been misrepresented; the true difference between them is poverty and wealth.

[1280ᵃ] Wherever men rule by virtue of their wealth, be they few or many, there you have oligarchy; and where the poor rule, there you have democracy. But it so happens, as I have said, that the rich are few and the poor numerous.[1] Few men are well off, whereas all have a share in freedom; and it is upon the grounds of wealth and freedom respectively that the oligarchical and democratic parties lay claim to power.

---

[1] Hence number is an accidental attribute of democracy and oligarchy.

C. DEMOCRACY, OLIGARCHY, AND
DISTRIBUTIVE JUSTICE

WE must next ascertain what are the marks of oligarchy and democracy as generally recognized by their respective advocates, and what are the oligarchical and democratic notions of justice. Both sides cling to justice of one kind or another, but their conceptions are inadequate and fail to express the idea in all its fullness. For example, justice is thought by the democrats to mean equality; so it does, but only for equals—not for all. Oligarchs, on the other hand, believe that justice means inequality; so it does, but only for unequals—not for all.[1] Both sides overlook the relation of justice to persons, and thereby go astray; they are passing judgment upon themselves, and men are notoriously bad judges in their own case. Justice is relative to persons as well as to things; and a just distribution, as I have explained in the *Ethics*,[2] implies the same ratio between the persons receiving as between the things given. Now the advocates both of democracy and of oligarchy agree as to what constitutes equality among *things*, but differ as to what constitutes *personal* equality. This is mainly due to the fact mentioned above, that they are poor judges in their own case, but also to the fact that both sides are referring to a limited and partial form of justice. The oligarchs believe that superior wealth gives them absolute superiority; while the democrats hold that equality in a single respect—e.g. of free birth—implies absolute equality. Both sides, however, ignore the crucial point—the purpose of the state. If men formed themselves into associations *for the sake of wealth alone*, their share in civic rights would be determined by the amount of their property, and the oligarchical theory would then appear the most tenable.[3] But the state exists for the sake of a *good* life, and not for that of

[1] 'Equality' and 'inequality' in these two sentences refer, of course, to the distribution of office.
[2] 1131ª14 sqq.
[3] It would seem unjust, for example, that a man who had contributed one mina should have the same share in a hundred minae (whether in the principal or in the interest) as another who had contributed the remaining ninety-nine. —(A.)

life *as such*; otherwise slaves and brute beasts might constitute a state—which they cannot in fact do, because they have no share in true felicity and the exercise of free will. Nor does the state exist for the sake of mutual defence against all and sundry, nor yet for the sake of commercial intercourse; otherwise peoples who, like the Etruscans and Carthaginians, are bound to one another by trade agreements, would be citizens of a single state. Certainly they have covenants regulating imports, concordats providing for the settlement of disputes without recourse to arms, and non-aggression pacts. There are, however, no magistracies common to the contracting parties; [1280^b] different states have each their own magistracies. Again, neither of the contracting parties is concerned with the moral welfare of the other; neither is interested in making sure that the other commits no crime or misdemeanour *of any sort*, but only in seeing that it suffers no injustice at the other's hands. Those, on the contrary, who have good government at heart look to the internal virtues and vices of the state. It is evident therefore that any state deserving of the name must concern itself with the promotion of virtue. Otherwise, the political association becomes a mere alliance differing only in respect of place from those alliances whose members live at some distance from one another; and the law becomes mere convention, 'a guarantor of mutual justice,' as the sophist Lycophron said, powerless to make the citizens into good and just men. This can easily be proved. (1) If separate places—say Megara and Corinth—were brought together so that their walls touched, they would still not form one state, not even if (2) their citizens had the right of intermarriage, which is peculiarly characteristic of states. Nor would they do so (3) merely on the strength of living within such distance of each other as did not preclude intercourse between them, and of having laws which forbade either side to wrong the other. Suppose, for example, that you have a total of 10,000 persons, one of whom is a carpenter, another a farmer, another a shoemaker, and so on; unless they have something more in common than trade and mutual defence, they will not form a state. Why is this? Certainly not on grounds of remoteness from one another. For even assuming (a) that such an association occupies one site, but (b) that each man's house is to all intents and purposes a state on its own, and (c) that they bind themselves to assist one another only against evildoers, no intelligent thinker will look upon them as constituting a state, for their mutual intercourse will be of the same character after as before their association.

Clearly, then, a state is not merely an association living on one site, established for the purpose of mutual defence and for the promotion of trade. These are admittedly conditions without which there can be no state; but they do not actually *constitute* a state. The state is an association of families and groups of families in a good life, for the sake of a perfect and self-sufficing existence, although this cannot be achieved unless the members dwell in a single place and intermarry. It was in order to provide those conditions that there arose in cities such institutions as fraternities, clubs, common sacrifices, and social entertainments. But these are the *business of friendship*,[1] i.e. of the will to live together; the *end or purpose of the state* is the good life, and they are the means thereto. The state itself is [1281ª] an association of families and villages in a perfect and self-sufficing existence, i.e. a life of true felicity and goodness.

We conclude, therefore, that political associations exist for the sake of good actions, and not of mere social life. Whence it follows that those who contribute most to an association of this kind have a greater share in the state than those who are equal (or even superior) to them in freedom or nobility of birth, but inferior as regards civic virtue, or than those who surpass them in wealth but are outstripped by them in virtue.

It is sufficiently clear from what I have said that, in advocating different forms of government, both democrats and oligarchs put forward an incomplete notion of justice.

Next we ask: What *should* be the sovereign body in the state? The masses? The wealthy? The better sort of men? The one best man? Or a tyrant? Each of these alternatives appears to involve unacceptable consequences.

(1) Surely it is unjust for the poor, on the strength of mere numbers, to divide among themselves the possessions of the rich. 'Of course not,' you may say; 'the supreme authority wills it and therefore it is just.' To which I reply, that if this is not the acme of injustice, what is? Again, taking men as a whole, irrespective of wealth and poverty, if the majority divide among themselves the possessions of the minority, the state will inevitably be ruined. But virtue does not ruin its possessor, nor is justice destructive of the state; and therefore such a law is

---

[1] As distinct from the purpose of a state.

beyond question unjust.   Otherwise every act of a tyrant must be just; for he uses his superior strength only to oppress others, in the same way as the masses would oppress the wealthy.

(2) Is it just that a wealthy minority should rule?   Suppose they behave in like manner, robbing and plundering the masses: what then?   Is that just?   If so, then the former case will be likewise just.   No; all such arrangements are manifestly wrong and unjust.

(3) Ought the better sort of men to enjoy supreme authority? If they do, everyone else will be excluded from office and thereby dishonoured.   The offices of state are recognized as honours, and if they are permanently held by the same group of men, the rest will be deprived of them.

(4) Is it better, perhaps, that the one best man should rule? Well, this is even more oligarchical; for still more persons are thus without honours.   It may be urged that, since every man is subject to the accidents of human passion, it is wrong that an individual, rather than the law, should hold supreme power. Yes, but suppose the law be oligarchical or democratic, how will that solve our difficulties?   Indeed it will not; the same results will follow.

Postponing further discussion of (2), (3), and (4) above,[1] let us go back to the first alternative, viz. that sovereignty should lie with the people at large rather than with a few persons of very high quality.   This view, although it involves some difficulty, is by no means indefensible, and seems to contain an element of truth.   The many, when taken *individually*, may be [1281b] quite ordinary fellows; but when they meet together they may well be found *collectively* better than the few.   A feast to which many have contributed is better than one provided from a single purse.   In the same way, each of those numerous individuals has some degree of virtue and moral prudence; and all of them met together may become as it were a single person combining many good qualities of character and intelligence, just as they form a unit having many hands, many feet, and many senses. This is why the many are better judges of music and poetry than the few; some appreciate one part, others another, so that all together can assess the true worth of the whole.   There is a similar combination of qualities in good men, who differ from the common run of their fellows; in them otherwise scattered

[1] See pages 86–100; 103–87.

elements are brought together.[1]   It is not clear, however, that this principle holds good of any and every group of men.   Of some it definitely cannot; for if it did, it would apply equally to brutes, between whom and certain classes of men there is little or no difference.   Our statement may nevertheless be true of *some* popular bodies; in which case we have solved the original problem,[2] and are on the way to solving another closely akin to it—viz.   What *extent* of sovereignty should be assigned to freemen, or the general body of citizens, who are not rich and have no claim to the reward of personal merit?   It is dangerous for such persons to share in the highest offices of state, for their folly may lead them into error, and their dishonesty into crime. On the other hand, it is risky to exclude them from such positions: a state in which many poor men are debarred from office cannot but have numerous enemies in its midst.   The only alternative is to allow them deliberative and judicial functions; and it was on these grounds that Solon [3] and other legislators assigned to them the power of electing magistrates and calling them to account, but *not* the right of holding office individually. When they all meet together their discrimination is sufficiently reliable, and combined with the better class they are useful to the state; [4] but each individual on his own is lacking in judgment.

Popular government of this kind, however, involves a number of difficulties.   (*a*) It might be argued that the best judge of whom to employ as a doctor is one who can himself here and now cure a man of disease and restore him to health—in other words a doctor.   The same rule may be applied to all other professions and arts; [1282ª] it may be argued that, just as a doctor should render an account of himself to a body of doctors, so should other professional men to members of their own calling.   But there are three classes of doctors: general practitioners, specialists, and those who, though not in practice, have been trained in the science of medicine.   In almost every art and science there is a class corresponding to these last, and we credit them with the ability to judge quite as well as the practitioners.   The same

[1] It is this assemblage of scattered elements which is also said to distinguish a beautiful person from one who is not beautiful, and works of art from everyday reality.   Taken separately, the eye of one person or some other feature in another might surpass an artistic representation.—(A.)
[2] *Sc*. What *persons* are to form the sovereign body?
[3] See pages 61, 62; 249–56.
[4] Just as a mixture of pure and impure food is more nourishing than a small quantity of the pure would be.—(A.)

principle would seem to hold good in the matter of elections, for a sound choice can be made only by those having the requisite knowledge.[1] Looking at the question from this angle, we must conclude that the masses should not be entrusted either with the election of magistrates or with the scrutiny of their administration. Perhaps, on the other hand, some of these objections may appear groundless in the light of our former thesis, that so long as the people are not utterly degraded, although individually they may be worse judges than those with special knowledge, collectively they are as good, if not better. Furthermore, there are certain arts in which the artists themselves are not the best, let alone the only, judges. Such are those whose products can be appreciated even by men who lack the skill to produce them. For instance, the builder is not the only one who can perceive the merits or demerits of a house; its user (i.e. the householder) will be a better judge, just as a pilot will be a better judge of a rudder than the carpenter, and a diner will estimate the quality of a meal better than the cook.

I think we may now claim to have disposed of this problem; but it leads directly to another.

(b) It is surely unreasonable that inferior persons should enjoy supreme authority in affairs of greater moment than those entrusted to men of outstanding merit. Now to elect magistrates and to audit their accounts are the most important duties; and yet these, as I said above, are assigned under some constitutions to the popular assembly, which has plenary powers in all such matters. Furthermore, the assembly, whose members are entitled to deliberate and to exercise judicial functions, includes men of any age and of little property; but a high qualification is attached to such great offices of state as those of treasurer and general. This difficulty may be overcome in the same way as the preceding, and the existing practice of democracies shown to be justified. It is not in individual members of the court, the council, or the assembly that authority resides, but in the court as a whole, the council as a whole, or the assembly as a whole; and each individual member is only a part of the particular whole. On these grounds the people can rightly claim sovereignty in affairs of greater moment than those entrusted to

---

[1] Those, for example, who understand geometry will be the ones to choose a geometer; and the choice of a pilot is best entrusted to men learned in the science of navigation. There may be certain occupations and arts in which non-scientific persons are qualified to judge; but they certainly cannot do so better than those who are fully trained in the subject.—(A.)

more distinguished minorities; for the popular assembly and the council and the courts consist of many individuals, and their property is collectively greater than the property of one or of a few persons holding high office. So much for that question.

[1282ᵇ] Our discussion of problem (a) shows nothing so clearly as that laws, when they are good, should be supreme, and that the magistrate or magistrates should exercise control in those matters alone upon which the laws fail to give a precise ruling.[1] But we have still to determine what are good laws. The merit or demerit, justice or injustice, of laws varies of necessity from one state to another according to the constitution. This, however, is clear, that laws must be adapted to constitutions, and not vice versa; in which case the right forms of government will inevitably have just, and the deviation forms unjust, laws.

The end or purpose of every art and science is some good. That of the most authoritative, i.e. of political science, is the greatest and most eagerly desired good—justice or, in other words, the common welfare. Now justice is recognized universally as some sort of equality. All men agree to some extent with the philosophical conclusions I have drawn on the subject of ethics;[2] for they admit that justice involves an assignment of things to persons, and that equals are entitled to equal things. But here we are met by the important question: Equals and unequals *in what*? This is a difficult problem, and entails philosophical speculation in the field of politics. It may be argued that offices of state should be distributed unequally on the basis of superiority *in any one respect whatsoever*, even though there be no difference between one citizen and the next in any other respect; and this argument may be founded on the assumption that those who differ from one another must have different rights.

But surely, if this is true, (1) a man's complexion, height, or any other such advantage will earn him a greater share of political rights. The error is plain for all to see, and may be illustrated from other arts and sciences. When a number of flautists are equally skilful players, there is no reason why those of them who are nobly born should receive the better flutes; they will play no better. It is the superior artist who deserves the superior instrument. If my point is not yet clear, it will become so by carrying the example a stage further. Take a man who is a

---

[1] It is difficult for general principles to cover all contingencies.—(A.)
[2] Cf. *Nic. Eth.* v. 3.

first-rate flautist, but of humble extraction and far from handsome. Blue blood and physical beauty may be greater assets
than the art of flute-playing, and may excel the latter in a higher
degree than our flautist excels others in his art; nevertheless, he
still has a claim to the [1283ª] best flutes—unless the advantages
of wealth and birth enhance the skill of an instrumentalist, which
they manifestly do not.

Furthermore, (2) every quality will be commensurable with
every other. If a given height is measurable against a given
degree of wealth or birth, then height in general can be measured
against wealth and birth in general. But if we are going to
allow that, in a particular instance, A excels in height more than
B does in goodness, and that, in general, height excels to a
greater degree than does goodness, then we shall have to allow
that all qualities are commensurable; for if amount P of a certain
quality is better than amount Q of another quality, then an
amount other than P must be equal to it. But since no such
comparison is admissible, there is clearly good reason why in
politics also men should not base their claim to office on any and
every kind of superiority. Some are slow and others swift, but
that does not entitle the former to little and the latter to much;
it is in athletic contests that such excellence takes the prize. No,
rival claims to office must be grounded exclusively on the
possession of those elements which go to form the state; and
therefore men of noble descent, free birth, or wealth may
fairly lay claim to office. Those who hold positions of this kind
must be freemen and taxpayers: a state can no more consist
entirely of poor men than of slaves. But if wealth and free
birth are necessary elements, so too are justice and valour;
without the former qualities a state cannot exist at all, and
without the latter there can be no good life.

If we have regard only to the existence of the state, then it
would seem that all, or some at least, of these elements may be
used to support a claim to office; but if we have in view the good
life, then, as I have already said,[1] education and virtue have yet
stronger claims. Those, however, who are equal (or superior)
in one sole respect do not deserve an equal (or superior) share in
everything; and it is therefore certain that all forms of government in which either of these principles is applied are deviation
forms. I have explained [2] that in one sense all men have a

[1] Cf. page 82, lines 19–24.   [2] Page 80, lines 1 sqq.

claim to office, but all have not an unqualified claim.   (1) The rich plead a larger share in the land, which is a matter of public interest; also, they are generally more reliable in the fulfilment of contracts.   (2) Freemen advance the same claim as those of noble birth, to whom they are closely akin.[1]   It is likewise true to say (3) that moral goodness has a claim; for we have recog-nized [2] justice (which implies all other forms of goodness) as a social virtue.   Again (4), the many may press their claims against the few; for when taken collectively and compared with the few they are stronger, richer, and better.

[1283^b] But, what if the good, the rich, the well born, and other citizen groups are all living together in a single state: will they, or will they not, agree as to who should govern?   There will be no dispute whatsoever as to who should do so under any of the constitutions we have already classified.   These constitu-tions differ from one another in respect of their governing bodies: sovereignty lies in one with the rich, in another with the good,[3] and so on.   Our problem, however, is to decide who shall govern when the different groups advance their claims simul-taneously.   Suppose the good are very few in number: ought we to consider their numbers in relation to the work they have to do, and ask whether they are sufficiently numerous to consti-tute, let alone govern, a state?   Here we meet a difficulty which confronts all claimants to political power.   There would appear to be no justice in the claim of those who take their stand on wealth or birth; otherwise, if one individual is wealthier or of better family than all the rest, justice will likewise demand that he shall be their ruler.   The same objection may be lodged with regard to personal merit in an aristocracy: if one individual be better than all other members of the civic body, the principle of justice will again require that he should govern them.   Finally, if the many are to be sovereign merely because they are stronger than the few, it follows that where one individual (or a minority group) is stronger than the rest of the many, he (or it) has a superior claim to rule.

All these considerations suggest that none of the foregoing principles, upon which men base their claims to govern and hold

---

[1] Men of good birth are more truly citizens than the low-born; and good birth is always esteemed in one's own country. Besides, men of good ancestry are likely to be better in themselves, for good birth implies goodness of one's whole stock.—(A.)

[2] Cf. page 8, lines 15–17.

[3] i.e. in an oligarchy and an aristocracy respectively.

all others in subjection, can be sound.   To those who claim
sovereignty on the strength of their personal merit or their
wealth, the many might fairly retort that there is nothing to
prevent themselves from being better and richer than the few—
not, of course, individually, but collectively.   This leads us to
another question, which can be answered along the same lines.
Assuming that the many are collectively better than the few,
what is the right course for a lawgiver who seeks to enact
perfectly just laws?   Should he legislate for the benefit of the
better sort or for that of the majority?   My answer is that *what
is right* is to be interpreted as *what is equally right*; and what is
equally right is that which benefits the whole state and advances
the common good of its citizens.   Citizens, in the ordinary
sense of the word, are all those who take their turn of ruling
and being ruled.   [1284ª] They vary from one constitution
to another, and in an ideal state they are those who are able
and willing to rule and to obey with the virtuous life as their
aim.

Suppose, however, that there is some individual (or several
persons, though not sufficiently numerous to make up the full
complement of a state) whose virtue is so outstanding that the
virtues or the political capacity of all the rest will stand no
comparison therewith; in that case he (or they) can no longer be
regarded as part of the state.   A man of such pre-eminence will
suffer injustice if he is reckoned as no more than the equal of
men who are so far inferior to him in virtue and political capacity; he must be counted rather as a god among men.   Hence it
is clear that law in general necessarily concerns itself only with
equals in birth and in capacity; and that there is no law for men
of transcendent superiority, for they are themselves a law.[1]
For this reason democratic states instituted the procedure
known as ostracism; equality is their principal aim, and therefore they used to ostracize [2] (i.e. banish from the city for a time)
those whom they considered too influential through their wealth,
their popularity, or some other political advantage.   There is a
legend that the Argonauts left Heracles behind for some such
reason; the ship *Argo* would not sail with him on board, fearing

---

[1] It would be foolish for anyone to attempt to make laws for them; their
reaction would probably be that of the lions in the fable of Antisthenes when
the hares began haranguing a council of the beasts and claiming equality for
all.   ['Where are your claws and teeth?']—(A.)
[2] Ostracism was not used at Athens after 417 B.C.   See J. Carcopino,
L'Ostracisme athénien (1935).

that he would outshine the rest of the crew. From this stand-point one can hardly approve those critics of tyranny who censure the advice given by Periander to Thrasybulus.[1] The story goes that Thrasybulus sent a messenger to ask for his advice. Periander spoke never a word; he merely levelled the surface of a corn-field by lopping off the outstanding ears. The messenger did not grasp the meaning of his action; but he reported it to Thrasybulus, who thereby understood that he must get rid of the outstanding men in his own state. This is a policy useful not only to tyrants, or in practice confined to them; it is equally desirable in oligarchies and democracies. Ostracism has more or less the same effect by restraining the most prominent citizens and driving them into exile. Major powers treat whole states and peoples in this way. Athens, for example, as soon as she had consolidated her empire, humbled the Samians, Chians, and Lesbians in defiance of existing treaties. [1284ᵇ] The kings of Persia, too, have repeatedly crushed the Medes, the Babylonians, and others who have presumed upon their former greatness.

The problem is universal; it concerns all forms of government, even right ones. For although deviation forms adopt this policy with an eye to their own benefit, those which have the common interest at heart do so likewise. The same thing is apparent in other arts and sciences. A painter, for instance, will never depict a man with one foot out of proportion, no matter how beautifully he may be able to paint such a foot; nor will a shipwright build the prow or any other part of the vessel unduly large or small, any more than a choir-master will allow a man whose voice is louder or better than all the rest to sing in his choir. And therefore there is no reason why monarchs who employ repressive measures of this kind should fall foul of their subjects, provided their government is otherwise beneficial. Hence, where you have any recognized form of pre-eminence, the argument in favour of ostracism is not altogether without political justice. True, it is better that the legislator should from the outset frame his constitution in such a way that there will be no need of such a remedy; but if the need *does* arise, the next best thing is that he should endeavour to correct the evil with some measure of the kind. Greek states, however, have not acted on this principle; ignoring the welfare of their own

[1] Periander was tyrant of Corinth (625–585 B.C.). Thrasybulus occupied a similar position at Miletus.

constitutions, they have used ostracism in a spirit of mere faction. It cannot be denied that under deviation forms of government, and from their special points of view, such a policy is both just and expedient; but we must also admit, I think, that it is not absolutely just. Under the ideal constitution, however, there must be grave doubts about its employment—not when it is used to deal with excess of political strength, wealth, personal popularity, and so on, but in the event of someone rising to pre-eminent virtue. What is one to do with such a man? No one will suggest that he should be driven into exile; on the other hand, he cannot be expected to remain a subject—that would be like claiming to rule over Zeus, by taking turns of government with him! The only alternative, and indeed the natural course, is that all should willingly obey the man of pre-eminent virtue, who will therefore be permanent king in his particular state.

D. KINGSHIP

1. FIVE FORMS OF KINGSHIP

WHAT I have just said leads us, by a natural transition, to the subject of kingship. This, as I have explained, is one of the 'right' forms of government. We must first inquire whether a state or a territory which is to have sound political bases will fare better under a kingship than under some other kind of constitution, or whether that will depend on circumstances. Before answering this question, however, we must ask ourselves whether there is only one or more than one variety of kingship.

[1285ª] It is, of course, easy to see that there are several varieties, and that the system of government is not the same in all of them.

Of constitutional kingships, (1) the Spartan type is thought by some to come nearest to the true pattern. But this is not really so. The kings of Sparta command the army on foreign expeditions, and may supervise religious worship; beyond that their sovereignty does not extend. This sort of kingship may accordingly be described as an independent and permanent generalship. It has never included the power of life and death, except that in ancient times a king, when on campaign, might execute a subject 'by right of superior force.' In Homer, for instance, we find Agamemnon showing no resentment when abused in the assembly, but when the army goes out to battle he has power even of life and death: 'If I find anyone,' he says, 'flinching from the fight, nothing shall save him from the dogs and vultures, for in my hands is death.' [1] So much for one type of kingship—military command on a life tenure, in some cases hereditary and in others elective.

(2) There is another type, which is not uncommon among barbarian peoples.[2] It closely resembles tyranny, except that it is constitutional and hereditary. The barbarians are more servile in character than Greeks,[3] and are therefore prepared to tolerate despotic government. Thus while such kingships bear

---

[1] *Iliad*, ii. 391–3. The words 'for . . . death' are not found in our version.
[2] It is to be understood that when Aristotle speaks of 'barbarians,' he is using the common term for all those outside the Greek-speaking world.
[3] Asiatics are likewise more servile than Europeans.—(A.)

the marks of tyranny because the people are by nature slaves,[1] their hereditary and constitutional nature ensures their stability. This last fact also explains why the royal bodyguard is such as a king rather than a tyrant would employ. It is composed, that is to say, of native troops and not of foreign mercenaries. Kings rule according to law and over a *willing* people, but tyrants over *unwilling* subjects; and so the former are protected *by* their subjects, the latter *against* them.

Besides these two forms of monarchy, there is another (3), which existed in ancient Greece and was known as dictatorship [*aesymnetia*]. Broadly speaking, this may be defined as an elective tyranny; like the barbarian type, it is constitutional, but differs therefrom in being non-hereditary. Sometimes the office was held for life, sometimes for a specified period or until certain duties had been discharged. At Mitylene, for example, the people chose Pittacus to lead them against the exiles under Antimenides and the poet Alcaeus.[2] The election of Pittacus is mentioned by Alcaeus in one of his drinking-songs, where he complains that 'they made the low-born Pittacus tyrant of the [1285b] lily-livered and ill-fated city, shouting his praise without a dissentient voice.'[3] These dictatorships have always been tyrannies inasmuch as they are despotic; but in so far as they are elective and willingly accepted by the people, they are kingships.

(4) There is yet another form of kingly rule—that of the heroic age—which was hereditary, constitutional, and exercised over willing subjects. The early chieftains were benefactors of the people both in arts and in arms: they either formed them into a community, or provided them with land and so became kings by general consent and transmitted their power to their descendants. They commanded the army in time of war and presided over the sacrifices, except when these latter were reserved to the priests. They also decided lawsuits (sometimes upon oath and sometimes not).[4] In ancient times their authority was comprehensive in both home and foreign affairs. At a later date, however, they relinquished some of their prerogatives, and others were taken over by the people, until in some states only the traditional sacrifices were left to them.

---

[1] Cf. page 6, lines 9–12.
[2] Pittacus held office from 589 to 579 B.C.
[3] Frag. 37, Bergk⁴.
[4] Their oath took the form of stretching out the sceptre.—(A.)

Even where their functions still entitled them to be called real kings, they retained no more than military command on foreign expeditions.

There are thus four types of kingship, differing from one another in the ways I have described. First, the kingship of the heroic age, which was exercised over willing subjects but limited to certain functions; the king was general and judge, and had jurisdiction in religious matters. Second, the barbarian type, hereditary and despotic, but constitutional. Third, the so-called dictatorship, an elective tyranny. Fourth, the Spartan type, which is in fact an hereditary generalship held for life.

But there is also (5) a fifth type, in which one man is sovereign in all matters, with the same authority that a tribe or a state enjoys in the control of its own public affairs. It corresponds to the rule of a father over his household; for as paternal government is kingly rule over a family, so this type of kingship is paternal government of a state, or of one or more tribes.

2. ABSOLUTE KINGSHIP

There are only two of these five types of kingship which we need consider—the Spartan variety and the one last mentioned. Most of the others lie somewhere between them, having more power than the first and less than the second. Our inquiry, therefore, turns upon two points: (1) Is it good for the state that a man should be general for life; and if so, should the office be confined to one family or be open to the citizens in turn? (2) [1286ᵃ] Is it expedient that one man should exercise sovereign power in all matters?

(1) The question as to perpetual generalship belongs rather to the study of laws than of constitutions, for the office is compatible with any form of government. We may accordingly dismiss the subject for the present.

(2) Absolute kingship, however, is a form of constitution; we must therefore examine it from the philosophical viewpoint, and take a glance at the difficulties it involves. We will begin by asking whether it is more expedient to be ruled by the one best man, or by the best laws.[1]

Those who favour kingship argue that, since laws are quite

[1] Cf. Plato, *Politicus*, 294 A–295 C.

general in their scope, and make no provision for unforeseen circumstances, it is ridiculous for any art to follow a written code. In Egypt a doctor may alter the prescribed treatment after the fourth day; if he does so before, it is at his own peril. In the same way and for the same reason a constitution which is bound by written laws is clearly not the best. No ruler, on the other hand, can dispense with the general principle of law; and law, which is wholly dispassionate, should be preferred to human judgment, seeing that passion is innate in the soul of every man. 'True,' you may reply; 'but an individual will be more clear-headed in particular cases.' Evidently then the one best man must be a lawgiver, and there must be a code of laws; but these laws, though generally supreme, must be revoked when they prove inadequate or unfair.[1] But when the law is wholly or partially incapable of determining a point, who is to decide—the one best man or the whole people? In modern practice popular assemblies have judicial and deliberative functions, and their decisions in either case refer to particular issues. Of course, any individual member of the assembly is inferior to the one best man; but the state is composed of many individuals, and just as a feast to which all the guests contribute is better than a dinner provided by a single man,[2] so the masses are often better judges than any individual.

Again, a large body of men is less easily corrupted than the few; in this respect it resembles a large volume of water, which is not so easily fouled as a small quantity. Whereas the judgment of a man in the throes of anger or some other passion is bound to be obscured, a great number of persons are most unlikely to be simultaneously led astray in this manner. Let us assume that the people are all freemen, that they never violate the law, and only supply what is inevitably deficient therein. Or, if such attainments are hardly possible in so large a body, let us suppose that many of them are good men and good citizens; and then let us go on to ask which will be more incorruptible, the one good ruler or these many. Surely the latter. [1286ᵇ] If you say they will be subject to faction, from which the one man will be free, I reply that their character is as good as his. We

---

[1] Aristotle began to discuss the choice between king and law. He has just declared for the time being in favour of law. At this point, however, he digresses to examine the claim of the 'one best man,' as against a body of men, to decide particular cases for which the law makes no provision. At 1287ᵃ (page 97) he will return to a more detailed study of King versus Law.

[2] Cf. page 83, lines 27–31.

may therefore conclude that if we define the rule of 'many good men' as aristocracy, and that of one man as kingship, then aristocracy will be better for a state than kingship (whether or not the king relies on the strength of a bodyguard), provided only that a number of men can be found who are all equally good.

The existence of kingship in early times was probably due to the fact that men of eminent virtue were few and far between, especially when states were small. Besides, kings were appointed because they were benefactors, and benefits can be conferred only by good men. However, when men of equal merit appeared in greater numbers, they would no longer tolerate the pre-eminence of one, but desired something in which they might all share and framed a constitution. Later, this ruling class deteriorated and enriched themselves from public funds; wealth became the road to honour, and so oligarchies sprang up. These were transformed into tyrannies, and tyrannies into democracies; for love of gain in the ruling classes tended unceasingly to diminish their numbers and so to strengthen the masses, who eventually turned upon their masters and established democracies. Now that states have been still further enlarged, it would appear virtually impossible, let alone easy, to establish any other form of government.

Assuming now that kingly rule is best for a state, what about the monarch's family: ought they to inherit his authority? This will be disastrous if they are no better than anyone else. A royalist may urge that the king, even if he has power to do so, will not in fact hand on his office to his children. But this is hard to believe nowadays; it is too much to expect of human nature. Next there is the question of what force the king is to have at his disposal: should he have a bodyguard with whose assistance he can overawe reluctant subjects? If not, can he exercise his office? Even though he were a sovereign who ruled according to law, doing nothing arbitrarily or illegally, he must still have some force wherewith to uphold the law. In the case of a limited kingship the answer is not far to seek: he must have such a force as will make him stronger than any individual or group of individuals, but not so strong as the whole people. The ancients acted on this principle when they allowed a bodyguard to anyone whom they appointed to govern the state as dictator or tyrant. For example, when Dionysius [1] requested a

---

[1] Dionysius I, tyrant of Syracuse (405–367 B.C.).

bodyguard, the Syracusans were advised to give him exactly such a number.

[1287ᵃ] ¹ We must now resume the main thread of our discussion. I have already explained that a kingship in which the sovereign's activity is bound by laws is not, properly speaking, a variety of constitution. Permanent military command, for instance, may exist under any form of government, including democracy and aristocracy; and one person is frequently entrusted with the civil administration subject to the rule of law, e.g. at Epidamnus and (with more limited powers) at Opus. But absolute kingship, i.e. the arbitrary and unrestricted rule of a king, is condemned by some theorists who think it altogether unnatural that one man should be sovereign over the whole citizen body in a state which is composed of equals. It is urged that those who are by nature equal must naturally have the same rights and worth; and that therefore to allow unequals an equal share (or vice versa) in the offices of state is no less detrimental than to apply the same principle to men with different physical attributes. It is therefore considered just that among equals everyone should obey as well as rule, and that consequently all should take their turn of office. Here at once we are in the realm of law, which is implied by an order of succession. The rule of law, so the argument continues, is preferable to that of an individual; and on the same principle, even if it be better that individuals should govern, they should be appointed only as guardians or ministers of the law. For although there must admittedly be magistrates, it is claimed that to bestow authority on any person when all are equal is unjust.

Furthermore, there may indeed be cases which the law appears unable to determine, but an individual is most unlikely to do better. Law certainly trains officials for this very purpose, leaves them to decide as best they can such matters as do not come within its scope, and permits them to make such alterations in its framework as experience may suggest. He, therefore, who would have law rule seems to advocate the exclusive rule of God and Reason; but he who would commit the government to a man adds a brutish element. Appetite is a wild beast, and passion perverts the minds of rulers, even when they are the best of men. Law may thus be defined as 'reason unaffected by passion '

¹ See page 95, footnote 1.

True, we are advised [1] when sick to call in a practising physician and not to rely on medical books. But the parallel of the arts is irrelevant here. A doctor never acts in defiance of right reason from motives of friendship; he merely cures his patient and takes his fee. Politicians, on the other hand, are not seldom actuated by spite or favouritism. If a man suspected his doctor of conspiring with his enemies to destroy him for a bribe, he would rather seek a remedy from books. Again, [1287ᵇ] doctors who are sick, and athletic trainers in training, call in other doctors and trainers, implying thereby that they are not good judges in their own case because they are influenced by their own feelings. Evidently, therefore, in seeking for justice men look for some neutral authority, which is the law. Now, customary laws have far more weight and deal with more important matters than do written laws; so the rule of a man may be safer than that of written law, without being safer than the rule of customary law.

Again, it is by no means easy for one man to supervise many things at once. He will therefore be obliged to appoint a number of subordinate officials. But what difference can it make if these officials are there from the outset instead of being appointed by him because he cannot do without them? If, as I said before,[2] the good man is entitled to rule precisely because he is better than others, then two good men are still better than one. Hence the phrase 'two getting together,' [3] and Agamemnon's prayer—'Would that I had ten such counsellors.' [4] And even to-day there are magistrates, such as judges, with jurisdiction in certain matters *which the law cannot determine*; I emphasize these last words because the law will unquestionably be the best ruler and judge within the limits of its competence. Some things can and others cannot be included in the scope of law; and this is the origin of that difficult question, whether the best law or the best man should be chosen to rule. Matters of detail, upon which men are liable to disagree, cannot be the subject of legislation; nor is it ever suggested that such matters should not be submitted to human judgment. But it *is* claimed that there should be many judges rather than one. Every office-holder trained by the law will be a sound judge; and it would surely appear strange that a man should see better with two eyes, hear better with two ears, or act better with two feet or

[1] Cf. Plato, *Politicus*, 296 B.   [2] Pages 88, lines 29–31; 91, lines 13–15.
[3] *Iliad*, x. 24.   [4] *Iliad*, ii. 372.

hands, than many with many.   Indeed, present-day monarchs make to themselves many eyes and ears and hands and feet in the shape of colleagues, who are friends of themselves and of their regimes.   Friends they must of necessity be, otherwise they will not do what the monarch requires.   But friendship implies likeness and equality, so that if he believes that his friends should hold office, he must also agree that his equals and peers should hold office on a level with himself.

Such are the main objections to kingship.   It seems to me, however, that while they are valid in some cases, they will not apply in others.   For despotic, kingly, and constitutional governments are all three just and advantageous according to circumstances; but the rule of a tyrant is never so—nor indeed are *any* of the deviation forms, because they are of unnatural origin.   Now what I have said makes it clear that among men who are equals [1288[a]] and peers it is neither expedient nor just that one person should be sovereign over all.   This is true whether there are laws, or whether there are no laws and the one man himself takes the place of law; it is true whether the one man is a good man ruling over good men, or a bad man ruling over bad men; and it is even true when the one man is of superior virtue, except in a particular case to which I have already alluded [1] and to which I shall now return. [2]

When a whole family, or some individual, happens to be of such outstanding merit that he surpasses all the rest, then it is just that they or he should enjoy kingly power over all.   This, as I said earlier on, [3] is not only in line with the principle of justice which all founders of states (whether aristocratic or oligarchical, or democratic) are accustomed to put forward, [4] but also with my earlier assertion [5] that no other course is expedient or natural.   It would surely be wrong to execute, banish, or ostracize a man of outstanding superiority, or to expect him to take his turn at being governed.   The whole is by nature superior to the part, and a man of such pre-eminence stands in the relation of a whole to its part.   The only alternative is that he should be obeyed and that his supremacy should not be

[1] Page 89, lines 3 sqq.
[2] For 1288[a]6–15 see Appendix II, page 237.
[3] Page 88, lines 28 sqq.
[4] They all recognize the claims of superiority, but disagree as to the *kind* of superiority.—(A.)
[5] Page 91, lines 9–15.

periodical but permanent. These, then, are our conclusions on the subject of kingship. They supply answers to the following questions: (1) What are the forms of kingship? (2) Is it, or is it not advantageous to states? and (3) If so, to which and under what conditions? [1]

---

[1] For the remaining portion of this Book see Appendix III, page 238.

Books IV–VI

THE INFERIOR CONSTITUTIONS

A. MORPHOLOGY OF THE STATE
(Book IV)

1. Subject-matter of Political Science

[1288ᵇ10] Every art and practical science which embraces the whole of any subject, and no longer studies it piecemeal, must consider the methods appropriate to each department of that subject. The science of gymnastic, for example, has to consider what sort of training is suited to various kinds of physique; what sort is absolutely the best, i.e. is suited to the ideal and perfectly equipped physique; yes, and also what common form of training is generally suited to most kinds of physique. Again, a man may have no wish to attain the standard of skill and fitness which would qualify him to take part in athletic contests; even so, the trainer and games master must be capable of imparting the particular standard he requires. And the same is obviously true in medicine, in shipbuilding, in tailoring, and so forth.

The science of politics, therefore, should be no less comprehensive. It must consider (1) which form of government is best in the absolute sense and what qualities that form must have in order to approximate most closely to the ideal when no external impediment intervenes. It must consider (2) which form of government is suited to particular states; for the absolute best is likely to be unattainable in many cases, and therefore the good legislator and true statesman must be acquainted also with that form which is best under present circumstances. It must consider (3) how a state may be constituted under any given conditions—how it is originally formed, and how, once in existence, it may be longest preserved.[1] Apart from all these functions, the science of politics must also discover (4) which kind of government is best suited to states in general; for most political writers, however sound their views in other respects, are unpractical.

What we have to do is to consider not only which constitution is best, but also which is practicable and most easily within reach

[1] I am thinking here of a state which, so far from having the ideally best constitution, lacks even the conditions necessary for it; one which has not even the best constitution possible under the circumstances, but one of an inferior type.—(A.)

of all.   Some modern authors (1) would have nothing but the supremely perfect, for which many natural advantages are required; others (2) speak of a more attainable kind, but ignore the various constitutions under which they themselves live, and extol, say, the Spartan.   [1289ᵃ] If any change of government is needed, it must be one which the citizens in question will be both able and ready to accept as evolving naturally from their present system.   For just as it is equally hard to unlearn as to learn a lesson, so there is as much difficulty in reforming an old constitution as in creating a new one.   Our statesman, therefore, besides the qualifications implied by (1) and (2) above, must be able, as already stated, to amend an existing constitution; and this he cannot do without knowing how many forms of government there are.   To-day, some people think there is only one kind of democracy or oligarchy.   But this is a mistake; in order to avoid it we must discover the several varieties of each constitution, and in how many ways they are compounded.   With the help of this same political insight it will also be possible to recognize which laws are absolutely best and which are *suited to particular constitutions*.   I use this last phrase because laws ought to be (as in fact they always are) adapted to the constitution, and not vice versa.   Here is the reason.   A constitution is an arrangement of offices in a state, appointing the method of their distribution, determining the sovereign authority, and prescribing the end to be pursued by all members of the association. Laws, as distinct from the principles of the constitution, are the rules according to which the magistrates should exercise their authority and proceed against offenders.   It follows that we must know the varieties, and the number of varieties, of each form of government, if only with a view to enacting laws; for since there is undoubtedly more than a single form of democracy′ and of oligarchy, the same laws cannot be suited to *all* oligarchies or to *all* democracies.

When first discussing [1] forms of government I distinguished three 'right' forms (kingship, aristocracy, polity) and three corresponding 'deviation' forms (tyranny, oligarchy, democracy).   We have already dealt with aristocracy and kingship,[2] explaining how these two differ from one another and in what

---

[1] Pages 76–9.
[2] [Pages 92–100.]   To study the ideal constitution is equivalent to discussing the two forms thus named, both of which imply a principle of virtue equipped with the means necessary for its exercise.—(A.)

circumstances kingship should be adopted. It remains, therefore, to describe *polity* (which bears the generic name of all constitutions) as well as the *deviation forms*—tyranny, oligarchy, and democracy.

It is obvious which of these latter is the worst and which comes next. The worst is necessarily the deviation form of the first and most godlike of 'right' constitutions, i.e. of kingship, [1289b] which, if it is anything more than an insubstantial name, must be founded on the king's great personal superiority. Tyranny, therefore, is the worst, and farthest removed from a 'right' form of government; oligarchy, being far removed from aristocracy, is the next worst; democracy is the most tolerable.

One of my predecessors [1] drew these same distinctions, but his viewpoint was not the same as mine. Believing that there is a good form of every constitution, he ranked the good form of democracy as the worst of all good forms, and the bad form of it as the best of all the bad. I maintain, on the other hand, that both constitutions are absolutely defective. We cannot properly describe one form of oligarchy as *better* than another; we can only say that it is *not as bad*.

But enough of this question for the present. We have now to determine (1) how many varieties of constitution there are, having already implied that there are several forms both of democracy and of oligarchy; (2) what constitution (short of the ideal) is most generally acceptable and most to be desired, and also whether there is any other well-organized constitution aristocratic in character but none the less suited to a majority of states; (3) which of the inferior kinds of government is suited to each kind of civic body, one of which may need democracy rather than oligarchy, and vice versa. Next, we have to consider (4) how those who wish to do so ought to go about constructing these various constitutions—I mean the different varieties of democracy and oligarchy. Lastly, having discussed these matters briefly to the best of our ability, we must try to ascertain (5) how constitutions generally, and each one in particular, are liable to be destroyed, how they can be preserved, and what causes them to produce these results.[2]

---

[1] Plato, *Politicus*, 302 E, 303 A.
[2] The first of these questions is dealt with on pages 106–116 *infra*; the second on pages 117–20; the third on pages 120–1; the fourth on pages 123–132, 172–83; the fifth on pages 133–71.

2. Varieties of Constitution

(A) *Democracy and Oligarchy*

The reason why there are many forms of government is that every state has a number of different elements. In the first place we find that all states consist of families. Secondly, in this group of families there are inevitably some rich, some poor, and some in a condition between the two; the rich are heavy-armed and the poor not. Thirdly, the common people are made up of agriculturists, tradesmen, and artisans. Fourthly, among the notables too there are differences of wealth in the sense of property; horse-breeding, for instance, can hardly be carried on except by very rich men.[1] Besides differences of wealth, there are differences of rank and merit, [1290^a] and others based on similar factors which I called 'elements which go to form the state' when discussing aristocracy.[2] Sometimes all these elements, sometimes only a few, and sometimes a majority of them, have a share in the government. So there must be many constitutions, differing in kind, since the parts of which they are composed differ likewise. For a constitution is an arrangement of offices, which the whole citizen body distribute among themselves either according to the power of those enjoying political rights, e.g. the rich or the poor, or according to some principle of equality which includes both. There must therefore be as many forms of government as there are ways of arranging the distribution of offices according to the relative superiorities and differences of the elements of the state.

It is commonly believed that there are only two constitutions. Just as the winds are commonly spoken of as north or south, the others being treated as mere deviations from these, so there are said to be only two constitutions—democracy and oligarchy. Aristocracy is considered as a form of oligarchy, and what we call polity as in fact a democracy—much as westerly winds are classified as northerly, and easterly winds as southerly. There are likewise said to be two musical modes, the Dorian and the Phrygian, other arrangements of the scale being included under one or other. But although this is the favourite view of

---

[1] This is why states whose strength lay in their cavalry were in ancient times the homes of oligarchy. The Eretrians, for example, the Chalcidians, the Magnesians on the Maeander, and many other peoples of Asia Minor, used cavalry in warfare against their neighbours.—(A.)

[2] Page 87, line 24.

constitutions, you will do better and come nearer to the truth in either case by recognizing, as I have done, one or two 'right' forms, and by treating the rest as deviations from the best, just as there are perversions of the properly tempered musical modes. These deviation forms, when oligarchical, may be compared with the abnormally severe and dominant modes; when democratic they are comparable with those that are gentle and relaxed.[1]

It must not be assumed, as some modern writers are pleased to do, that democracy and oligarchy can be defined without qualification as forms of government in which the greater number and the few respectively are sovereign; for the majority [2] is always sovereign, even in an oligarchy.   Imagine a total population of 1,300 souls, 1,000 of whom are rich and allow the 300 poor no share in government, although the latter are freeborn and their equals in all other respects.   No one would maintain that this was a democracy.   Suppose, on the other hand, there are only a few poor who dominate the well-to-do majority, excluding them from office: no one could call this an oligarchy.   It is better, therefore, to call [1290b] democracy a form of government in which the free-born are sovereign, and an oligarchy one in which the wealthy rule.   It is merely accidental that the free-born are many and the rich only a few.   If the difference were one of number alone, we should have an oligarchy, say, if offices were distributed on a basis of stature (as is said to be the case in Ethiopia) or looks; [3] for the number of tall or good-looking men is everywhere small.   However, it is not sufficient to distinguish oligarchy and democracy by the sole criterion of riches and free birth; since there are more elements than one both in a democracy and in an oligarchy, we must carry our analysis further.   We cannot, for example, maintain that there is democracy where a few men of full citizen birth rule a majority who are not free-born, as was once the case at Apollonia on the Ionian Gulf and at Thera.[4]   Nor can we recognize an oligarchy where the rich are sovereign merely because they are more numerous than the poor, as they once did

[1] The former of these modes was the Dorian, the latter the Phrygian.

[2] i.e. the majority of those having constitutional rights.

[3] For the criterion of stature in Ethiopia see Herodotus iii. 20; for that of looks, Athenaeus, 566 C.   But in each case the reference is to choice of *kings*, not magistrates.

[4] In both these states honours and offices were reserved to those of noble birth, i.e. to those who were descended from the original colonists, though they were only a handful of the entire population.—(A.)

at Colophon, where a majority of the citizens owned large estates before the Lydian war. No, you have democracy when government is in the hands of a free-born and poor majority, but oligarchy when it is in the hands of a rich and high-born minority.[1]

[1291[b]14] Having established the fact, and explained why, there are a number of constitutions, let me now explain that there are several forms both of democracy and of oligarchy. This indeed is clear from what I have already said, viz. that the common people and the so-called notables vary among themselves. With regard to the common people, they include agriculturists, artisans, retail traders, and the seafaring class which is subdivided according as its members belong to the navy, the mercantile marine, the ferry service, or the fishing fleet.[2] To these may be added unskilled labourers, those whose slender means allow them no leisure, those who are not free-born of two citizen parents; and even these may not complete the list. The notables, in their turn, may be classified according to wealth, birth, merit, education, and so forth.

(1) The following are varieties of democracy: (a) That which claims to be founded on strict equality. The law in this case declares equality to mean that the poor enjoy no more advantage than the rich: neither is sovereign, both are on the same level. And quite right too; for if liberty and equality are, as some maintain, to be found chiefly in democracy, this is most likely to be true where all enjoy a full share of constitutional rights. A constitution of this order is necessarily a democracy, because the common people are a majority, whose will is decisive. So much for the first type of democracy. (b) That in which the distribution of offices is based on a property qualification, albeit a small one: those who have the requisite amount of property must be admitted to office, and those who alienate it are excluded. [1292[a]] (c) That in which all citizens *of unimpeachable descent* can share in office, subject, however, to the overriding sovereignty of law. (d) That in which *everyone*, provided only he is a citizen, can share in office, subject to law as above. Lastly (e), there is another form which is similar to (d), except that here the

---

[1] For 1290[b]21–91[b]13 see Appendix IV, page 239.
[2] In many places one or other of these groups forms quite a large population: the fishermen do at Tarentum and Byzantium, the naval crews at Athens, the merchant seamen at Aegina and Chios, and the ferrymen at Tenedos.—(A.)

people are above the law, which they supersede by their decrees.[1] The people then becomes an autocrat, a single composite autocrat, with the many playing sovereign—not, of course, individually, but collectively.   Homer says that 'the rule of many is not good'; but whether he refers to this collective rule, or to the rule of many individuals, is uncertain.   Be that as it may, a democracy of this kind, having all the characteristics of an autocrat and being uncontrolled by law, seeks to exercise autocratic powers.   It grows despotic; flatterers are esteemed; and the democracy itself becomes analogous to the tyrannical form of one-man government.   Both have the same spirit; both behave like despots to the better class of citizens; the decrees of the people correspond to the edicts of the tyrant; and the demogogue is the same as, or at any rate analogous to, the flatterer.   Both of these have enormous influence—flatterers over tyrants, and demagogues over the people whom they lead.   It is, in fact, owing to the demagogues, who refer everything to the popular assembly, that its decrees override the laws.   The power of these men rests on the universal sovereignty of the people who lend them a ready ear and thus enable them to control the voting. Furthermore, those who lodge any complaint against the magistrates say that it is for the people to pass judgment—an invitation welcomed by the people; and so the authority of every official is undermined.   There is indeed a good deal to be said for the view that such a democracy is no constitution at all; for where the laws are not supreme, there is no constitution.   Law should be sovereign in all matters, the magistrates and citizen body confining themselves to decisions on points of detail.   The conclusion, therefore, is plain for all to see: democracy may be a genuine form of government; but this particular system, under which everything is regulated by decree, is not even a democracy in any true sense of the word, for no decree can be a general rule. These, then, are the varieties of democracy.

(2) Here now are the different kinds of oligarchy: (a) That in which offices are assigned on the basis of a property qualification so high as to exclude the poor (although they form a majority) from any share in office, but allowing constitutional rights to all those who satisfy its requirements.   [1292^b] (b) That in which

---

[1] This is due to the activity of demagogues, who always make their appearance in democracies where the laws are not supreme; there are no demogogues in those which obey the law and in which the better class of citizens are predominant.—(A.)

the holding of office is dependent on a high property qualification, and those who are to fill vacant offices are chosen only *by* those who satisfy its requirements.[1] (*c*) That in which son succeeds father. And fourthly (*d*) another hereditary kind, in which the magistrates are supreme and not the law. This variety holds a place among oligarchies corresponding to that of tyranny among monarchies and to that of the last mentioned form of democracy among democracies; it is known as a 'dynasty'[2] or family clique.

Such, then, are the different forms of oligarchy and democracy. It should be noted, however, that in many states the constitution although not *legally* democratic, is administered on democratic lines owing to the habits and training of the people. Conversely, in other states the constitution as by law established inclines to democracy, but functions rather according to oligarchic principles for the same reasons. This is especially so after a revolution. There is no immediate change; the victorious party is at first content with small encroachments on the former regime. Old laws therefore remain in force, even though the revolutionary party is in power.

My earlier remarks [3] are sufficient in themselves to prove that there must be all the above forms of democracy and oligarchy,[4] for either *all* those various groups must share in constitutional rights or some must share while others do not. (1) When people of moderate means, e.g. the agricultural class, are constitutionally supreme, they govern according to law. Compelled to work for a living, they have no leisure; so they make the law supreme and meet in assembly only when it is absolutely necessary. The rest of the population are entitled to a share in constitutional rights whenever they have attained the property qualification determined by law. Absolute exclusion of any class from constitutional rights is a step towards oligarchy; hence all who qualify are admitted to a share in those rights, but the want of sufficient means deprives them of leisure. This then is one form of democracy, and these are the causes which

[1] If the choice is also made *from* the whole body of qualified persons you have something like an aristocracy; but if from a privileged section, the constitution tends rather to oligarchy.—(A.)

[2] The word *dynasteia* occurs several times in the following pages. It denotes a group of families enjoying hereditary and absolute power.

[3] Page 108, lines 11–19.

[4] Up to this point Aristotle has been distinguishing varieties of oligarchy and democracy on the basis of their *political structure*; he now does the same on the basis of their *social make-up*.

produce it.   A second form (2) is based on the distinction which comes next in order—that of birth.   Here, all those of irreproachable birth share theoretically, but do so *in practice* only when they can find the necessary leisure.   In such a democracy, therefore, the laws are supreme, because the state has no means of buying leisure for its citizens.   Under a third form (3) all men of free birth enjoy constitutional rights, but do not in fact exercise them because they lack the requisite means; here again, therefore, the law is necessarily sovereign.   The fourth form (4) of democracy [1293ª] is chronologically last in the development of states.   Modern states have far outgrown their original size, and their revenues have increased proportionately.   Under this twofold influence, and owing to the numerical superiority of the masses, not only do all enjoy constitutional rights, but all take an active part in public life—even the poor, for whom leisure is secured by state payment.   A paid proletariat, indeed, has more leisure than any other group; for they are not subject to the demands of private property, which occupy the wealthy to such an extent that they have no time for the assembly or for the courts.   In these circumstances the state is governed by a majority of poor folk, and not by the laws.

These, then, are the various kinds of democracy, and the causes which give rise to each.   Now for the different forms of oligarchy.   The first (1) is that in which the majority of citizens are property owners, though not on any large scale, and all who possess the required amount are entitled to share in constitutional rights.   Since those who thus enjoy constitutional rights are a numerous body, it follows that sovereignty is vested in the law rather than in persons.   Such an oligarchy is something very different from monarchy; and as its members have neither so much property that they can enjoy leisure free from the cares of business, nor so little that they need state support, they will inevitably ask the law to rule on their behalf, instead of claiming sovereignty for themselves.

The second form (2) of oligarchy arises where property owners are fewer than in the former case, but have larger holdings.   They claim a share of constitutional rights proportionate to their greater power; and with this end in view they themselves select those members of the other classes who are to be admitted to the civic body—not, of course, as an arbitrary measure (for they are not yet strong enough to rule without law), but by virtue of a law which they themselves enact.

When this power is intensified by a further diminution of their numbers and a corresponding increase in the size of their holdings, a third form (3) of oligarchy arises. Here the members of the governing class keep the offices in their own hands by means of a law which provides that sons shall succeed to their fathers.

The fourth form (4) of oligarchy, analogous to extreme democracy, results from the possession of enormous wealth and influential friends. It is a 'dynasty' closely akin to monarchy; individuals are supreme, and not the law.

(B) *Aristocracy*

Besides democracy and oligarchy, there are still two forms of government which go to make up the quartet of generally recognized constitutions, viz. kingship (with which I have already dealt) and the so-called aristocracy.[1] But there is also a fifth, known by the generic name of polity. Owing to its infrequent occurrence, it has been overlooked by those who set out to enumerate the different kinds of constitution; like Plato in the *Republic*,[2] they confine themselves to the above four-fold classification. [1293^b] The only form of government to which the term 'aristocracy' can be applied *in its strict sense* is the one mentioned in an earlier section.[3] For it is the only constitution where the members are 'best' in an absolute sense, and not merely 'good' in relation to some given standard; here alone the good man is absolutely identical with the good citizen, whereas in all other constitutions the good citizen is a good man only relatively to the particular form of government under which he lives. On the other hand, there are certain forms which differ both from oligarchies and from the so-called polity in such a way that they *may be described as* aristocracies. Under them magistrates are chosen on a basis not only of wealth but also of moral worth. Constitutions of this kind differ from the two just mentioned, and are justly called aristocracies; for even in those states which do not make goodness a matter of public concern, there still exist men esteemed for their evident virtue. Accordingly, when a constitution has regard to wealth, to goodness, and to numbers, as at Carthage, it may be called an aristocracy; so too may a constitution like that of Sparta, which has regard only to goodness and numbers; and the same may be said

---

[1] i.e. aristocracy as *not* coincident with the best constitution.
[2] viii, ix.   [3] Pages 78, line 8; 96, line 2.

where the principles of democracy and aristocracy intermingle. In addition, therefore, to the first or best constitution there are these two forms of aristocracy, not forgetting a third represented by those varieties of 'polity' which show a marked leaning towards oligarchy.

(C) Polity

We have yet to deal with the constitution known as polity, and with tyranny. I mention them together in this way, despite the fact that polity is no more a deviation form of government than are the aristocracies referred to above. It must, however, be recognized that they one and all fall short of the most perfectly 'right' constitution, and so may be reckoned among the deviation forms, which last (as explained in an earlier section [1]) are in turn deviation forms of them. Finally, I shall have a word or two to say about tyranny by way of rounding off our study of constitutions; it naturally comes last in the series, for no other is so far removed from a right form of government.

Having explained my reason for adopting this method, I must now go on to deal with polity, the character of which will be clearer in the light of what has been said about oligarchy and democracy. Polity may be described generally as a fusion of oligarchy and democracy; but the term is most often used of those constitutions which incline towards democracy. Those tending more towards oligarchy are known as aristocracies, because culture and breeding are usually associated with wealth; besides, the well-to-do are commonly supposed to enjoy those material advantages for lack of which others take to crime, and are therefore called 'gentlemen' or 'notables.' Well then, since aristocracy aims at giving pre-eminence to the best of the citizens, there is a tendency to describe oligarchies likewise as states governed by notables.

Moreover [1294a] it is considered impossible that the rule of law should prevail in a state which is governed by the worst rather than by the best of its citizens, and equally impossible that aristocracy should prevail in a state not subject to the rule of law. But there is no rule of law where the laws themselves, however good, are not properly obeyed. We must therefore recognize

[1] Pages 77, 78. In that place, however, oligarchy (to which Aristotle is mainly referring here) is described as a deviation form of *pure* aristocracy and of polity.

the phrase 'rule of law' as having two senses: (1) obedience to
any laws that are in force, and (2) *goodness* of the laws which are
obeyed.[1] The latter sense is capable of further subdivision:
obedience may be rendered (*a*) to laws which are the best in
given circumstances, or (*b*) to laws which are absolutely the best.

Aristocracy, again, is thought to consist especially in the distribution of offices according to merit; its criterion is merit, as
that of oligarchy is wealth, and that of democracy free birth.
The principle of rule by a decision of the majority is found in *all*
constitutions: in oligarchies, in aristocracies, and in democracies the decision of a majority of those having constitutional
rights is final. The form of government known as 'polity' is
called by another name in most states. The fusion attempted
involves only the rich and poor, or wealth and free birth; but the
rich are commonly held to occupy the place of gentlemen.[2] In
point of fact, however, there are *three* grounds upon which it is
possible to claim an equal share in the mixed form of government: free birth, wealth, and merit.[3] Obviously then we should
use the term 'polity' for a fusion of the two elements, rich and
poor; 'aristocracy' we should apply to a fusion of all three elements, which is more of an aristocracy than any other form so
called—except the first and true form.

So far I have proved that there are forms of government other
than kingship, democracy, and oligarchy; I have explained
what they are, how aristocracies differ among themselves, and
polities from aristocracies; and lastly I have shown that aristocracies and polities are not far removed from one another.

Let us now go on to consider how, side by side with democracy and oligarchy, the so-called polity comes into being, and
how it should be organized. It will become clear in the process
what are the characteristic marks of democracy and oligarchy;
for in order to construct a polity one has to discover the difference between them, take something of each, and put the two
together like the parts of an indenture. Now there are three
different modes of effecting this combination or fusion. The
first (1) is to take and combine the rules governing oligarchies on
the one hand and democracies on the other with regard, say, to
jury service. In this case, under an oligarchy, the rich are

---

[1] Obedience can also be rendered to bad laws.—(A.)
[2] And therefore what is in fact polity comes to be called aristocracy.
[3] A fourth, described as 'good birth,' is a corollary of the last two, consisting of *inherited* wealth and merit.—(A.)

liable to a fine if they do not sit in the courts, but the poor are not paid to do so. Under a democracy, however, the poor receive wages for their service, but the rich are not penalized for non-attendance. The fusion of these two sets of regulations is a common or middle term between them; it is therefore character-istic of a polity, [1294ᵇ] combining as it does the two forms of government. There you have one method of fusion. Another (2) is to adopt a mean between two distinct rules. One con-stitution, for example, requires no property qualification, or only a very small one, for membership of the assembly, while the other requires a high one. In this case both rules cannot be employed to provide a common term, and we have to take a mean between the two. The third method of fusion (3) is to combine elements of both, taking something of the oligarchical rule and something of the democratic. For example, the appointment of magistrates by lot is commonly held to be characteristic of democracy, whereas the process of election for that purpose is looked upon as oligarchical. Again, the absence of property qualification is considered democratic, its presence as oligarchical. Here, accordingly, the method appropriate to an aristocracy or a polity is to take one element from each—choice of magistrates by vote from oligarchy, absence of pro-perty qualification from democracy.

Having explained the different modes of fusion, we may add that one criterion of a satisfactory blend of oligarchy with democ-racy is the possibility of describing a single constitution both (1) as a democracy and (2) as an oligarchy. Those who do so evidently feel that the fusion is a good one—as is generally true of a mean between two extremes, both of which can be detected therein. The constitution of Sparta is a case in point. (1) It is often described as a democracy because it embodies many demo-cratic features. In the first place (a) with regard to the up-bringing of children, the sons of the rich are treated in the same way as those of the poor, and their education is such as the latter may also attain. The same system of equality prevails in adolescence and onwards into manhood. There is no dis-tinction between rich and poor: they all eat the same food at the public tables, and the rich wear such clothing as any poor man could provide for himself. Moreover (b) the people elect to one of the two great institutions (the senate), and are themselves eligible for the other (the ephorate). (2) Others describe the Spartan constitution as an oligarchy, because here again many oligarchical features may be detected. Such are (*a*) the appointment to all offices by vote and not by lot, (*b*) the narrow circle of those entitled to inflict death or banishment, and so on. A properly fused polity should at once manifest both democratic and oligarchical elements, and yet seem as if it contained neither. It should owe its stability to its own intrinsic strength and not to external support; and its intrinsic strength should be due not to the goodwill of a majority (which might be so even in the case of a depraved constitution), but to the fact that there is not one class in the state willing to change the present form of government. So much for the correct organization of a polity and of the so-called aristocracies.

(D) *Tyranny*

[1295ª] It remains now to speak of tyranny; not that there is much to say about it,[1] but since I have reckoned it as a form of government it must find a place in our inquiry.

In an earlier section [2] I dealt with kingship [3] in the most usual sense of the word, asking whether it is beneficial or prejudicial to states, what sort of person should be king, from what source he should be drawn, and how established. In the course of that discussion I was led to distinguish two forms of tyranny, because they function in obedience to law, and their nature accordingly overlaps to some extent with that of kingship. (1) Some barbarian peoples elect monarchs with absolute power; and (2) there sometimes arose among the early Greeks monarchs of the same type, known as dictators. These two differ from one another in certain respects; but they have the marks of *kingship* inasmuch as their rule is based on popular consent, and of *tyranny* by virtue of their arbitrary rule, like that of a master over his slaves. There is also (3) a third form of tyranny, which is regarded particularly as such and is the counterpart of absolute kingship. It exists automatically where a single person exercises irresponsible rule over men who are all his peers or superiors, and does so with a view to his own advantage rather than to that of his subjects. It is consequently a regime of force, because no freeman is prepared to tolerate such government.

There you have the several kinds of tyranny and their distinctive characteristics.

[1] In Book V, however, Aristotle deals with tyranny at considerable length, though from another point of view (pages 161–169).
[2] Pages 92–100
[3] Of which tyranny is a deviation form.

3. THE BEST CONSTITUTION IN NORMAL CIRCUMSTANCES

We have now to inquire what is the best constitution for the majority of states, i.e. the best way of life for the majority of men? [1]   In doing so we shall not assume a standard of excellence beyond the reach of ordinary men, or a standard of education calling for exceptional gifts of nature and fortune, or, yet again, an ideal form of government.   No, we shall confine ourselves to the sort of life which most men are able to share, and a constitution to which most states can attain.   Some of the so-called aristocracies mentioned above are beyond the reach of most states, while others are so closely akin to the constitution known as polity that both must be treated as one.   The question asked above may be answered by reference to a single set of principles.   If I was right when I said in the *Ethics* [2] that a happy life is one lived in freedom without impediments, and that goodness consists in a mean, it follows that the best way of life is a mean, a mean which can be attained by everyone.   These same criteria must be used to judge the excellence or otherwise of a constitution, which is, so to speak, the life of a state.

[1295^b] Every state has three parts: the very rich, the very poor, and the middle class.   Now it is admitted that moderation and the mean are best, from which we must infer that a middle state will invariably be best in the possession of the gifts of fortune.   For (1) it is in these circumstances that men most readily lend an ear to reason.   One who is excessively handsome, excessively strong, excessively well born, excessively rich, or who, conversely, suffers from abject poverty, abject weakness, abject lowliness of birth—such a man, I say, finds it difficult to obey the voice of reason.   Those in the first group tend to become violent and major criminals, the others to become rogues and petty offenders; violence and roguery are the twin sources of wrongdoing.

(2) The middle class is least likely to shirk or to covet the responsibility of government, both of which attitudes are harmful to the state.

(3) Those whom fortune has endowed with too many advantages, whether of strength, riches, friends, or the like,

[1] See page 105, footnote 2.   Note also that whenever Aristotle uses the word 'best' in this section we are to understand him as meaning 'best for the majority of men.'
[2] *Nic. Eth.* 1098^{a}16; 1153^{b}10; 1177^{a}12.

neither will nor can obey; the trouble starts at home, where children are so pampered that they never learn discipline even at their lessons.   Those, on the other hand, who suffer too great want of these advantages are mean-spirited creatures.   The net result is that while one class is unable to rule, but only to obey like slaves, the other is incapable of obedience and can only rule as a master rules his slaves.   Thus you get a state consisting not of freemen, but of masters and slaves, the former contemptuous and the latter envious.   All of which is far removed from friendliness and the true spirit of a political society.   Society springs from friendliness; enemies will not even travel in one another's company.   The state aims at being, as far as possible, a society of equals and likes; and this ideal comes nearest to fulfilment in the middle class.   Therefore, of course, a state which rests upon the middle class is the best constituted in respect of those elements which, in our opinion, constitute a state.

(4) The middle classes are more secure than any other. They do not, like the poor, covet their neighbours' goods; nor do others covet theirs, as the poor do those of the rich; and since they neither plot against others, nor are themselves plotted against, they live out their lives in safety.   Hence the admirable prayer of Phocylides: [1] 'A middle-class citizen fain would I be; such folk enjoy so many blessings.'   All this goes to show that the best political society is one where power lies with the middle class.   And it is equally clear that good government is attainable in those states where the middle class is sufficiently large to outnumber both the other classes or at least each of them singly; for in this last case its addition will turn the scale and prevent either extreme from having its own way.   Blessed the state, therefore, whose citizens own property sufficient for their needs but in moderation.   [1296^a] For wherever some have great possessions, and others nothing at all, you get extreme democracy or pure oligarchy.   Either extreme, on the other hand, may produce tyranny, which is liable to spring alike from rampant democracy and from oligarchy, though not from the middle constitutions and those akin to them.[2]

Again (5), the middle type of constitution is clearly best inasmuch as no other is free from faction.   Where you have a large middle class there is least likelihood of faction and civil

---

[1] Phocylides of Miletus (6th cent. B.C.), a gnomic poet.
[2] [1296^{a}5, 6].   I will explain why later on [Book V, page 151, lines 22–31] when dealing with revolutions.—(A.)

discord.   And large states are less liable to faction for the same reason—a large middle class.   In small ones, on the other hand, it is easy for the whole population to be divided into two classes —rich and poor with little or no mean between them.   Democracies are generally safer and more permanent than oligarchies because they have a middle class which is more numerous and enjoys a larger share in government than under an oligarchy. In those democracies which have no middle class and the poor far outnumber the rich, trouble ensues and the state soon goes to pieces.

(6) Another proof of the value of the middle classes may be seen in the fact that they have produced the best legislators. Solon [1] was one, as his own poems show; so was Lycurgus,[2] who, by the way, was *not* of royal descent; so too were Charondas [3] and most other lawgivers.

What I have been saying serves also to explain why the majority of constitutions are either democratic or oligarchical. (1) In a majority of states the middle class is small, with the result that as soon as one or other of the main parties (rich or poor) gains an advantage, it oversteps the mean, handles the constitution according to its own whims, and thereby establishes either a democracy or an oligarchy.   (2) Factions arise, the rich fall foul of the poor, and the victorious party, no matter which it may turn out to be, refuses to establish a constitution founded on justice and equality; it considers political supremacy as the prize of victory, and sets up a democracy or an oligarchy as the case may be.   Finally (3) the two states [4] which at one time or another have enjoyed the hegemony of Greece, being concerned exclusively with their own particular forms of government and their own interests, have instituted democracies and oligarchies respectively in the states under their control.

These are the reasons why the middle form of government has rarely ever existed, and in very few states.   One man, and only one,[5] of those who have hitherto dominated the Greek world has let himself be persuaded to favour the introduction of such a type.   And now [1296[b]] it has become the habit in individual

[1] *c.* 639–*c.* 559 B.C.
[2] See page 52, footnote 1.
[3] See pages 62, 63.
[4] Athens and Sparta.
[5] The reference is perhaps to Antipater, whose ascendancy coincided with Aristotle's second Athenian residence, to which this Book belongs.   He had probably been persuaded of the value of such a constitution by Aristotle himself some years earlier.

states to reject the principle of equality; all men seek dominion, or, if beaten, are ready to submit.

The foregoing study enables us to determine which is the best form of government for the majority of states, and why. Having done so, we shall not find it difficult to arrange the other constitutions [1] in their correct order of merit. That which is nearest to the best must always be better than the remainder, and that which is farthest from the mean must always be worse, provided we are not judging relatively to particular circumstances.[2]

4. APPROPRIATE CONSTITUTIONS

The next question on our list is as follows: What and what kind of constitution is appropriate to what and what kind of persons? [3] Let us begin by assuming a general principle common to all governments, viz. that the part of a state which desires the permanence of the constitution should be stronger than the part which does not. Now every state is a compound of quality (free birth, wealth, culture, nobility of descent) and quantity (superiority of numbers). Quality may belong to one of the classes making up the state and quantity to another. For example, the low-born may be more numerous than the high-born, the poor than the rich; and yet their numerical superiority may fail to counterbalance the superior quality of the opposite group, and therefore quantity must be weighed against quality.

(1) Where the number of the poor outweighs the superior quality of the other side, there will naturally be a democracy, varying in form according to the sort of people who possess this numerical superiority. If they are agriculturists, you will have the first kind of democracy; [4] if they are mechanics and day-labourers, extreme democracy [5] will result; and so with the intermediate forms between those two.

---

[1] Sc. the different kinds of democracy and oligarchy which we have agreed to recognize.—(A.)

[2] I use the phrase 'relatively to particular circumstances,' because although one constitution may be preferable in itself, there is nothing to prevent another being more suitable in a given case.—(A.)

[3] See page 105, footnote 2.

[4] See pages 108, line 20; 110, line 24.

[5] See pages 108, line 36; 111, line 10.

(2) Where the rich and the notables excel in point of quality more than they fall short in point of quantity, there will be an oligarchy; and this again will vary in form according to the degree of superiority manifested by the oligarchical body.[1]

(3) Where the middle class outnumbers both or only one of the extremes, a durable polity can be established. For in such a case there is no risk [1297ᵃ] of the wealthy uniting with the poor against the middle class. Neither of them will ever agree to be subject to the other, and if they look for a form of government more in their common interest than is polity, they will not find one. Mistrust of one another would always lead them to reject a system of alternate rule. A neutral arbitrator enjoys more confidence than anyone else, and that is exactly what your 'man in the middle' is. The better the mixture of its elements, the more durable a constitution will prove to be. In this connection, many of those who desire to establish aristocratic constitutions go astray, not only by giving too much power to the wealthy, but also by deceiving the people; for there inevitably comes a time when illusory privileges give rise to undoubted evils, since the encroachments of the rich do more to destroy the constitution than those of the people.

The devices employed in oligarchies for hoodwinking the people are five in number: they concern the assembly, the magistracies, the law courts, the possession of arms, and athletic exercises.

(1) *The assembly* is open to all alike, but fines for non-attendance are incurred only by the rich, or incurred by them at a far higher rate.

(2) As regards the *magistracies*, those who possess ratable property may not decline office upon oath,[2] but the poor may do so.

(3) As regards the *law courts*, the rich are fined for non-attendance while the poor absent themselves with impunity; or else, as under the laws of Charondas, the rich incur a heavy fine, and the poor only a light one. In some states all who have registered themselves may attend both the assembly and the

[1] The legislator should always have regard to the middle class in his constitution; if the laws he makes are oligarchical, he should extend their benefits to the middle class, and if they are democratic he should try to attach that class to his laws.—(A.)

[2] An oath swearing that one lacked the means necessary to fulfil the duties of office.

courts; once they have registered, attendance is obligatory under pain of a heavy fine. The purpose of this rule is to stop men registering through fear of the fines to which they may become liable, and thereby to exclude them from the courts and the assembly.

As regards (4) the *possession of arms*, and (5) *athletic exercises*, similar regulations are laid down. The poor need not have arms, but the rich are fined for not having them. Likewise the poor are subject to no fine for non-attendance at the gymnasium, but the rich are; and consequently the latter attend in order to escape the fine, while the former, having nothing to fear, absent themselves.

These are the devices of oligarchical legislation. Democracies have their counter-devices: the poor are paid for attending the assembly and the law courts, but the rich are not fined for being absent.

It is obvious, therefore, that in order to achieve an equitable mixture of the two principles one must combine elements from both, paying the poor for attendance, and fining the rich for non-attendance. Under such a system all will take part in the assembly and in the administration of justice; otherwise the constitution is a one-sided affair. [1297^b] Although the constitution of a polity should give citizen rights only to those who possess arms, it is impossible to define absolutely the property qualification thus involved, or to say that it must consist of a fixed amount in all cases. We must try to discover in each case, and appoint for each, the highest amount that can be required while still enabling those who enjoy citizen rights to outnumber those who do not. As for the poor, they are ready to keep quiet, even when excluded from office, provided they are not subjected to violence or to confiscation of their property. But this is no easy thing to ensure, because the ruling class is not always humane. In time of war, for example, the poor generally begrudge their services if they are not granted a subsistence allowance to save them from destitution. Grant them that, and they are quite willing to fight.

In some states the citizen body is made up not only of those doing military service, but also of retired veterans. In Malis, for example, it consisted of both; but the magistrates were drawn from those actually on service. The earliest form of government in Greece, after the abolition of kingship, was one in which the citizen body was drawn exclusively from the warrior class, represented at first by cavalry.[1] But as states grew larger and the strength of infantry divisions increased, more persons were allowed political rights; and this extension of the franchise explains why the constitutions we now call polities were at that time called democracies. As might have been expected, the old constitutions were oligarchical or monarchical. While their populations remained small, they had no large middle class; and the people as a whole, weak both in numbers and in organization, were all the more ready to obey.

I have now explained (1) why there are several forms of government, and why there are forms other than those commonly recognized.[2] I have also explained the differences between those several forms, and the causes underlying the character of each. I have shown (2) which is the best constitution for the majority of states. And with regard to the other constitutions, I have explained (3) which kind is appropriate to which kind of civic body.

5. Methods of Framing Constitutions

We must now go on to deal with the next subject,[3] both generally and in relation to particular forms of government, first laying down a suitable basis of discussion.

All constitutions have three elements, and a good legislator must take account of what is expedient for each of them under these several heads. So long as they are properly constructed, so is the constitution as a whole; and according as they differ from one another, so will constitutions differ among themselves. The first element (A) is the deliberative, concerned with public affairs; [1298ᵃ] second (B), the executive; [4] and third (C), the judicature.

(A) *The Deliberative Element*

The deliberative element is supreme first in deciding upon war or peace, and for making or dissolving of alliances; secondly in enacting laws; thirdly in cases involving a sentence of death,

[1] Military strength and superiority depended at that time on cavalry. Infantry is useless without the science of tactics; this did not exist in ancient times, and therefore the strength of an army lay in its cavalry.—(A.)

[2] Both democracy and the other constitutions have more than one form. —(A.)

[3] See page 105, footnote 2.

[4] The question here is what the magistracies are to be, what the extent of their jurisdiction, and how they are to be filled.—(A.)

exile, or confiscation; and fourthly in choosing magistrates and calling them to account when they retire from office. Now this element can be arranged in any one of three different ways: (1) *all* the above powers may be assigned to *all* the citizens; (2) *all* may be assigned to *some* of them;[1] or (3) *some* powers may be assigned to *all* the citizens, while *others* are allowed only to *some*.

(1) It is characteristic of democracy to assign *all* matters of deliberation to the *entire* citizen body; the sort of equality implied thereby is exactly what the people demand. But there are several ways in which this can be done.

(*a*) All the citizens may deliberate, not in a single body, but in relays,[2] and only for the purpose of enacting laws, deciding constitutional matters, and hearing the announcements of magistrates.

(*b*) All the citizens may deliberate in a single body, but only to choose magistrates and call them to account, to enact laws, and to decide issues of war and peace. Other matters will be left to the deliberation of specially appointed boards chosen from the whole citizen body either by election or by lot.

(*c*) The citizens may meet in a single body to appoint and examine magistrates, and to deliberate questions of war and foreign alliance, while other matters are left to the control of highly qualified magistrates appointed, as far as possible, by election.

(*d*) All may meet to deliberate on all matters, nothing being left to the boards of magistrates excepting preliminary inquiries. Extreme democracy is now run on these lines; it is a form analogous, as I have argued,[3] to the 'dynastic' form of oligarchy and the tyrannical form of monarchy.

All these ways of ordering the deliberative element are democratic.

(2) Deliberation by *some* of the citizens on *all* matters is characteristic of oligarchy; and here again there are several ways in which it may be effected.

(*a*) Membership of the deliberative body is based on a moderate property qualification, and that body is accordingly

[1] By assigning (*a*) all to one magistracy or board of magistracies, or else (*b*) different ones to different magistracies.—(A.)

[2] This was done in the constitution framed by Telecles of Miletus. In other constitutions the boards of magistrates meet together for deliberation as a single body, but the citizens become members of those boards in relays (drawn from the tribes and the smallest units thereof) until all have served their turn —(A.)

[3] Pages 109, lines 9–14; 110, lines 5–9; 112, lines 6, 7.

large; it makes no changes contrary to the law; and all who possess the required amount of property are allowed to take part in its proceedings. This is in fact an oligarchy, but inclines to polity by virtue of its moderation.

(b) Membership of the deliberative body is not open to everyone [1298ᵇ] who can satisfy a fixed property qualification, but only to selected persons, who rule, as above, in accordance with the law. This is an oligarchical arrangement.

(c) Those who possess the power to deliberate recruit their own number by co-optation, or merely succeed by heredity; in either case they are entitled to override the laws. Here, definitely, you have an oligarchical system.

(3) Where *some* of the citizens deliberate on *some* matters only,[1] the constitution is aristocratic. It may be, on the other hand, that some matters are submitted to the deliberation of persons chosen by election, others to persons chosen by lot;[2] or all matters may fall under the cognizance of a single body consisting of persons chosen partly by vote and partly by lot. Such arrangements are partly characteristic of polity inclining towards aristocracy, and partly of pure polity.

These are the several forms of the deliberative element, corresponding to the several constitutions. Each constitution is framed according to one or other of the systems I have just outlined.

(1) *Democracy*, as now most commonly conceived,[3] would do well (a) to raise the standard of its deliberative body by adopting the regulations applied by oligarchies to meetings of the law-courts. Under these regulations all who are wanted for jury service must attend or pay a fine, as against the democratic system of paying the poor for their attendance. I say this oligarchical practice should be applied to meetings of a democratic assembly, because that body will deliberate more satisfactorily when they do so all together—the common people along with the notables, and vice versa. A democracy of the type in question will also do well (b) to choose its deliberative body, either by vote or by lot, in equal numbers from the different

[1] Whereas *all*, for instance, may deliberate such questions as war and peace and the examination of magistrates, other matters are reserved to elected magistrates.—(A.)

[2] By lot, that is to say, either from the whole citizen body or from previously selected candidates.—(A.)

[3] I refer to the type in which the people can overrule the laws.—(A.)

parts of the state. It is likewise an advantage (c), when the common people far outnumber the notables who have political experience, not to pay all the citizens for attending the assembly, but only so many as will balance the number of the notables, or else to eliminate by lot those who are in excess of this number.

(2) It is in the interest of *oligarchies* (a) that some members of the deliberative body be co-opted from the common people; or else that a board of magistrates be set up, such as exists in some states under the name of 'preliminary council' or 'council of legal supervision,' and the citizens left to deal only with such matters as have first been considered by that board.[1] Again (b) it is in the interest of oligarchies either that the common people should vote only for measures introduced by the government, or at any rate not contrary thereto; or else that the people as a whole should act in a consultative capacity; the magistrates forming the deliberative body. If the second of these last alternatives is chosen, it should function on opposite lines to those followed in polities: the people should be sovereign when rejecting, but not when passing proposals; and any which they pass should be referred back to the magistrates. In polities things are done the other way round: the magistrates are sovereign when passing, but not when rejecting proposals; and any which they pass are referred back [1299a] to the people.

These then are our conclusions regarding the deliberative and sovereign element of the constitution.

(B) *The Executive*

And now we pass on to consider the executive. This is another element of the constitution which is capable of manifold arrangement, in respect of (1) the number of magistracies; (2) their functions; (3) length of tenure in each case; [2] and (4) the method of appointment with reference to three questions—who should be eligible, who should appoint, and how? We must discover first the true extent of that 'manifold arrangement,' and then go on to explain what particular magistracies are suited to particular constitutions.

---

[1] In this way the people at large will have a deliberative voice, without being able to make constitutional changes.—(A.)

[2] Some are appointed for six months, others for a shorter period; some for a year, others for longer. So we have to ask whether they should be held for life, or for a long term of years; and if for neither, whether or not the same person should hold office more than once.—(A.) [He does not discuss these questions in detail.]

But at the very outset we are up against a difficulty: what is to be included in the term 'magistracy'? So many officials are required by a political association that we can hardly describe as 'magistrates' anyone and everyone who has been elected or chosen by lot. To begin with, the priesthood must be considered something quite different from a political magistracy; so must the offices of choregus, herald, ambassador. 'Official duties' are first *political* when they extend to the whole citizen body in a particular sphere of action (e.g. as a general commands the state militia in the field), or to some section of that body (e.g. as inspectors of women and children supervise their respective charges); second *economic*, like those of officials elected to measure out public issues of corn; and third *menial*, such as wealthy cities impose on their slaves. But on the whole, it is best to describe as 'magistrates' only those officials whose duty it is, in some definite field, to deliberate, to decide, and to give instruction—but above all to give instruction which is the special domain of a magistrate. Not that all this is of any significance in practice; there is no judicial ruling on the meaning of the word, and the whole question is merely of speculative interest.

In discussing any constitution, particularly those of small states, it is more important to ask what kind and number of magistracies are necessary to a state's existence, and what kind (even though not necessary) help to make a good constitution. In large states it is possible for each individual function to be in the hands of a separate magistracy; the size of the population ensures a plentiful supply of eligible candidates for office, and thereby enables some offices to be held by the same person at very long intervals or only once in his lifetime. Besides being possible, it is *desirable* that this should be so; for a task is always carried out more efficiently when the man responsible can give it his undivided attention.

[1299^b] A different situation arises in small states, where numerous functions must be concentrated in the hands of a few individuals. Owing to the small population, it is difficult for many to be in office at one time; if there were, who could be found to succeed them? I grant that small states do sometimes need the same magistracies as large ones, and the same laws governing their tenure and administration. But the point is that large states need those magistracies most of the time, whereas small ones experience the need at long intervals. Accordingly there is no reason why a small state should not oblige its magistrates to undertake several duties at once. They will not interfere with one another; and in any case, when the population is small the magistrates will just have to take on a variety of tasks.

In order to determine how many magistracies can be safely entrusted to one man, it will be useful (1) to obtain a clear idea of how many magistracies a state *must* have, and how many it *ought* to have even though they are not necessary. Nor (2) must we overlook the question as to which matters should fall within the authority of local magistracies, and which should come under the control of central government. For example, should one person be responsible for maintaining order in the market-place and another in another place, or should a single person exercise that function in every place? We have also to inquire (3) whether duties should be assigned according to the type of function or to the human groups involved. I mean, for instance, ought a single magistrate to be appointed to deal with the whole business of preserving order, or should one take charge of the children and another of women? (4) What about differences of constitution? Is the government to consist of the same magistracies in a democracy, in an oligarchy, in an aristocracy, and in a monarchy? [1] Or do the magistracies, as well as the magistrates, vary from one constitution to another, except perhaps in so far as in some cases the same magistracies are suitable while in others they are not? [2]

True, some magistracies are peculiar to certain forms of government. Such is the 'preliminary council,' which is not democratic, whereas the council *is*. There must indeed be some kind of body to undertake preliminary deliberation on behalf of the people, who will otherwise be unable to attend to their normal business. But if this body is small, it is oligarchical in character; a preliminary council is inevitably small, and therefore inevitably oligarchical. But when you have a council *and* a 'preliminary council,' the latter serves as a check on the

---

[1] I say 'the same,' bearing in mind, of course, that they are not drawn in each case from the same, or even a similar, stratum of society, but come from a different one under each different constitution: e.g. from the cultured in an aristocracy, from the rich in an oligarchy, from the free-born in a democracy.—(A.)

[2] Thus in some constitutions it is appropriate that magistracies should have extensive powers, in others a more limited authority.—(A.)

former, because while the council is democratic the 'preliminary council' is oligarchical.   Even the authority of the council, however, is undermined in an extreme democracy, where the people themselves meet to transact every kind of business. [1300ª] And meet in this way they generally do when they are well paid for their attendance.   In such circumstances they have plenty of leisure, and therefore hold frequent meetings and decide everything for themselves.   Supervisors of women and children, and suchlike officials, are more characteristic of an aristocracy than of a democracy, for it is impossible to prevent poor men's wives from wandering abroad.   Nor do they fit into an oligarchy, where the wives of the ruling class are too sensitive to endure control.

But I have said enough on this subject, and must now try to explain the order of appointing magistrates.   The varieties in the mode of this procedure depend on three determining factors —who appoints, who is eligible, how they are appointed—and the combinations of these give us all possible different ways. Each of the three admits in turn of three varieties: (A) *All* the citizens, or (B) only *some*, appoint.   Either (1) the magistrates are chosen *from all* or (2) *from some*.[1]   They may be appointed either (a) by *vote* or (b) by *lot*.   Again, these several varieties may be coupled; I mean (C) some magistrates may be appointed *by some*, others *by all*, and (3) some again *from some*, and others *from all*, and (c) some by *vote* and others by *lot*.

Each variety of these admits of four modes.   For either (A 1a) all may appoint from all by vote, or (A 1b) all from all by lot, or (A 2a) all from some by vote, or (A 2b) all from some by lot;[2] or again (A 1c, A 2c) to some magistracies in the one way, to some in the other.   Again, if it is only some who appoint, they may do so either (B 1a) from all by vote, or (B 1b) from all by lot, or (B 2a) from some by vote, or (B 2b) from some by lot, or to some magistracies in the one way, to others in the other, i.e. (B 1c) from all, to some magistracies by vote, to

[1] Distinguished either by a property qualification or birth or merit; or else for some special reason, as in the unique case of Megara, where only those were eligible who had returned from exile and fought together against the democracy.—(A.)   [The reference may be either to the revolution of 424 B.C., or to the withdrawal of Megara from the Athenian alliance in 447.]

[2] If from all [A 1a and A 1b], either by sections, as, for example, by tribes and wards and phratries, until all the citizens have served their turn; or the citizens may be in all cases eligible indiscriminately.—(A.)

some by lot, and (B 2c) from some, to some offices by vote, to some by lot.

Thus the modes that arise, excepting two (C 3) out of the three couplings, number twelve. Of these systems two are democratic: that all should appoint from all (A 1a) by vote or (A 1b) by lot—or (A 1c) by both. It is characteristic of polity that all should not appoint at once, but should appoint from all or from some either by lot or by vote or by both,[1] or appoint to some magistracies from all and to others from some. It is also characteristic of polity (though more oligarchical than the former method) that (B 1c) some should appoint from all, to magistracies by vote, to others by lot. And it is characteristic of a polity inclining to aristocracy to appoint (A 3a, b, c, B 3a, b, c) from both, to some magistracies from all, to others from some. [1300^b] It is oligarchical that (B 2) some should appoint from some; so too is it (B 2b) that some should appoint from some by lot (even if this does not actually occur), or (B 2c) that some should appoint from some by both. That (B 1a) some should appoint from all, and that (A 2a) all should appoint from some, by vote, is aristocratic.

Such are the different ways of appointing magistrates, corresponding to different forms of government. Which is suitable to which, and how they should be established, will appear when we have determined [2] the nature of their prerogatives.[3]

(C) *The Judicature*

It remains to say something about the last of the three constitutional elements—the judicature, with regard to which we must follow the same plan.[4] The factors which give rise to differences between the courts are again three in number: membership, jurisdiction, and appointment of members. In other words, are the courts recruited from the whole citizen body, or only from one section? How many kinds of court are there? Are the members chosen by vote or by lot?

Well, let us start with the second of these questions. There are eight kinds of law-court, as follows. (1) The court of

---

[1] 'By both': i.e. to some magistracies by lot, to others by vote.—(A.)

[2] He does not discuss this question.

[3] By the prerogative of a magistracy I mean the authority it exercises over, say, the revenue or defences of a state. The authority of a general, for instance, is not the same as that of market commissioners [See *Ath. Con.*, LI].—(A.)

[4] i.e. the same as was employed under the heading *Executive*.

audits.   (2) The court which deals with anyone who commits an offence against any public interest.   (3) That which tries cases of high treason.   (4) That which hears disputes arising from the imposition of penalties, and to which magistrates as well as private persons may have recourse.   (5) That which tries cases of contract between private persons where large sums are involved. (6) That which tries cases of homicide, which are of several kinds: (a) premeditated homicide; (b) involuntary homicide; (c) cases in which the facts are admitted, but the guilt is disputed; and (d) cases in which murderers who have been exiled for involuntary homicide from justice are arraigned for premeditated murder on their return.[1]   (7) The court which hears suits (a) between one alien and another, and (b) between aliens and citizens.   Besides all these there is (8) a court for petty suits involving sums from one to five drachmas or a little more; cases of this sort do not require many jurors, but they have to be tried all the same.

We need dwell no longer on (7) (b) and (8), since we are concerned rather with those courts which have a more immediate bearing on public life, and which, when mismanaged, are liable to cause faction and constitutional upheavals.

Now if (1) *all* the citizens are eligible to sit upon *all* the different kinds of cases distinguished above, they may be appointed (a) by *vote*, or (b) by *lot*, or (c) *sometimes by lot* and *sometimes by vote*. If *all* are likewise eligible to sit on only *some* cases, they may be appointed (d) some by *vote*, and some by *lot*. [1301ᵃ] These then are the four modes of appointing judges from the whole citizen body.   There will also be four modes if (2) only *some* of them are eligible: they may be appointed (a) *from some* by *vote* to sit on *all* cases; or (b) *from some* by *lot* to sit on *all* cases; or (c) partly by *lot* and partly by *vote*;[2] or (d) *some courts* may be composed of members, some of whom are appointed by *lot* and some by *vote*, the jurisdiction of both classes being the same.   These modes then, as I said, correspond to those previously mentioned.

Furthermore, (3) these methods of appointment may be coupled.   I mean, some members may be chosen from the whole citizen body, others out of some, and some out of both. For instance, a single court may be composed of some chosen

---

[1] e.g. the so-called Court of Phreatto at Athens.   Cases of this sort, however, are rare, even in large cities.   The different kinds of homicide may be tried by the same or by different courts.—(A.)
[2] This is a combination of (1) and (2)

from the whole citizen body, and of others chosen out of some only, either by lot or by vote or by both.

So much for the ways in which the courts of law can be constituted. The first way, in which the members are drawn from all the citizens, and the courts have jurisdiction in all matters, is democratic. The second way, in which the members are drawn from one section only, and the courts have jurisdiction in all matters, is oligarchical. The third way, in which the members of some courts are drawn from the whole citizen body, and those of others from one section only, is a feature of aristocracy and polity.[1]

[1] At this point Aristotle leaves the fourth point of his programme, but returns to it by a somewhat different approach in Book VI (see page 105, footnote 2).

B. PATHOLOGY OF THE STATE (Book V)

1. General Causes of Sedition and Constitutional Change

[1301a19]. We have now almost completed our programme. It remains,[1] however, to discuss the following points: first, the general causes of constitutional change, together with their number and nature; secondly, the ways in which each constitution is liable to degenerate, i.e. from what and into what it usually changes; thirdly, the policies which will best ensure the permanence of constitutions both collectively and individually, and the actual means which will serve that purpose in the case of each particular constitution.

I have already explained [2] the reason why there are several forms of government: it is that whilst all men agree in paying tribute to justice and proportionate equality, they fall short of it in practice. This truth must form the starting-point of our discussion. Democracy arose from the assumption that those who are equal in any respect whatsoever are equal in *all* respects; men think that because they are all equally free-born they are absolutely equal. Oligarchy derives from the assumption that those who are unequal in one respect are wholly unequal; men of superior wealth consider themselves to be absolutely superior. The democrats accordingly claim that, since they are equal, they should have equal shares of everything; while the oligarchs expect to get more on the strength of their alleged inequality (i.e. superiority). Both these forms of government embody an element of justice, but they both fall short of absolute justice; and this is why democrats and oligarchs alike have recourse to sedition [3] whenever their share of constitutional rights does not measure up to the preconceived idea of justice which they happen to entertain. [1303b3–7] In oligarchies the masses turn to sedition on the grounds already noted, viz. that they are

---

[1] See page 105, footnote 2.

[2] Page 86, lines 15–30.

[3] The word 'sedition' (Greek *stasis*) occurs repeatedly in this Book. It denotes the formation of a group (or that group itself) for the accomplishment of some political end, whether by legal or illegal means. The result may be political change within the framework of the constitution, or revolution.

unjustly denied equal rights notwithstanding their *de facto* equality. In democracies, on the other hand, it is the notables who take this course, objecting that they have no more than equal rights notwithstanding their *de facto* superiority. [1301ᵃ39] Those who are pre-eminent in merit have the best right of all to attempt sedition, for [1301ᵇ] they alone can be fairly considered superior in an absolute sense; and yet they are the very last to do so. There is also some excuse for those who claim more than an equal share on the strength of their superior birth, which is commonly held to mean descent from virtuous and wealthy ancestors.

Here then, so to speak, are the sources or well-springs of sedition, resulting in two kinds of constitutional change. (1) Sometimes it aims to effect a transformation of the existing form of government: to turn democracy into oligarchy, or vice versa; or democracy and oligarchy into polity and aristocracy, or the latter into the former. (2) Sometimes, however, it is not directed against the existing constitution. (*a*) The seditious party may choose to maintain the present establishment (an oligarchy, for instance, or a monarchy), but to administer it in their own way. Or (*b*) the issue may be one of degree: they may seek to render an oligarchy more, or less, oligarchical; to make a democracy more, or less, democratic; or to apply similar treatment to some other form of government. Again (*c*), sedition may be directed towards change in one department only of the constitution, e.g. the creation or abolition of a particular office. At Sparta, for example, some authorities tell us that Lysander attempted to abolish the kingship,[1] and King Pausanias [2] the ephoralty. At Epidamnus, too, the constitution underwent a partial change when a council was substituted for the assembly of tribal heads; yet even to-day the magistrates are the only members of the civic body who are obliged to attend the public assembly when it meets to vote on an official appointment. Another oligarchical feature of the Epidamnian constitution until recent years was the existence of a single archon.

At all events, whatever the aim of sedition may be, it stems in every case from inequality, though there is no inequality if unequals are treated in proportion to their mutual inequality.[3]

---

[1] i.e. the hereditary kingship of the Heracleidae.

[2] He was not legally king, but only agent for his cousin Pleistarchus, who was an infant at the date in question (*c.* 480 B.C.).

[3] For this reason hereditary kingship involves no inequality except when it exists among equals.—(A.)

The desire for equality, therefore, is the mainspring of sedition. But equality is of two kinds—numerical and proportionate to desert. Numerical equality implies that one receives exactly the same (i.e. equivalent) number of things or volume of a thing as everyone else. Equality proportionate to desert implies treatment based on equality of ratios. Here is an illustration of what I mean. Arithmetically, the excess of 3 over 2 is equal to that of 2 over 1; but proportionally, the excess of 4 over 2 is equal to that of 2 over 1, because 2 is the same fraction of 4 as 1 is of 2. Now although men agree that absolute justice consists in proportion to desert, they differ, as I noted above, as to the principle of desert. Some think that if men are equal in one respect they are equal in all; others maintain that if they are superior in one respect then they are entitled to superiority in everything. Hence the frequent occurrence of two constitutions—democracy and oligarchy. [1302ª] While poverty and wealth abound, good birth and merit are rare. You will find a hundred virtuous men of noble family in few, if any, states; but there are many which harbour that number of rich men. No form of government, however, can be satisfactory when based exclusively on either the oligarchical or the democratic notion of equality. That much is proved by experience: no such constitution has ever survived. Why not? Because anything that originates in error is doomed to failure. The right way, therefore, is to employ in some cases the principle of numerical equality, and in others that of equality proportionate to desert. Nevertheless, democracy is manifestly safer, and less troubled by sedition, than oligarchy. In oligarchies there is the twofold danger of the oligarchs falling out among themselves, *and* of becoming embroiled with the popular party. In democracies, on the other hand, you have the single threat of a clash with the oligarchical party; there is only the remotest likelihood of internal dissension among the democratic groups themselves. Democracy, too, is more closely akin than oligarchy to that form of government which is based on the middle classes and which is the most enduring of all forms short of the ideal.

In considering the rise of sedition and constitutional change, we must begin with a general survey of their origins and causes. We may say that these are three in number, each of which must first be described in outline. We want to know (1) what is the state of mind leading to sedition, (2) what are the objectives in view, and (3) what are the occasions giving rise to political upheaval and mutual strife?

(1) I have already spoken [1] of the general and principal cause of that state of mind which disposes men to revolution. In some cases it is a craving for equality on the part of those who believe they are the equals of those more highly privileged than themselves. In other cases it is a craving for inequality, i.e. superiority, on the part of those who conceive that despite their superiority they enjoy no advantage over others, compared with whom they are treated as equals or even inferiors.[2] Inferiors have recourse to sedition in order to achieve equality, equals in order to achieve superiority.

Such, then, is the state of mind leading to sedition. (2) The objectives are profit and honour—and also the fear of their opposites, for the instigators of political sedition are often trying to save themselves or their friends from a fine or from disgrace.

(3) The occasions which give rise to disturbances, inasmuch as they produce the frame of mind which disposes men to seek the objectives aforesaid, may be counted as seven or more, according to one's point of view. Two of them are identical with two of the objectives mentioned above, but acting in a different way. As *objectives*, (a) profit and (b) honour create dissension because, as I have explained, men desire those things for themselves; [1302ᵇ] but as *occasions*, they do so because men see others enjoying—whether justly or unjustly—more than they themselves possess. Other occasions are: (c) insolence, (d) fear, (e) superiority in some shape or form, (f) contempt, (g) disproportionate increase in some part of the state. The following may also create dissension, though in a different way: (h) election intrigues, (i) wilful negligence, (j) neglect of apparently insignificant changes, and (k) dissimilarity of the state's component parts.[3]

The part played by *insolence* [4] and *profit* in fostering sedition is not far to seek. When those in office are overweening and grasping,[5] sedition rears its head, not only between one party and

---

[1] Pages 133, line 25; 134, line 36.
[2] Either of these cravings may or may not be justified.—(A.)
[3] Aristotle now deals with these occasions in the following order: (c) and (a), (b), (e), (d), (f)–(k).
[4] For historical examples see pages 139–41.
[5] Magistrates prey sometimes on individuals, and sometimes on the general public.—(A.)

another, but also against the constitution which makes these abuses possible.

Nor is it difficult to understand how *honour* can beget sedition among those who, while they are themselves dishonoured, see others honoured—justly or unjustly in either case according as honour and dishonour are deserved or undeserved.

Superiority opens the door to sedition when some person or group of persons has grown too powerful for the constitution and can defy the civic body.   From situations of this kind either a monarchy or government by a family clique is likely to result, and therefore some states (e.g. Athens and Argos) have adopted the measure known as ostracism.[1]   But it is more satisfactory to ensure at the outset that such powerful elements have no place in the state, than to allow their development and only then to seek a remedy.

Fear may be the immediate cause of sedition among those who dread the consequences of their own misdeeds, or who are anxious to forestall some threatened injustice.   At Rhodes, for example, the notables were driven to conspire against the people by fear of the lawsuits in which they had become involved.[2]

Contempt may call forth sedition and rebellion in an oligarchy when those who lack constitutional rights are more numerous, and therefore believe themselves stronger, than those who have them.   In a democracy it may have similar results when the rich come to despise the disorder and anarchy which they see rampant in the state.   At Thebes, for instance, after the battle of Oeonophyta,[3] the democracy perished through misgovernment, as did that of Megara in consequence of a defeat occasioned by disorder and anarchy.   At Syracuse the democracy was already in decay before the tyranny of Gelon,[4] and at Rhodes before the above-mentioned insurrection.

Disproportionate increase of any part of the state is another likely source of constitutional change.   Consider the human body.   It is made up of parts, which must grow proportionally if symmetry is to be preserved; otherwise it perishes.[5]   Or again, it may assume some other animal form if the disproportionate increase is qualitative as well as quantitative.   Now the state

[1] See page 89.
[2] See page 142.
[3] 456 B.C.
[4] Gelon became tyrant of Syracuse in 485 B.C.
[5] This will happen if the foot, say, is fifteen feet long, and the body itself eighteen inches.—(A.)

also is composed of parts, [1303ᵃ] one of which may increase imperceptibly and out of all proportion to the others. In democracies and polities, for example, the poor may become too numerous, sometimes owing to an accident. Thus at Tarentum, soon after the Persian wars, many of the notables fell in action against the Iapygians, and the polity was turned into a democracy.[1] At Argos, following the slaughter of 'the Seventh' [2] by King Cleomenes of Sparta,[3] it was found necessary to admit a number of the serfs into the citizen body. At Athens, again, the obligation of military service imposed on all registered citizens during the Peloponnesian War led to the depletion of the notables: for Athens suffered heavily by land. Disproportionate increase may affect democracies likewise. If the rich become more numerous, or if properties increase, then democracies may well be changed into oligarchies and family cliques.[4]

Election intrigues may lead to constitutional changes without previous sedition. At Heraea, for example, the lot was substituted for the vote, because it was discovered that elections were too often decided by intrigue. *Wilful negligence may have* the same effect by allowing the highest magistracies to come into the hands of men who have no wish to uphold the constitution. Take the case of Oreus: [5] here the oligarchy was destroyed when Heracleodorus was admitted to office and forthwith erected a democracy—or, I should say, a polity. Yet another occasion is *neglect of apparently insignificant changes*. Important alterations in the field of written law may grow up almost unperceived if minor changes are overlooked. In Ambracia, for example, there was originally a small property qualification for office; but even this vanished in course of time, because there appeared little difference between a small one and none at all. *Disparity of elements in the composition of a state* is also conducive to sedition. This is true of (*a*) national heterogeneity, at any rate until the elements have had time to coalesce.[6] For this reason most of the states which have admitted persons of another

---

[1] c. 480 B.C.

[2] The meaning is uncertain; it may refer to a date or to a tribe.

[3] He was son of Anaxandrides, and held office from 520 to 487 B.C.

[4] For further historical examples see page 141.

[5] Oreus, or Hestiaea, in Euboea. The episode referred to occurred in 377 B.C.

[6] A state cannot be formed from any random body of persons, or within any random period of time.—(A.)

nationality [1] either (i) at the time of their foundation, or (ii) later, have been troubled by sedition.   (i) the Achaeans colonized Sybaris along with the Troezenians,[2] but drove them out when their own numbers increased, and thereby involved Sybaris in a curse.   At Thurii the Sybarites quarrelled with their fellow settlers; and, claiming to be owners of the territory, and therefore entitled to superior privileges, they were expelled from the colony.

(ii) At Byzantium the later settlers were found out in a conspiracy against the original colonists, and were driven out by force; and the same fate overtook the refugees from Chios who had been welcomed by the people of Antissa.   At Zancle, however, the first colonists were themselves forced into exile by the Samians whom they had invited.[3]   At Apollonia on the Black Sea the admission of new settlers led to sedition.   Syracuse conferred citizenship on foreign [1303^b] mercenaries soon after the abolition of tyranny, and the result was sedition,[4] leading to civil war; while most of the original citizens of Amphipolis were driven out by Chalcidian settlers whom they had admitted to the colony.[5]

Another occasion of sedition is (b) territorial heterogeneity, which is found wherever the territory is unsuited to the formation of a united state.   At Clazomenae the inhabitants of Chytrus fell foul of the islanders; and there was similar trouble between Colophon and Notium.   There are, in fact, such differences within the Athenian state; for those who live in Peiraeus are more democratically minded than their neighbours in the city.   Just as a phalanx in action must break ranks before crossing even the narrowest ditch, so every difference is liable to create a division.   The widest gap, undoubtedly, is that between virtue and vice; the next, between wealth and poverty; and so on, down to and including that caused by difference of territory.

Sedition may result [6] from trifles, but the issues at stake are far from trifling.   Even the most insignificant quarrel may have enormous consequences when it begins in high places, as appears from an incident that occurred long ago at Syracuse

---

[1] Aristotle is not referring here to non-Hellenic elements, but only to members of another Greek state.

[2] 720 B.C.

[3] The account given by Herodotus (vi. 22 ff.) is different.

[4] Because the Syracusans made them citizens (c. 465 B.C.), *but at the same time excluded them from office* (*see* Diodorus, xi. 72, 3), not because they were of different nationality.

[5] Probably c. 367 B.C.   See also page 145, lines 35–7.

[6] The next two paragraphs give examples of sedition arising from insolence.

and led to revolution.[1]   Two young magistrates fell foul of one another over a love affair.   While X was absent from home, Y seduced the affections of his own colleague's boy-favourite, and the injured party retaliated by seducing the other's wife.   The whole civic body was drawn into the subsequent dispute, and Syracuse was split into two factions.   The story goes to show how important it is to guard against the initial stages of such feuds, and to forestall the machination of influential leaders. Remember the proverbs: 'An error lies in its beginning' and 'Well begun is half done'; a small error, therefore, is a kind of half-way house to its ultimate consequences.   Quarrels among members of the notables, in particular, and no matter what their pretext, are likely to involve the whole state.   Consider, for instance, what happened at Hestiaea [2] after the Persian wars, when two brothers fell out regarding the division of an inheritance.   One of them declined to render accounts of the estate and of a treasure which their father had discovered.   The poorer of the two thereupon rallied the commons to his side, while the other, who was already a wealthy man, engaged the sympathies of the rich.

[1304ᵃ] At Delphi, also, there was trouble over a wedding, which was the origin of all later seditions.   A bridegroom who had come to fetch his bride interpreted some chance occurrence as an evil omen, and fled from the scene without her.   His prospective in-laws took his conduct as an insult; while he was offering sacrifice they put some of the sacred treasure among his belongings, and then slew him on the grounds that he had robbed the temple.[3]   At Mitylene, a dispute about heiresses was the beginning of many evils and led to a war with Athens,[4] during which Paches took their city.   A gentleman named Timophanes left two daughters, whom Dexander tried unsuccessfully to obtain for his own sons.   He therefore stirred up sedition, and used his position as proxenus of the Athenians to secure their intervention.   Another quarrel about an heiress, this time in Phocis, between Mnaseas, father of Mnason, and Euthycrates, father of Onomarchus, led to sedition and ultimately to the Sacred War.[5]   Matrimonial interests, again, once

----

[1] c. 486 B.C.
[2] In Euboea.   The incident occurred between 479 and 446 B.C.
[3] For this story, and that of the Syracusan magistrates above, see Plutarch, Reip. Gerend. Praec., c. 32.
[4] 428 B.C.
[5] 355–346 B.C.

fired the train of revolution at Epidamnus. In this case one of the citizens married his daughter to a man whose father ultimately became a magistrate and fined the girl's father. The latter was filled with wrath, and plotted with the unenfranchized to overthrow the constitution.

The [1] various forms of government may also change—whether towards oligarchy, democracy, or polity—as the result of a single magistracy or a section of the people enhancing its power or reputation. At Athens, for example, the Council of Areopagus was so high in public esteem during the Persian wars that the constitution began to look like an oligarchy. But the common people, serving in the fleet, were responsible for the victory at Salamis; they gave Athens her sea-power, which in turn secured her empire, and thereby saved the democracy. At Argos the notables distinguished themselves against the Spartans at the battle of Mantinea,[2] and attempted to overthrow the democracy; while at Syracuse the people, who were mainly responsible for victory in the war with Athens,[3] changed the pre-existing polity into a democracy. At Chalcis the people combined with the notables to remove the tyrant Phoxus, and forthwith seized the government.[4] At Ambracia the people likewise helped to get rid of the tyrant Periander,[5] and, having done so, established a popular form of government. Do not forget this universal truth: Any person or persons who enhance the power of a state —any private citizen, board of magistrates, tribe, or indeed any section or group whatsoever—are likely to arouse sedition, either because others are jealous of their pre-eminence, or because their own vanity will not allow them to continue on a basis of equality with their fellow men.

Revolutions may also occur when seemingly opposite groups, e.g. the rich and the common people, are evenly balanced [1304^b] and there is, to all intents and purposes, no middle class; for if either side is clearly far superior in strength, the other will not risk an attack upon it. This is why men of outstanding merit seldom if ever have recourse to sedition: they are a mere handful against many.

Such, in general, are the occasions which give rise to sedition

---

[1] In this paragraph Aristotle gives further examples of constitutional change resulting from a disproportionate increase of some part of the state.
[2] 418 B.C.
[3] Thucydides, vii.
[4] Nothing more is known of Phoxus.
[5] See page 159.

and constitutional change in all forms of government, though we may add a final word in this connection. Political revolutions are brought about sometimes by force and sometimes by fraud. Force may be brought to bear either at the beginning or at a later stage. Fraud, again, may be employed (1) initially or (2) later on. (1) The conspirators sometimes beguile men at the very start to acquiesce in a change of the constitution, and then, despite opposition, hold on by force to the advantage they have won. Thus the Four Hundred at Athens, having deluded the people with an assurance that the Persian king would provide money for the war against Sparta, followed up the initial lie by attempting to retain their hold on the constitution.[1] (2) Sometimes, however, the people are deceived into acquiescence from the very start, and their continued allegiance is secured by repeated acts of deception.

2. PARTICULAR CAUSES OF CONSTITUTIONAL CHANGE

(A) *Causes of Revolution in Democracies*

In the light of the general principles just outlined, we must now take the different types of constitution separately and see what happens in each.

Change in democracies is due principally to the unrestricted licence of demagogues, who sometimes launch their calumnious attacks upon rich men *individually*, thereby compelling them to unite,[2] and sometimes urge the people against the well-to-do *as a class*. There are many examples to illustrate the consequences of such behaviour. At Cos the democracy was overthrown by the rise of unprincipled demagogues who drove the upper classes to combine against them. At Rhodes the demagogues, having introduced a system of payment, withheld the sums due to the trierarchs; and these latter, faced with a series of lawsuits, were driven to join forces and overthrow the democracy.[3] At Heraclea, soon after that colony's foundation,[4] democracy was ruined by the conduct of demagogues. The notables, who had

[1] 411 B.C.

[2] Even the bitterest enemies are united by a common threat.—(A.)

[3] The 'system of payment' refers to payment for attendance at the popular assembly. In order to secure the necessary funds, the demagogues withheld from the trierarchs (who were themselves 'notables') sums due to them for work done by the shipbuilders on their instructions; and the builders accordingly sued the trierarchs for the money.

[4] Heraclea on the Black Sea was founded from Megara *c.* 560 B.C.

been driven out by the injustices of these men, at length made common cause, returned to Heraclea, and abolished the democracy. At Megara itself democracy likewise came to grief. There the demagogues, eager for an excuse to confiscate their property, drove out so many of the notables that the exiles were able to return in strength, defeat the popular forces in battle, and set up an oligarchy. A similar fate overtook the democracy [1305ᵃ] at Cyme, to which Thrasymachus put an end.[1] You will find, indeed, that revolution has followed this pattern in a majority of the other Greek states. Sometimes the demagogues, wishing to curry favour with the masses, drive the notables to combine against their unjust imposition of public services, which, if they do not result in the actual break-up of estates, at least diminish their revenues. Sometimes, on the other hand, your demagogue will bring unfounded accusations in the courts, hoping thereby to obtain some grounds upon which to confiscate the property of well-to-do citizens.

In ancient times, when a single man was both demagogue and general, democracy often changed into tyranny. Most of the early tyrants had originally been demagogues, and the reason why this is no longer so must be attributed to the progress of oratory. While that art was yet virtually unknown, demagogues were drawn exclusively from among the generals. To-day, with the development of rhetoric, skilled orators are the demagogues; but such men, lacking experience of war, make no effort to become tyrants—though perhaps one could point to a few isolated instances here and there. Another reason why tyranny is now so much less common is the fact that in early times the greater magistracies were held by individuals. The tyranny at Miletus, for example, arose from one man [2] holding the office of prytanis, which carried numerous and important prerogatives. Again, at that period there were no large cities. Most of the people were country folk, who had little time for anything but work on their farms; so that any headman with a flair for military leadership was qualified to establish a tyranny. Whenever this occurred it was on the strength of popular support, which your would-be tyrant enlisted by proclaiming his detestation of the rich. Thus, at Athens, Peisistratus won his way to tyranny by leading a faction against the party of the

---

[1] Nothing further is known of the occurrence, and it is uncertain to which Cyme Aristotle refers.
[2] Thrasybulus, c. 600 B.C.

Plain.[1] Theagenes was accepted as tyrant of Megara after slaughtering the cattle of wealthy landowners, which he found grazing by the river.[2] And Dionysius owed his position to having denounced Daphnaeus[3] and other rich men, and thereby convinced the people of his democratic principles.

Finally, the traditional kind of democracy may be transformed into the most modern type. Where offices are filled by universal suffrage, without any property qualification, candidates tend to play the demagogue, and go so far as to exalt the people even above the laws. A more or less complete remedy for this state of affairs is to limit the right of voting to the separate tribes, instead of conferring it on the whole people. So much, then, for the principal causes of change in democracies.

(B) Causes of Revolution in Oligarchies

There are two situations which are obviously most liable to transform an oligarchy. One is the oppression of the masses by the government. Any leader is acceptable to them at such times, particularly when that leader happens himself to be a member of the government.[4] [1305[b]] Seditions originating (1) *outside* the governing body may assume a variety of forms. Sometimes an oligarchy is destroyed by those who, notwithstanding their wealth, are excluded from office. This happens where the magistracies are very few, as at Massilia, Istros, Heraclea,[5] and elsewhere. In all these places those who were debarred from office created one disturbance after another until the privilege was extended first to the elder brothers of a family, and then to the younger also.[6] The final result was that the oligarchy at Massilia became more like a polity; that of Istros ended as a democracy; while that of Heraclea was enlarged from a mere handful to the number of six hundred men. At Cnidos too the oligarchy underwent a change in consequence of sedition among the notables themselves. Few of them were admitted to office; and the aforementioned rule applied, viz. that if a father were admitted his son was not, and only the eldest of several

---

[1] 560 B.C.

[2] The incident is otherwise unknown.

[3] A Syracusan general who failed to prevent the Carthaginian occupation of Acragas. Dionysius the Elder became tyrant of Syracuse in 405 B.C.

[4] A case in point is that of Lygdamis [6th cent. B.C.], who afterwards became tyrant of Naxos.—(A.)

[5] i.e. Pontic Heraclea, on the Black Sea.

[6] In some states father and son, in others an elder and younger brother, may not hold office together.—(A.)

brothers was eligible. The people took advantage of this sedition to choose themselves a leader from among the notables. They attacked and defeated the oligarchs, who, being divided, were inevitably weak. In ancient times the Basilidan oligarchy at Erythrae was thoroughly efficient; but the people resented its exclusiveness and altered the constitution.

Oligarchies are sometimes upset (2) *from within* (a) owing to personal rivalry among their members, who are led thereby to play the demagogue in one of two ways. (i) They may practise on the governing body itself; for the narrowest of circles is no bar to the rise of demagogues like Charicles and Phrynicus at Athens, who led their followers to power by currying favour with the Thirty and the Four Hundred respectively.[1] Or (ii) members of the government may play on the feelings of the masses. Such was the case at Larissa, where the police chiefs habitually fawned upon the masses, by whom they were elected. Indeed this generally happens in oligarchies, such as that of Abydos, where the election of magistrates is not confined to those who are themselves eligible, but where the whole army, say (or even the entire people), have a right to vote, though with eligibility limited to those with large estates or the members of political clubs. Similar disturbances occur when the law-courts include members other than those who belong to the civic body. When this is so men play the demagogue in order to secure a verdict, and ultimately succeed in changing the constitution, as at Pontic Heraclea. Dissension may also follow upon an attempt by some members of an oligarchy to make it more exclusive; for in such cases those who desire equality of rights are obliged to invoke popular assistance.

(b) An oligarchy may also undergo change from within in consequence of its members dissipating their goods by riotous living. Persons of this kind are always eager for revolution, and either attempt to make themselves tyrants or [1306ª] set up someone else. Hipparinus advanced Dionysius in this way at Syracuse. At Amphipolis a man named Cleotimus introduced Chalcidian settlers,[2] and then raised a sedition between them and the rich. At Aegina, too, the same motive caused the man who undertook negotiations with Chares to attempt a constitutional change.[3] Such men sometimes make a direct bid for political change. Sometimes, on the other hand, they set to work by embezzling public funds, which leads eventually to sedition,

---

[1] i.e. in 404 and 411 B.C.   [2] See page 139, footnote 5.   [3] c. 367 B.C.

either on the part of the criminals themselves or of those who would resist their depredations. We have an instance of this at Apollonia on the Black Sea. An oligarchy at one with itself is not easily ruined from within; as witness the constitution of Pharsalus, where the governing body, though very small, is able to control a large population because its members conduct themselves well towards one another.

(c) Then again, oligarchies may be undermined from inside when a second oligarchy is created within the original one, i.e. when the whole body of those qualified for office is small, and yet not all of those few are admitted to the highest magistracies. Take the case of Elis. At one time that state was ruled by a small group of senators; but only a mere handful of men were ever appointed to the senate, owing to the fact that there were only ninety members, all of whom held office for life and were elected (rather like the Spartan senators) from a limited number of families.

(d) Oligarchies may be changed from within both in war and in peace. This happens in time of war when the oligarchs cannot trust the people, and therefore employ mercenary troops. If the command of these mercenaries is given to one man, he is as likely as not to become a tyrant, as did Timophanes at Corinth.[1] If it is entrusted to several persons, they often transform themselves into a governing clique. An oligarchy is sometimes driven by fear of such consequences to employ an army composed of its own subjects, and therefore to allow the masses a share of constitutional rights. Peace-time changes occur when mutual suspicion causes the oligarchs to entrust the defence of their state to mercenary troops and a neutral arbiter, who not seldom ends as master of both factions. This happened at Larissa under Simias the Aleuad,[2] as well as at Abydos in the days of the political clubs,[3] one of which was led by Iphiades.

(e) Seditions also arise within an oligarchy from marriages or lawsuits, which result in the humiliation of one party by another and thereby create dissension. I have already given some examples of sedition due to matrimonial affairs.[4] There was a similar instance at Eretria, where Diagoras destroyed an oligarchy of the knights because he had been cheated over an intended marriage.[5] A sedition at Heraclea and another at Thebes both resulted from judicial verdicts on charges of

[1] 346 B.C.   [2] fl. 344 B.C.   [3] 4th cent. B.C.
[4] Pages 140, 141.   [5] Probably before the Persian wars.

adultery. In each case [1] the sentence, though just in itself, was carried out [1306ᵇ] in a party spirit; for such was the animosity of their enemies that both defendants were pilloried in the agora.

(*f*) Many oligarchies too (e.g. at Cnidos and Chios) have been overthrown by members of the ruling class who resented their excessive despotism.

(*g*) Lastly, constitutional changes may result from accidental causes. This is true of so-called polities, and of those oligarchies under which membership of the council, the law-courts, and other official bodies is dependent on a property qualification. It may be that the amount of this qualification was originally fixed on the basis of existing circumstances, in such a way as to restrict constitutional rights to a few in oligarchies and to the middle classes in polities. Then perhaps you get an era of prosperity, due to the return of peace or some other good fortune; with the result that a given property is now assessable at a value many times greater than before, and every citizen sooner or later becomes eligible for every office. So much for the causes of sedition and revolution in oligarchies. [2]

(C) *Causes of Revolution in Aristocracies and Polities*

In aristocracies sedition may occur as a result of limiting office to a mere handful of the population. I have already shown [3] how this cause produces the same effect in oligarchies; and that it should do so in aristocracies is quite understandable when we realize that an aristocracy is a kind of oligarchy. [4]   (1) Sedition owing to the above-mentioned cause is particularly liable to occur under the following conditions:

(*a*) When the rank and file of a people are exalted by the idea that they are just as worthy as their rulers. At Sparta, for instance, the so-called Partheniae (who were the sons of Spartan peers) determined to vindicate their rights; but their conspiracy was found out, and they were sent to colonize Tarentum. [5]

---

[1] That of Eurytion at Heraclea, and that of Archias at Thebes.—(A.)
[2] With regard to both democracies and oligarchies in general, it should be noted that they occasionally give place, not to the opposite type of constitution, but to another variety of their own class. For example, those democracies and oligarchies which are regulated by law may turn into arbitrary forms, and vice versa.—(A.)
[3] Page 144, lines 21 sqq.
[4] An aristocracy may be considered as an oligarchy, because in both the ruling class is small, though not for the same reason.—(A.)
[5] 708 B.C.

(b) When great men who are also second to none in merit are dishonoured by those higher in office, as was Lysander by the kings of Sparta.[1]

(c) When a high-spirited individual, like Cinadon, is excluded from honours. He it was who led the conspiracy against the Spartan peers during the reign of Agesilaus.[2]

(d) When some of the governing class are very poor and others very rich—a state of affairs arising especially in time of war. This happened at Sparta during the Messenian war,[3] as appears from Tyrtaeus's poem [1307ᵃ] *The Rule of Law*, in which he speaks of men impoverished by the war demanding a redistribution of land.

(e) When an individual who is great, and might be still greater, wishes to be sole ruler. Pausanias, who commanded the Greek forces in the Persian war, is one example at Sparta; Hanno at Carthage is another.

(2) Aristocracies, and polities too, are most likely to suffer complete ruin owing to some deviation from justice in the constitution itself. In polities this flaw is an imperfect fusion of democratic and oligarchical elements; in aristocracies it is the failure properly to combine those elements *plus* the element of merit, but especially the former two—i.e. the democratic and oligarchical, which are the only elements which polities and most of the so-called aristocracies actually attempt to fuse. The only difference between aristocracies and what we call polities lies in the different method of effecting the combination. And this also explains why the former are less stable than the latter. Those constitutions in which the combination inclines them more towards oligarchy are called aristocracies; those in which it tends to make them favour the masses are called polities. This, I say, is the reason why the latter are more stable than the former. There is strength in numbers, and men who have equal rights are generally contented. Well-to-do people, on the other hand, take advantage of their constitutional superiority to become arrogant and avaricious. On the whole, it is true to say that a constitution will change in the direction towards which it already inclines, according as the party representing this inclination grows stronger: a polity, for example, will turn into a democracy, and an aristocracy into an oligarchy.

---

[1] Pausanias and Agesilaus.   [2] 401–360 B.C.
[3] The second Messenian war lasted from 685 to 668 B.C.

It is quite possible, however, that the process may be reversed. Aristocracy may change into democracy because the poorer classes, under the impression that they are treated unfairly, give it a twist in the opposite direction. Polities likewise may be changed into oligarchies on the ground that proportionate equality (i.e. the principle whereby each enjoys rights in proportion to his desert) is the only guarantee of stability. This is in fact what happened at Thurii. The property qualification for office was too high; it was lowered, and the number of offices increased. But the notables had illegally bought up all the land,[1] which led in turn to civil war; and during the ensuing hostilities the people became such expert soldiers that they wore down the civic guard, and obliged the landowners to surrender their ill-gotten gains.

It should be noted that the oligarchical leanings of all aristocratic constitutions tend to arouse avarice among the notables. At Sparta, for instance, where property is concentrated in the hands of a few, these people are too free to do as they like and to marry whom they please. A situation of this kind was responsible for the fate of Locri,[2] thanks to the marriage of Dionysius with the daughter of one of its citizens.[3] Such a thing would never have happened in a democracy or a well-compounded aristocracy.

[1307b] I have already observed [4] of constitutions in general that even trifles may beget revolution; and this is particularly true of aristocracies, which are liable to suffer imperceptible change through being gradually undermined. Let an aristocracy sacrifice just one part of the constitution, and the way is smoothed to depriving it of a slightly more important feature; and so the process continues until the whole fabric of the state is altered. This is what happened to the constitution of Thurii. There was a law that no retiring general might hold the office again until five years had elapsed. But some of the younger men, who were admired by the soldiers of the guard as first-rate officers, took it into their heads to abrogate this law. Despising the authorities, they foresaw no difficulty in achieving their purpose and enabling the generals to serve continuously; the people, as they well knew, would gladly re-elect them over

---

[1] The oligarchical tendency of the constitution gave free rein to their avarice.—(A.)

[2] Locri Epizephyrii, in southern Italy, which received a Syracusan tyranny.

[3] 396 B.C.

[4] Page 139, line 31.

and over again.   The magistrates forming the Board of Councillors, whose duty it was to examine the proposal, at first determined to resist; but on second thoughts they came to the conclusion that concession on this one point would leave the constitution otherwise intact.   Other changes, however, were put forward in due course; all their attempts at opposition now proved futile; and the whole constitutional system passed into the hands of a revolutionary clique.

Constitutions generally are destroyed either from within or from without.   The external agency is a constitution of opposite type, which is either a near neighbour or powerful even though remote.   Examples are the Athenian and Spartan empires: Athens everywhere put down oligarchies, while Sparta did the same to democracies.

(D) *Methods of Stabilizing Democracies, Oligarchies, Aristocracies, and Polities*

Having described the causes of sedition and revolution, we must now go on to explain the methods of preserving constitutions in general, and each one separately.   In the first place, it is clear that once we know the causes which destroy constitutions, we also know the causes which preserve them; for opposite causes produce opposite effects, and destruction is the opposite of preservation.   Bearing this fact in mind, we may draw the following conclusions.   (1) In properly blended constitutions there is nothing more important than to foster respect for the law, and especially to guard against minor transgressions.   Lawlessness of this kind creeps in unnoticed until at length it overwhelms the state, just as small expenses will gradually engulf a whole fortune.   Such disbursements are not made all at once, and are therefore unperceived; they mislead the mind in the same way as does the logical puzzle according to which 'if each is small, all are small too.' [1]   This, then, is one precaution we should take, viz. to prevent the beginnings of unrest.

(2) No reliance should be placed on those constitutional devices [1308ª] which are intended to outwit the masses, and which I have already described.[2]   They are always shown up for what they are.

[1] In one respect this is true, but not in another.   'All,' understood as 'the whole,' is not small, even though it is made up of little units.—(A.)

[2] Pages 121, 122.

(3) Some states, oligarchies no less than aristocracies, owe their permanence not to the essential stability of their constitutions, but to the fact that successive magistrates are on good terms both with (a) those who have no constitutional rights and with (b) the civic body.   (a) The unenfranchised, so far from being unjustly treated, see their most distinguished members advanced to the enjoyment of full civic status; and while the ambitious among them are never wronged where honour is at stake, the rank and file suffer no harm to their pockets.   (b) The magistrates and other members of the governing class behave towards one another in that spirit of equality which is characteristic of democracies. The measure of equality which democrats seek to confer upon all the masses should at least include those who are genuinely 'peers,' and that not only on grounds of justice, but also of expediency. The presence, therefore, of a large governing class calls for a number of democratic institutions. It will be advantageous, for example, to restrict the tenure of office to six-monthly periods, so that everyone who belongs to the class of 'peers' may take his turn. A numerous class of 'peers' is by its very nature a sort of democracy; and that is why, as I have already observed,[1] it is so often the nursery of demagogues. Brief tenure of office, and other measures of the kind, reduce the likelihood of oligarchies and aristocracies falling into the hands of family cliques. Short-term officials, unlike those who are members of the executive for long periods at a time, cannot easily do harm; it is long tenure of office that gives rise to tyranny in oligarchies and democracies. Aspirants to tyranny, under both types of constitution, are either the leading figures in the state (demagogues in democracies, heads of great families in oligarchies), or else the higher magistrates who have been in office for some considerable time.

(4) Constitutions are preserved not only by their remoteness from a source of peril, but also, on occasion, by their very proximity thereto; for the dread of present danger drives a state to keep a firmer hold on its constitution. Those, therefore, who are interested in its stability should even invent causes for alarm, so as to keep the citizens perpetually alert and on their guard, like sentinels on night duty. In other words, they must bring distant peril near.

(5) Legislation is another means which should be employed to guard against animosity and sedition among the notables, and

[1] Page 145, lines 7 sqq.

to ward off the spirit of contention from those not yet involved. No ordinary man can detect the first stirring of trouble; only a true statesman can do that.

(6) Oligarchies and polities may suffer change in consequence of the assessments necessary to discharge the requirements of a property qualification. This will tend to happen, for example, when the qualification itself remains unaltered but there is far more money in circulation; and the best way of preventing it will be to make a comparison at stated intervals between the present sum total of all assessments and their sum total on the last occasion. In those states where the assessment is annual the comparison should likewise be made annually, [1308^b] and in larger states every third or fifth year. If the sum total is then discovered to be (a) many times greater, or (b) many times less, than on the last occasion when the assessments demanded by the constitution were fixed, a law should be passed to raise or lower the qualification correspondingly. In oligarchies and polities where this is not done change is bound to follow. In case (b) polity will be transformed into oligarchy, and oligarchy into a family clique; in case (a) polity will become democracy, and oligarchy either polity or democracy.

(7) Here now is a rule that should be followed by democracies, by oligarchies, and indeed by all constitutions alike: Raise no man too high above the level of his fellow citizens; [1] better to confer small honours over a long period than great ones in rapid succession. If this rule is not observed, and a man is to be loaded with honours all at once, take care at least not to deprive him of them at a single stroke, but by degrees. Aim, above all, by means of legislation, to prevent any man becoming too influential either through his friends or through his wealth; failing which, anyone who has climbed too high should be dismissed and cleared right out of the country.

(8) Men are just as likely to become revolutionaries through the circumstances of their *private* lives; and a magistracy should therefore be created to keep an eye on those who live in a manner that does not harmonize with the spirit of the constitution, be it a democracy, an oligarchy, or any other form of government. For the same reasons a watch should be kept over the social group which happens to be particularly flourishing at any given time. The best way of forestalling trouble from that quarter is either (a) always to entrust the management of affairs, i.e. the

[1] Men are easily spoilt; not everyone can wear prosperity.—(A.)

holding of office, to the opposite group,[1] and so to aim at a fusion of the rich and the poor, or else (*b*) to attempt a strengthening of the middle class, which will put a stop to dissensions arising from inequality.

(9) It is of paramount importance that the laws, and indeed the general administrative system, should be framed in such a way that no magistracy can be used as a stepping-stone to wealth. This matter is of greater consequence in oligarchies than in any other type of constitution. For while the masses take no great offence at. being excluded from office,[2] they strongly object to the idea of their rulers embezzling public funds and thereby depriving them of profit as well as of constitutional rights. Furthermore, if a means could be found to prevent the use of office for personal gain, then (and only then) it would be possible to create a satisfactory blend of democracy and aristocracy, in which [1309ᵃ] both the notables and the masses would get what they desire. All would be *qualified for* office, which is the goal of democracy, and the notables would *actually hold* office, in accordance with the principles of aristocracy. I say that an arrangement of this kind can be brought about by divorcing office from profit, because the poor will rather devote themselves to private business than seek offices that hold out no rewards, and the rich will be able to afford the expense of public life without drawing on public funds. The poor will thus have a chance to become wealthy by their own diligence, and the upper class will not be subjected to government by persons of inferior standing. As a further precaution against embezzlement, outgoing magistrates should hand over public funds in presence of the whole civic body, and duplicates of their accounts should be deposited with each class, ward, and tribe. There should also be statutory rewards for magistrates of notorious incorruptibility.

(10) In democracies the rich should be spared. Not only should their estates be left intact, but the revenues of those estates should be equally secure, and not distributed according to a custom which is creeping into certain states. It is also good policy not to allow wealthy citizens, however willing they may be, to undertake such costly but useless public services as equipping a dramatic chorus, paying for a torch-race, and so on. In

[1] By opposite groups I mean here the gentry and the masses, or the rich and the poor.—(A.)

[2] On the contrary, they may even be glad of this opportunity to look after their private affairs.—(A.)

oligarchies, on the other hand, the poor should be particularly well treated. They should be allowed to hold the lucrative offices; and if they suffer violence at the hands of a rich man, that man should be punished more severely than if he had wronged a member of his own class. Inheritances should pass by right of descent, and not by bequest; nor should one individual ever receive more than one inheritance. These provisions will ensure a more even distribution of estates, and will enable more of the poor to reach a state of affluence. Apart from matters of property, it will not be out of place to allow those who enjoy fewer constitutional rights[1] a position of equality or even precedence, excepting always the supreme offices of state, which should be entrusted exclusively, or almost exclusively, to those having *full* constitutional rights.

Three qualifications are necessary in those who are to fill the supreme offices: (1) Loyalty to the established constitution; (2) outstanding administrative capacity according to the office; and (3) the virtue of justice in a form suited to the particular constitution involved.[2] But suppose these three qualifications are not found together in a single person: [1309b] the question then arises, how is the choice to be made? One man, for example, may be a good general, but a bad man and disloyal to the constitution; another may possess no more than justice and loyalty. How are we to choose? Well, two points, I think, call for consideration: which is the commoner qualification, and which the rarer? Thus, in choosing a general, we should have more regard to military experience than to moral virtue, because military genius is not so common as personal goodness. The opposite rule applies in the choice of a trustee or a treasurer; more than average strength of character is necessary for the execution of such duties, whereas all men have the requisite ability.

It may perhaps be asked: What need is there of moral virtue if a man is endowed with the appropriate capacity and is loyal to the constitution? Will not these two qualifications alone guarantee the public interest? No: a man who possesses the two qualifications may still lack self-control; and he who cannot

---

[1] i.e. the rich in a democracy, and the poor in an oligarchy.—(A.)

[2] If the principle varies from one constitution to another, the quality of justice must differ also.—(A.)

govern his own passions will fail to serve the public interest, just as he will fail to serve his own interest which he understands so well and which he has so much at heart.

Speaking generally, we may say that constitutions are preserved by adhering to all the legal provisions suggested above as conducive to their stability. Of paramount importance, however, is the principle to which I have several times referred: [1] Make sure that those who favour the constitution outweigh those who do not. Then again do not forget the mean, which is too often overlooked in the deviation forms of government. Much that is considered democratic is the ruin of democracies, and much that is reckoned oligarchical is fatal to oligarchies. The champions of democracy and oligarchy, who can see no good outside the constitutional principles which they respectively uphold, push matters to extremes. They do not understand that lack of proportion is no less harmful to a constitution than, say, to a nose. A nose may deviate from the ideal of straightness towards hooked or snub, and yet remain well shaped and pleasing to the eye; but there is a limit beyond which it may develop so far in one direction, and so far away from the opposite, that it ultimately ceases to look like a nose at all. The same applies to other parts of the body, and likewise to constitutions. Oligarchy and democracy, though deviations from the ideal, may be adequate forms of government; but if you carry either of them too far, you will first cause it to deteriorate, and end by turning it into something that can no longer be described as a constitution.

Legislators and statesmen should therefore know which democratic measures preserve, and which destroy, a democracy; similarly they should be able to recognize those oligarchical institutions which stabilize or ruin an oligarchy. Neither form of government can exist or continue to exist without including both the rich and the poor. If equal ownership is introduced, the constitution will inevitably be transformed [1310a] as a result of this radical legislation which eliminates wealth and poverty.

There is another mistake common to both democracies and oligarchies. In those democracies where the people are above the law demagogues cleave the state in two with their constant attacks upon the rich. Their duty, however, is quite the opposite: they should always pretend to speak on behalf of the rich. The same applies in oligarchies: members of the ruling

[1] Cf. page 120, lines 14–17.

class should profess to speak for the poor and should take oaths in opposite terms to those now in use. In some modern states the oath runs as follows: 'I will bear ill will to the people and will do them all the harm I can.' The intention which they should both entertain *and express* is just the opposite; their oath should contain the declaration: 'I will in no way do wrong to the people.'

But the most powerful factor of all those I have mentioned as contributing to the stability of constitutions, but one which is nowadays universally neglected, is the education of citizens in the spirit of the constitution under which they live. You may have an unsurpassed legal system, ratified by the whole civic body; but it is of no avail unless the citizens have been trained by force of habit and teaching in the spirit of the constitution according as the laws are democratic or oligarchical. For self-discipline may be lacking in a state no less than in an individual. To have been 'educated in the spirit of the constitution,' however, does not mean that your citizen does what pleases the advocates of oligarchy or democracy. It means rather that he behaves in such a way as is conducive to the stability of one or the other. Under present-day oligarchies the sons of magistrates are brought up in luxury, while those of the poor, hardened by exercise and daily toil, are more disposed and better able to engage in revolutionary activity. Extreme democracies—those, namely, which are considered patterns of the democratic type [1]—have adopted a policy which runs counter to their real interest; and this is due to a false idea of liberty. Two principles are generally regarded as characteristic of democracy: the absolute sovereignty of the masses and individual liberty. Justice is believed to consist in equality, equality in mass supremacy, and liberty in doing exactly what one likes. In extreme democracies, therefore, everyone lives as he pleases, or, as Euripides says, 'for any end he happens to desire.' [2] But this is an altogether unsatisfactory conception of liberty. It is quite wrong to imagine that life subject to constitutional control is mere slavery; it is in fact salvation.

Such in general are the causes leading to the change of constitutions; [3] such also are the means to their preservation and stability.

---

[1] See page 125.　　　　　　　　　　[2] Frag. 891, Nauck[2].
[3] i.e. of democracy (see page 105, footnote 2), oligarchy, aristocracy, and polity.

(E) *Causes of Revolution in Monarchies*

I have yet to describe how monarchies [1] may be overthrown and how preserved. My remarks [1310^b] on constitutions properly so called [2] are, generally speaking, true also of kingship and tyranny. Kingship has much in common with aristocracy. Tyranny is a compound of two evils—oligarchy and democracy carried to their furthest lengths; and the fact that it combines the errors and perversions of both explains why it is more injurious to its subjects than any other form of government. The two kinds of monarchy stem from wholly different roots. Kingships have been created by the gentry as a bulwark against the common people, the ruler being chosen from among the upper classes themselves because of his own or his family's pre-eminence in character and conduct. Tyrants, on the contrary, are drawn from the lower strata of society in order to protect them against the notables and to prevent these latter treating them unjustly. Historical evidence, indeed, tends to prove that the great majority of tyrants were originally demagogues who curried favour with the masses by their attacks upon the well-to-do. Tyrannies have had such beginnings at any rate since the emergence of large states. Before that time, however, they sprang up under a variety of influences. (1) Some were due to the ambition of kings who sought to overstep traditional boundaries with a view to absolutism. (2) Others were established by men who had been elected to the highest magistracies, and who took advantage of an ancient custom whereby certain democracies appointed their 'craftsmen' and 'overseers' [3] for long periods at a time. (3) Others again owed their existence to the practice, followed by oligarchics, of placing all major offices under the supervision of a single person. In any of these three ways an ambitious man would find his purpose easy of attainment, since he already enjoyed a measure of power, either as king or as holding some position of honour. Pheidon of Argos, [4] for example, to name one out of many, began as a king

---

[1] Whether kingships or tyrannies.
[2] Notice that Aristotle here distinguishes monarchy from constitutions *properly so called*, contrary to the classification adopted in Book III.
[3] These were terms applied to magistrates in Peloponnesian states. Cf. page 69, line 13.
[4] Fl. 668 B.C.

and ended as a tyrant. Phalaris [1] and the Ionian tyrants seized
the opportunity afforded by their official rank; while Panaetius
at Leontini, Cypselus at Corinth, Peisistratus at Athens,
Dionysius at Syracuse, and several others who later became
tyrants, began as demogogues.

As I was saying, the pattern of kingship is similar to that of
aristocracy. It is based on merit (whether of an individual or
of a family) in the shape of moral virtue, benefits conferred, or
these last two *plus* capability. Those who have been raised to
the dignity of kingship have all been men who had benefited, or
were in a position to benefit, their city or their country. Some,
like Codrus,[2] had saved their fellow citizens from bondage as
prisoners of war; others, like Cyrus,[3] had been liberators; others
again, like the Spartan, Macedonian, and Molossian kings, had
settled or acquired the territory of their respective states. A
king looks upon himself as protecting [1311ª] owners of property
from unfair treatment, and defending the poor against insult and
oppression. A tyrant, as I have said more than once,[4] has no
regard whatsoever to the public interest, except as it may serve
his private ends. The aim of a tyrant is pleasure; that of a king
is the good. Hence a tyrant covets riches, while a king seeks
what redounds to honour. A king employs a bodyguard of
citizens, a tyrant one of mercenary troops.

That tyranny includes the vices of both oligarchy and democracy cannot be denied. From (1) oligarchy it derives (a) its
end—riches, which alone enable a tyrant to maintain his bodyguard and live in luxury; (b) mistrust of the people, which leads
the tyrant to deprive them of arms; (c) oppression of the masses,
who are driven from the capital and dispersed over the countryside. From (2) democracy it derives (a) its hostility towards
the upper classes; (b) its policy of destroying them secretly or
openly; (c) its practice of driving them into exile, not only as
rivals and hindrances to its power, but also as the source of
conspiracies on the part of those who seek either to rule or to
escape from subjection.[5]

I have already intimated that the *origins* of revolution must be

[1] Tyrant of Acragas (Agrigentum), 570–554 B.C.
[2] Traditional last king of Athens.
[3] Cyrus the Great of Persia, 559–529 B.C.
[4] Pages 78, lines 20, 21; 116, lines 30–6.
[5] Hence the advice [see page 90] given to Thrasybulus by Periander, who
lopped the outstanding ears of corn in order to suggest the constant need of
removing all distinguished citizens.—(A.)

reckoned the same in monarchies as in other forms of government; many attacks upon sovereign rulers by their subjects are due to ill treatment,[1] to fear, or to contempt. The *aims* of revolution are likewise the same in respect of tyranny and kingship as of regular constitutions; monarchs enjoy great wealth and honour, both of which are coveted by all mankind. The attacks themselves are directed sometimes against the person of the sovereign, and sometimes against his throne. Those which are provoked by insult are made upon his life.

(1) Insult, whatever form it may assume, invariably begets anger; and an angry man usually strikes for the sake of revenge, not from ambition. (*a*) The Peisistratidae, for example, were attacked because of a public insult directed at the sister of Harmodius, and the latter's consequent humiliation. Harmodius acted for his sister's sake, Aristogeiton out of love for his friend.[2] A conspiracy was formed against Periander, tyrant of Ambracia, because he once asked a favourite, [1311[b]] with whom he was drinking, whether he was not yet with child by him. Philip of Macedon was assassinated by Pausanias,[3] upon whom he had allowed Attalus and his circle to heap the worst indignities; so too was Amyntas the Little by Derdas, whose youthful charms he claimed to have enjoyed. Evagoras of Cyprus, too, was killed by a eunuch whose wife [4] had been ravished by the tyrant's son.

(*b*) Many conspiracies have originated (i) in unnatural attempts by monarchs on the persons of their subjects, as in the case of Archelaus [5] and Crataeas. Archelaus, whom Crataeas had long detested for this reason, had promised him in return the hand of one or other of his daughters. He broke his word. Hard pressed in war with Sirras and Arrabaeus, he married the elder to the king of Elimeia; the younger he gave to his own son Amyntas.[6] Crataeas, left empty-handed, used this slight as a pretext for his attack on Archelaus. No such provocation, however, was in fact required; the real source of trouble between the

---

[1] The most common form of ill treatment is insult, another is confiscation of property—(A.)

[2] 514 B.C.

[3] 336 B.C.

[4] For other examples of married eunuchs cf. the Septuagint version of Genesis xxxvii. 36; Juvenal, i. 22; and Montesquieu, *Esprit des Lois*, xv. 19.

[5] King of Macedonia, 413–399 B.C.

[6] The idea in this case was to deter Amyntas from quarrelling with Archelaus's son by Cleopatra.—(A.)

two men was Crataeas's dislike of the king's unnatural pro-
pensities. Young Hellanocrates of Larissa joined this conspiracy for the same reason. Archelaus had dishonoured the
young man, but had undertaken to restore him to his country
from which he had been exiled. Finding that the king made no
effort to fulfil his promise, Hellanocrates came to the conclusion
that Archelaus had been moved, not by affection, but by sheer
lust begotten of power. Again, Parrhon and Heracleides of
Aenos murdered Cotys to avenge their father,[1] while Adamas
rebelled against the same monarch in revenge for the outrage he
had suffered as a child when Cotys ordered his mutilation.
(ii) Many, too, have been roused to anger by the humiliation of a
flogging, and have killed or attempted to kill even magistrates
and court officials. At Mitylene, for example, Megacles and
his friends assassinated most of the Penthelidae [2] who were
going about armed with clubs and beating up inoffensive citizens. At a later date Smerdis killed Penthilus who had had him
flogged and forcibly separated from his wife. The assassination
of Archelaus [3] was inspired and led by Decamnichus, whose
anger had been roused when Archelaus handed him over to
Euripides to be scourged in revenge for having made some
reference to the poet's foul breath.[4] Many other murders and
conspiracies have arisen from such causes.

(2) Fear, again, as I have said, is one of the motives behind
rebellion in monarchies no less than in more popular forms of
government. Artabanus, for example, murdered Xerxes
through fear that he would be accused of having had Darius
hanged without instructions from Xerxes, assuming that the
latter would forget what he had said while in his cups and would
therefore condone the assassination.[5]

(3) Contempt is yet another motive. [1312[a]] Sardanapalus
was killed by a man who saw him carding wool with his harem;[6]
and Dionysius II [7] was attacked in the same spirit of contempt
by Dion, who saw that the tyrant was equally despised by his
own subjects because of his habitual drunkenness. [1312[a]17–20]

[1] 359 B.C. Cotys was a Thracian king.
[2] They were the ruling clan in the early oligarchy of Mitylene.
[3] See *supra*, page 159.
[4] Cf. Martial, xi. 30.
[5] There are several variations of this story in ancient writers. The
assassination of Xerxes by Artabanus occurred in 465 B.C.
[6] That, at any rate, is the story. If it is not true of Sardanapalus, it may
well be so of another monarch.—(A.)
[7] 357–356 B.C. Dionysius was exiled, not assassinated.

Attempts of this kind are generally carried out by men of natural audacity, who have received high military honours from the sovereign. Power going hand in hand with courage leads to determination, and their alliance causes men to rebel in the assurance of an easy victory. [1312ᵃ6] Even the friends of a monarch will sometimes attack him because they despise him; the very confidence he reposes in them stirs their contempt and persuades them that their purpose will go undetected. Confidence of being able to seize power is also a form of contempt leading to rebellion; a man is ready to strike without thought of consequences, because he feels himself strong. This is what sometimes causes a general to attack his sovereign. Cyrus, for example, attacked Astyages[1] because he despised that monarch's life as effeminate and his power as in decline. The Thracian Seuthes when he was general attacked Amadocus for the same reason.[2]

(4) Some rebellions are due to more than one of these causes, as, for instance, in the case of Mithradates who contrived the overthrow of Ariobarzanes,[3] partly out of contempt and partly from avarice.

(5) Thirst for glory as a motive for rebellion is of quite a different character from any of the foregoing. Anyone who decides to risk rebellion through love of fame behaves quite differently from those who attempt the lives of tyrants for the sake of great wealth or high honours. The latter are moved simply by greed or ambition; but the man who thirsts for glory will attack a monarch in the same spirit as when confronted with any other extraordinary task, looking for renown rather than a throne. The number of those actuated by such motives is, of course, very few indeed. Their conduct presupposes an utter disregard for their personal safety in the event of failure. They must resolve, like Dion, when he set out on his expedition against Dionysius with a mere handful of troops:[4] 'Whatever I may manage to achieve, I am content to have advanced thus far in my undertaking; if I die as soon as I have landed—why, then I shall welcome death.' To those heights few can rise.

Tyranny, in common with all other forms of government, may be destroyed (1) *from without* [1312ᵇ] by some opposite and

[1] Astyages was deposed by Cyrus in 559 B.C.
[2] Between 390 and 386 B.C.
[3] Probably Ariobarzanes, satrap of Pontus, who was succeeded by his son Mithradates II in 336 B.C.
[4] 357 B.C.

more powerful type of constitution.   There will obviously be a
conflict of ideologies, since the two are opposed in principle, and
when determination is backed by power it must always succeed.
Now democracy is antagonistic towards tyranny; for in its
extreme and latest form it is *closely akin thereto*, and, as Hesiod
says, 'Potter is at loggerheads with potter.'   Kingship and
aristocracy are no less antagonistic to tyranny, because they are
altogether different kinds of constitution.   This is why so many
tyrannies were overthrown by Sparta, and by Syracuse also in
the heyday of her political life.[1]

Tyranny may also be destroyed (2) *by internal influences*, when
the reigning family is divided against itself.   Such a fate overtook the tyranny established by Gelon and, more recently, that
of Dionysius.   In the first of these cases Hieron's brother
Thrasybulus, having designs upon the throne, flattered Gelon's
son and seduced him into a life of pleasure.[2]   Whereupon
the relatives formed a party to get rid of Thrasybulus and save
the tyranny; but this party saw their chance and drove
out the whole family.   In the second case, Dion led an
expedition against his brother-in-law, Dionysius, and expelled
him with popular support; but he himself was afterwards
assassinated.[3]

Hatred and contempt are the two main causes of rebellion
against tyranny.   Hatred of tyrants is inevitable, but it is often
due to contempt that tyrannies are actually destroyed.   There
is evidence of this truth in the fact that most tyrants who have
attained power by their own efforts have managed to retain it.
Their successors, on the other hand, lose it almost at once; their
luxurious lives bring them into contempt and afford many
opportunities to would-be assailants.   Hate must be considered
as including anger, the effects of which are more or less the same.
Anger, indeed, is often more effective; an angry man attacks the
more ferociously, in that his passion is unreasoning.[4]   Hate is
more rational: it is devoid of pain, which is the accompaniment
of anger and impedes the use of reason.

Briefly, all the causes which I have mentioned as liable to

[1] *c.* 465–*c.* 413 B.C.
[2] Gelon was succeeded by his brother Hieron in 478.   On the latter's
death (467 B.C.) his brother Thrasybulus led astray the next heir, Gelon's
son.   The name of this son is unknown.
[3] 353 B.C.
[4] There is nothing so exasperating to a man as insult; to which cause must
be attributed the overthrow of the Peisistratidae and many other tyrants.
—(A.)

destroy oligarchy in its unmixed and ultimate form, and also the
extreme form of democracy, must be reckoned as no less fatal to
tyranny; indeed those forms are merely collective tyrannies.
Kingship is seldom destroyed by external causes, and is therefore lasting. The causes of its destruction are nearly always
internal, and that destruction may come about in two ways:
(1) [1313ª] members of the royal family may quarrel among
themselves; or (2) the king may attempt to govern on tyrannical
lines, by claiming too many prerogatives over and above those
conferred by law. Kingships rarely emerge in these days; and
when they do they are no better than the tyrannical form of
monarchy. Kingship is a form of government by consent,
having sovereign authority in affairs of major consequence.
Equality is now widespread, and no one is sufficiently outstanding to assume the majesty and prerogatives of royalty.
For this reason men will not submit to such a form of government, and anyone who wins a throne by force or fraud is immediately regarded as a tyrant. Kingships limited to a single
family are liable to be overthrown by another cause in addition to
those already mentioned. A ruler is often despised by his subjects for outrages committed in spite of the fact that, while
possessing the dignity of a king, he lacks the power of a tyrant.
In these circumstances his overthrow presents no difficulty. A
king ceases to be a king when his subjects renounce their
allegiance, though a tyrant may hold his ground even against
recalcitrant subjects. These and similar causes are responsible
for the overthrow of monarchies.

(F) *Methods of Stabilizing Monarchies*

Monarchies generally speaking are preserved by the opposite
means to those which tend to destroy them. If we consider
them separately, (1) kingship can be made to last by the restriction of its authority. The more limited a king's power, the
longer it will endure unimpaired; he will act with greater
moderation and more like an equal toward his subjects, who will
therefore envy him the less. This is why kingship has lasted
for so long among the Molossians; and the survival of the Spartan
kingship must be attributed partly to its original division
between two members, partly to the limitations introduced by
Theopompus, of which the most outstanding was the ephoralty.
While restricting the royal prerogative, Theopompus established
the monarchy on a more durable basis, and thereby, if anything,

enhanced its greatness.   The story is told that on one occasion his wife asked him if he were not ashamed to bequeath his sons less power than he had inherited from his father.   To which he replied: 'Certainly not; I am bequeathing them a power that will endure much longer.'

(2) Tyrannies are preserved in two ways which are diametrically opposed.   One of them (*a*) is traditional; it is the method of government still followed by the majority of tyrants.   Many of its features are said to have been introduced by Periander of Corinth,[1] but quite a number also may be derived from the Persian regime.   To this method belong some of the practices referred to above as helping to preserve a tyranny, so far as this is possible; e.g. the 'lopping off' of outstanding men and the removal of bold spirits.   Here now are some others: (i) The prohibition of common meals, clubs, [1313^b] education, and the like; in a word, the avoidance of all likely sources whether of high spirit or of mutual confidence.   (ii) The exclusion of cultural societies and other such gatherings, and indeed the employment of whatever means help to prevent people getting to know one another; for mutual acquaintance breeds mutual confidence.   (iii) The adoption of all those Persian or barbarian practices which bolster up a tyranny.   Chief among these is the custom of obliging every resident in the capital to appear regularly in public and to hang about outside the palace gate.   This enables your tyrant to keep an eye on the doings of his subjects, who develop humility through their constant servitude.   (iv) The endeavour to obtain information about every man's words and actions through the agency of spies, like the female detectives at Syracuse, or the eavesdroppers sent by Hiero to all social gatherings and public meetings.[2]   (v) The sowing of mutual discord by setting friend against friend, the common people against the notables, and the rich against one another.

Finally (vi) it is the practice of tyrants to impoverish their subjects in order to prevent them maintaining a civic guard, and also to make sure that they are so busy earning their daily bread that they will have no time for conspiracy.   The Egyptian pyramids illustrate this policy, as do the lavish offerings made by the family of Cypselus,[3] the building of the temple of

---

[1] 625–585 B.C.

[2] Men who go in fear of spies are less outspoken; and if they do venture to speak their minds, they are less likely to get away with it.—(A.)

[3] At Delphi and Olympia.

Olympian Zeus by the Peisistratidae,[1] and the monuments erected at Samos by Polycrates.[2] All these works were undertaken with a single end in view—to keep the people busy and ensure their poverty. Taxation has the same effect. At Syracuse, for example, within a period of five years during the reign of Dionysius, his subjects were made to pay their entire property into the exchequer. A tyrant is also a war-monger: here again his purpose is to keep his subjects occupied and continually in want of a leader.

The power of a king is sustained by his friends. A tyrant, on the contrary, distrusts them above everyone else, because he knows that while all his subjects would like to get rid of him, his friends are in the best position to do so. And so the methods of extreme democracies are likewise characteristic of tyrannies. Women are permitted to domineer over their families, in the hope that they will inform against their husbands; and the same motive accounts for the indulgence shown towards slaves. Slaves and women do not plot against tyrants, under whom, indeed, they prosper, and towards whom they are for that reason inevitably well disposed—just as they are ready to support democracies, where the people assume the role of monarch. This is why flatterers rank high under both forms of government. While democracies admire demagogues, who are in fact the 'courtiers of democracy,' a tyrant loves the [1314ª] calculated flattery of his obsequious retinue. Tyranny is therefore a regime which favours bad men. It rejoices in flattery, to which no one with the spirit of a freeman can ever stoop; good men, of course, are capable of friendship, but certainly not of flattery. Bad men are also useful instruments of iniquity; 'nail knocks out nail,' as the proverb says. Tyranny is characteristically averse to men of dignity and independence. The tyrant likes to think of himself alone as possessing these qualities; anyone who asserts a rival dignity, or behaves independently, appears to encroach on his prerogative, on his supremacy, and is loathed accordingly as hostile to his power. It is also characteristic of tyrants to prefer the company of foreigners to that of citizens, both at table and at social gatherings; they take the view that while citizens are enemies, they need fear no opposition from foreigners.

---

[1] This great temple at Athens was not completed until the reign of Hadrian (A.D. 132).
[2] Polycrates was tyrant of Samos (532–522 B.C.).

Such are the arts employed by tyrants, and such the props of their authority; wickedness can go no further. They may be summed up under three main headings which correspond to the threefold aims of a tyrant. First, the humiliation of his subjects, on the grounds that a man whose spirit has been broken will never conspire against anyone; second, to create mutual distrust among them, bearing in mind that tyranny is never overthrown until men begin to have confidence in one another;[1] third, to render their subjects incapable of action, for nobody attempts the impossible, and therefore nobody will try to overthrow a tyranny when he is powerless to do so. Under these three headings, then, the policies of a tyrant may be reduced, and to one or other of them all his measures may be referred: to sow mistrust among his subjects; to render them powerless; and to break their spirit.

So much, too, for (a) the first method of preserving tyrannies. The second method (b) works on lines almost exactly the reverse; its nature will be better understood if we remind ourselves of those causes which underlie the fall of regal government. Just as kingship may be destroyed, among other ways, by inclining too far in the direction of tyranny, so the latter may be preserved by tending more towards kingship—subject, however, to one indispensable condition. The tyrant must retain sufficient power to govern with *or without* the consent of his subjects: let him once relax his hold and he is lost. With this all-important proviso, he should act, or appear to act, the part of a right royal king. (i) He must show himself [1314^b] anxious to protect the public funds. He must avoid making those lavish gifts which are apt to cause discontent among the masses when they see their hard-won earnings wrung from them only to be squandered on prostitutes, foreigners, and artists. He should also render an account of his income and expenditure, as many tyrants in the past have done. By following their example he will appear more like a steward than a tyrant; and so long as his authority remains secure he need have no fear that he will ever want for money. In point of fact, when tyrants are away from home it is better for them to leave behind a deficit than a well-filled treasury; the regents will then be less likely to attempt

---

[1] This is also the reason why tyrants are always at loggerheads with the good. They feel that good men constitute a threat to their authority, not only because such men reject despotic government, but also because they are loyal to all their fellows as well as among themselves, and will not denounce one another or anyone else.—(A.)

usurpation.[1]   He should levy taxes and require special contributions in such a way that they are manifestly intended for the upkeep of public services or, in case of need, for the emergencies of
war.   In all his dealings with the revenue he should behave as
guardian, or treasurer, of public funds, not handling them as
though they were his private fortune.

(ii) A tyrant should appear grave, but not harsh; and those
who meet him should be filled with awe, though not with dread.
This is unlikely to happen if he inspires no respect; and therefore, whatever virtues he may choose to neglect, he should cultivate a soldierly bearing and give the impression of military
competence.   Both the tyrant himself and all his associates must
be free from suspicion of sexual offences of any kind against any
of his subjects, male or female.   His womenfolk must exercise
the same self-control towards other women; female insolence
has proved fatal to many tyrannies.   With regard to other kinds
of self-indulgence, he should be the opposite of some modern
tyrants, who not only start at dawn and carry on for days at a
time, but even wish others to see them doing so and to applaud
their happy, blissful state.   No, indeed, our tyrant should be
moderate in this respect.   At any rate, he should *appear* to shun
excess.   It is your drowsy drunkard, not the sober and watchful
ruler, who is readily despised and easily attacked.   A tyrant's
conduct should, in fact, be the opposite in nearly all respects of
that which I have described above as characteristic of his kind.
He should plan and adorn his capital as if he held it in trust,
rather than as an autocrat.   He should also show the utmost zeal
in matters of ritual worship.   Men are less afraid of suffering
injustice at the hands of their ruler [1315ᵃ] when they look upon
him as a god-fearing man; nor are they so likely to conspire
against him if they believe that the gods themselves are on his
side.   At the same time, his zeal must never incur ridicule.
Our tyrant should also honour good men in any walk of life,
and he should do so in such a way as to convince them that they
could not have been more highly honoured by their fellow
citizens under a non-tyrannical regime.   He should distribute
such honours in person, but should delegate the infliction of
punishment to the magistrates or courts of law.   All monarchs,
on the other hand, are careful not to exalt one individual above

---

[1] Regents are more formidable than the citizen body to a tyrant campaign-
ing abroad; they remain at home, while the rank and file of the people
accompany him to war.—(A.)

the rest.   If any such dignity is conferred, it should be granted
to several persons, who will then keep an eye on one another.
However, if it becomes absolutely necessary to promote an
individual, he should not be a man of bold spirit; such characters
are always the most liable to strike in every sphere of action.
Again, if it is decided to curtail someone's power, this should be
done gradually, not at a single stroke.   A tyrant ought to shun
every form of outrage, especially these two—physical violence
and indecent assault on the young.   He should be particularly
cautious in his behaviour towards those who prize their honour.
A man of high principles will resent any slight to his good name,
just as a miser is upset by any diminution of his wealth.   A
tyrant, therefore, should abstain from such acts.   At the very
least, his punishments should seem to flow from the exercise of
paternal discipline, and his intimacy with young people from
true love rather than from the insolence of power.   In any case,
he should make good his apparent disrespect with the reward of
even higher honours.

The most dreaded and most dangerous of would-be assassins
are those who set out to fulfil their purpose without caring
whether they perish in consequence.   This is why special precautions are required against those who believe that they themselves, or others dear to them, are the victims of outrage.   Those
who strike under the influence of blind passion do so regardless
of their fate: as Heracleitus used to say, 'it is difficult to fight
blind passion, for it will pay the price of life.'

(iii) Bearing in mind that all states are composed of two
elements, viz. the poor and the rich, a tyrant should do everything he can to convince both groups that his rule alone secures
their position and protects them from injustice at one another's
hands.   He should also enlist whichever is the stronger as his
particular supporters; with them at his side he will have no need,
for instance, to emancipate slaves or disarm the citizens.   Either
group added to his existing power will make him more than a
match for any assailant.

But it is superfluous to discuss these matters in detail; what I
am driving at is plain.   First, a tyrant should appear to his subjects not as a tyrant [1315^b], but as a steward or a king, acting not
in his own interest but as a trustee on their behalf.   Second, he
ought to shun excess and practise moderation in his way of life.
Third, he should cultivate the society of the notables, but also
curry favour with the masses.   In this way his rule will assuredly

be nobler and more enviable, because his subjects will be better men, men of unbroken spirit; and he himself will no longer be an object of hatred or of fear. His power, too, will be more lasting; and his own character, if not completely disposed to virtue, will be at any rate half good—partially bad, of course, but not entirely so.[1]

(G) *Critical Notes on Plato's Theory of Constitutional Change*

I have now dealt with practically all the causes responsible for the destruction and preservation both of constitutions and of monarchies.[2] [1316ᵃ] In Plato's *Republic* Socrates has something to say about constitutional change; but his treatment of the subject is quite unsatisfactory, for he mentions no cause of change peculiar to his first and ideal constitution. After saying that the cause is that nothing abides, and that everything changes in a given period, he states [3] that the source of such change is to be found in a numerical system 'where the ratio 4: 3 married with 5 produces two harmonies,' meaning that this happens when the arithmetical value of the diagram is cubed.[4] What he implies here is that nature sometimes produces men of a low type who are incapable of education. And in doing so he may not be far wrong; for it is possible that there are individuals who cannot be educated and turned into good men. But why should this cause of change be peculiar to the ideal state described by Plato, rather than one common to all states, and even to all existing things? Then again, is it as a result of time (which he says is the universal cause of change) that things which did not begin simultaneously end simultaneously? For instance, does a thing which came into existence on the day before the close of a cycle change simultaneously with things that originated long before?

Furthermore, why should the ideal state change into one like that of Sparta? All constitutions tend to assume an opposite rather than a cognate form. The same reasoning applies to

[1] For 1315ᵇ11–39 see Appendix V, page 242.
[2] See page 157, footnote 2.
[3] *Republic*, viii. 546.
[4] The numbers 4 and 3 'married with 5' denote a right-angled triangle having its sides as 3, 4, 5. Cube the diagram, either by adding the cubes of the sides or by cubing the area, and we get the number 216. Now 216 days is the minimum period of human gestation; and therefore the number 216 is fancied by Plato to be the source of degeneration. The 'two harmonies' are a square with sides of 3,600, and a rectangle with sides of 4,800 and 2,700. In each case the area is 12,960,000, i.e. $(3 \times 4 \times 5)^4$.

other constitutional changes.   Plato represents the Spartan type
as changing into oligarchy, oligarchy into democracy, and democracy into tyranny.   But the process may be reversed: democracy, for example, is even more likely to change into oligarchy
than into monarchy.

On the subject of tyrannies, he leaves us in the dark as to
whether they do or do not change; nor, if they do, does he tell
us why, or into what form of government they change.   The
reason for his silence is that he would have been at his wit's end
for an answer: the matter cannot be determined in the light of
his theory, according to which a tyranny would have to change
into the first and ideal constitution in order to perpetuate the
cycle.   In point of fact, however, a tyranny may change into
(1) another form thereof, just as at Sicyon that of Cleisthenes [1]
superseded the tyranny of Myron.   It may likewise change into
(2) oligarchy, as did that of Antileon at Chalcis; into (3) democracy, like the tyranny of Gelon's house at Syracuse; [2] or,
finally, into (4) aristocracy, as happened to that of Charilaus [3] at
Sparta and . . .[4] at Carthage.   Tyranny itself may take the place
of oligarchy, as it did that of most ancient oligarchies in Sicily.
For example, the oligarchy at Leontini gave way to the tyranny
of Panaetius; at Gela to that of Cleander; and at Rhegium to that
of Anaxilaus.   The same kind of thing happened in several other
states.

It is absurd for Plato to imagine that the change into oligarchy
is due to the magistrates becoming money-lovers and profit-
makers, [1316^b] rather than to a feeling among the wealthiest
class that it is unfair to grant the have-nots an equal share of
constitutional rights with those who own property.   The fact is
that in quite a number of oligarchies profit-making is forbidden,
and forbidden by law; but at Carthage, where the government is
democratic,[5] profit-making *is* carried on, and the constitution
has so far remained unaltered.

It is also absurd for Plato to maintain that an oligarchical state
is really two states—one of the rich and another of the poor.   Is
this truer of oligarchy than of the Spartan or any other form of
constitution where property is not equally distributed, or where

[1] He died *c.* 576 B.C.
[2] See page 162, footnote 2.
[3] Traditional ruler, placed on the throne by Lycurgus.
[4] There would appear to be a small lacuna at this point.
[5] But see pages 59–61 and 112, line 37.   The word *demokratoumene* here is
probably a mere slip of the pen.

all men are not equally good? Once the poor are in a majority, an oligarchy may change into a democracy without anyone having become a whit poorer than he was before. Similarly, if the well-to-do are stronger than the masses, and are energetic while the latter are indifferent, democracy may change into oligarchy.

Although there are many possible causes of the change from oligarchy to democracy, Plato mentions only one, viz. impoverishment through extravagance and debt. He seems to think that all men, or nearly all, are rich at the outset; but this is not true. It *is* true, on the other hand, that when any of the leading men lose their property they dream of revolution; but others may do so without any serious consequences, and the change which follows is no more likely to result in democracy than in any other form of government. Further, if men are excluded from the honours of office, or are subject to injustice or insult, they may have recourse to sedition and constitutional change, even though they have not frittered away their property through the right to 'do what I please with my own,' which Plato attributes to excessive freedom.

While there are several varieties of oligarchy and of democracy, Socrates is made to speak of their changes as if there were only one variety of each. . . . [*Unfinished.*]

C. POSTSCRIPT TO BOOK IV
(Book VI)[1]

1. Introductory

[1316^b34] I have discussed (1) the number and nature of the varieties found in (a) the deliberative and supreme constitutional body, (b) the distribution of offices, (c) the structure of the law-courts, and have explained which of these varieties is appropriate to each constitution.[2] I have likewise dealt with (2) the occasions and causes which result in the overthrow and preservation of the several constitutions.[3] Since, however, there is more than one species both of democracy and of other governmental forms, it will not be out of place to round off the subject by determining the mode of organization which is appropriate and advantageous to each. Further, we shall do well to investigate possible ways of combining the different modes whereby (a), (b), and (c) above-mentioned may be organized; [1317^a] for these combinations give rise to the overlapping of constitutions, so that, for example, aristocracy becomes tinged with oligarchy, and polity inclines to democracy.

The combinations to which I refer as due for study, though hitherto left out of the picture, may be illustrated by these examples. The deliberative body and the method of choosing magistrates may be planned on an oligarchical basis, while the structure of the judiciary is characteristic of aristocracies; or the judiciary and the deliberative body may be organized on oligarchical lines, while the magistrates are chosen according to the principles of aristocracy; or, again, some other arrangement may

---

[1] In Book IV (pages 123–32) Aristotle began to deal with the last part of his programme enunciated on page 105. Having discussed the construction of constitutions with special reference to the deliberative, executive, and judicial elements, he broke off to deal with the Pathology of the State in Book V. In this latter book (pages 150, 163) he inserted a digression on the *preservation* of constitutions *as they stand*; and now, by way of a postscript to Book IV, he turns to the *construction* of constitutions *with particular reference to their greater stability*, but gets no further than democracy and oligarchy.

[2] Pages 123–32.

[3] Pages 133–69.

be adopted whereby the several departments of state differ from one another in their framework.

I have already explained [1] what variety of democracy is suited to what kind of citizen body, what type of oligarchy to what kind of society, and which of the other forms of government is appropriate to which sort of population. It is necessary, however, not only to make clear which of these constitutional varieties is best for each state, but also to explain succinctly how they and their sub-forms are to be *constructed*.

2. CONSTRUCTION OF DEMOCRACIES

Let us take democracy first; it will throw light upon the opposite form of government, which is usually described as oligarchy. For the purposes of this inquiry we must keep in view the attributes of democracy, and everything commonly associated therewith. Taken together they will account for the several types of democracy—for the existence of more than one type, and also for the particular differences between them.

Now there are two reasons why democracy takes a variety of forms. I have already mentioned [2] the first of these, viz. the difference in character between the people of one state and another. The popular element may consist of farmers, or of mechanics and day-labourers; and if farmers are added to mechanics, and day-labourers to both, the resulting difference is not merely one between better and worse, but between totally different things. The second reason why democracy takes a variety of forms lies in the different possible ways of blending its salient features which are accepted as its attributes. One form will include fewer of them, another more, and yet another all of them. There is an advantage in studying each and every one of these attributes, for the purpose, that is to say, of constructing a new form of democracy, as well as of remodelling existing types. The founder of a constitution often attempts to synthesize all the attributes connected with the idea on which his constitution is based; but this is a mistake, as I remarked [3] above when speaking of the destruction and preservation of constitutions.

I turn now to the principles, the ethical character, and the aims of democratic constitutions. The idea underlying the

[1] Pages 120–1.   [2] Pages 108, 110.   [3] Pages 155–6.

democratic type of government is *liberty*,[1] one form of which provides that all the citizens shall rule and be ruled in turn. The democratic notion of justice is that all should enjoy numerical rather than proportionate equality on the basis of merit.   On this view, the masses are of course supreme; whatever the majority decides must be the perfect embodiment of justice.   It is argued that each and every citizen should be on a level with his neighbour; and therefore in a democracy the poor have more authority than the well-to-do, because they constitute a majority whose decisions are *ex hypothesi* supreme.   Such, then, is one note of liberty, which all democrats recognize as the goal of their constitution.   The other consists in living as one likes.   Such, they maintain, is the function of a freeman, just as the function of a slave is *not* to live as he likes.   This is the second goal of democracy, resulting, if possible, in absolute freedom from governmental control, or, at most, intermittent subjection; and so it contributes to the system of liberty based on equality.

Such being the underlying principle of democracy, the following institutions are democratic: (1) Election of officers by all and from all; (2) the system whereby all rule over each, and each in his turn over all; (3) appointment by lot to all offices, or at any rate to such as require no experience or particular skill; (4) absence of property qualification for office, or at any rate a very low one; (5) the rule providing that offices (other than military ones) should never be held twice by the same man;[2] (6) the short tenure of all offices, or at least of as many as possible; (7) a judiciary consisting of all the citizens, or of members chosen from the whole civic body, and empowered to decide all cases, or at any rate the most important, involving, for example, the scrutiny of public accounts, constitutional issues, and private contracts; (8) supremacy of the popular assembly in all (or at least the most vital) concerns, while the magistrates enjoy such authority in none or at any rate in the fewest possible;[3] (9) payment for services—ideally in all three departments (popular assembly, law-courts, and magistracies), but failing that, at least

[1] It is often held that this can be enjoyed only in a democracy; and this, it is also [1317b] maintained, is the aim of every democracy.—(A.)

[2] Except infrequently and in the case of only a few offices.—(A.)

[3] The council is the most popular of magistracies in a democracy which lacks the means to pay all its citizens for attending the popular assembly. But where such means exist, even the council is deprived of its authority; for once the people are adequately paid, they begin, as I remarked in the previous section [Book IV, page 129], to monopolize the whole sphere of administration.—(A.)

for attending the courts, the council, and stated meetings of the assembly, and also for serving on a board of magistrates, or at least on such boards as are obliged to keep a common table; (10) the exclusion of perpetual magistracies, or at any rate curtailment of the powers attached to any such office [1318ᵃ] as may have survived some early constitutional change, and appointment to such offices by *lot* instead of by *vote*.

These are the attributes common to all democracies. But democracy in its truest form, and the typically democratic populace, are traceable rather to the notion of justice which is recognized as the democratic notion, viz. equality of rights on a numerical basis. Such equality *seems* to imply that the poor should enjoy no more authority than the rich—that sovereignty, so far from being held exclusively by the poor, should be evenly distributed on a numerical basis.[1] On this view the advocates of democracy might well believe their constitution to embody freedom and equality.

Next comes the question, how is such equality to be achieved? Should the assessed properties be divided into two groups, so that those of a thousand owners will be equal in value to those of five hundred, and should the one thousand have equal voting power with the five hundred? Or, as an alternative, should equality in this respect be calculated in some other way, e.g. by dividing assessed properties as above and then taking an equal number from each group and giving them control of the elections and the courts? Which is the juster form of government according to the democratic notion of justice—one based on property or one based on numbers? Democrats say that justice is that which is decided by a majority *of persons*. Oligarchs hold it to consist in the will of a majority of *property owners*; they maintain that all issues should be decided according to weight of property. Both these opinions involve inequality and injustice. If justice is the will of the few, the door is open to tyranny; for any one man who possesses more than all the other property owners put together should, on the oligarchical notion of justice, be sole ruler. Conversely, if justice is the will of a majority of persons, they will, as I have already said,[2] unjustly confiscate the property of the rich minority. We have therefore to examine the definitions of justice put forward by both sides, in order to discover a form of equality acceptable to both.

Now democrats and oligarchs alike affirm that what is decided

---

[1] Cf. pages 108, 109.   [2] Page 82, lines 32–4.

upon by the majority of citizens should be final.   However true
the statement may be, we cannot let it pass without some qualification.   Because the state is composed of two elements, rich
and poor, we may recognize sovereignty as vested either in the
will of both parties, or in that of a majority of each.   But if these
parties reach opposite decisions, sovereignty may then be
allowed to the will of a majority of persons who are at the same
time the owners of a majority of property.   Let us take an
example.   Suppose you have ten rich men and twenty poor,
and suppose that six of the former have reached a decision
opposed to that taken by fifteen of the latter, meaning that four
of the rich have sided with the poor, and five of the poor with
the rich.   In such a case sovereignty ought to lie with the will of
that side whose members, when both its elements are added
together, have more property than those of the other side.   If
both sides turn out to be running neck and neck, the situation
need be considered no more difficult than it is at present, when,
if the assembly or the court is equally divided, [1318^b] the
matter is decided by lot or some such method.

Although it may be very difficult in theory to discover exactly
where equality and justice lie, it is nevertheless easier to do this
than to restrain those who can, if they so desire, indulge their
selfishness.   The weaker always long for equality and justice;
the stronger care for none of these things.

Of the four varieties of democracy the best, as I remarked in
an earlier section of this inquiry,[1] is (1) that which comes first in
order.[2]   It is also the most ancient of the four; but I call it
'first' in accordance with the degree of excellence assigned to
different kinds of populace.   The finest democratic material is
a populace of farmers; there is no difficulty in constructing a
democracy where the masses live by arable or pastoral farming.
Not having much property, they have no time for frequent
attendance at the popular assembly.   Wanting the necessities of
life, they are always hard at work and do not covet their neighbours' goods; indeed they find more enjoyment in work than in
politics and the cares of government, except maybe when the
perquisites of office are considerable.   The masses are more
greedy for gain than for honour, as is proved by the fact that they
endured the ancient tyrannies, and still live contentedly under
an oligarchy provided they are allowed to get on with their work

[1] Pages 110–11.   [2] i.e. the agricultural.

and are not robbed of their property.   Left alone, some of them will soon grow rich, while others at least rise above the level of penury.   If the masses are at all ambitious, their craving will be satisfied with the right of electing magistrates and calling them to account; and in some democracies they have been content to forgo the elective privilege [1] so long as they exercised the power of deliberation.   Even such a system, as exemplified at Mantinea, must be reckoned as democratic.

Hence it is expedient as well as customary in the above-mentioned type of democracy that all should elect the magistrates, call them to account, and exercise judicial functions, while the most important offices are filled by election and open exclusively to those who have a property qualification related in value to the dignity of each particular office.   On the other hand, there may be no such qualification, in which case only men of special ability will be appointed.   A state governed in this way is bound to be well governed.[2]   The upper classes and the notables, too, will inevitably be satisfied; for while the obligation of rendering an account to others will ensure that they govern justly, they themselves will not be subject to the rule of their inferiors.   It is a good thing to be responsible to others and not to be free to do whatever one pleases; for the power of arbitrary behaviour leaves one without protection [1319a] against the evil which is present in us all.   The principle of responsibility carries with it an incalculable advantage under any constitution: the best type of men will govern without misrule, and the masses will lack none of their just rights.

This form of democracy is evidently the best; and the reason too is no less clear, viz. the character of the populace.   In creating an agricultural community some of the laws governing a majority of states at an early period will be found useful; e.g. the absolute prohibition of acquiring landed property beyond a certain amount, or within a certain distance of the capital and its immediate environs.   It was also laid down in many ancient states that none might sell the land originally allotted to his family; while the effect of a law attributed to Oxylus [3] was to forbid the raising of a mortgage on a certain

---

[1] At Mantinea, for example, it belonged to representatives selected in rotation from the whole civic body.—(A.)

[2] Because the magistracies will always be held by the most worthy men, and with the consent of a people which bears no grudge against the higher ranks of society.—(A.)

[3] An early ruler of Elis on the west coast of Peloponnesus.

proportion of any landed estate. The Aphytean law may be employed as a useful corrective in the absence of any such laws. Aphytis [1] has a large population and not much land; the population, however, is exclusively agricultural. This is because their estates are not treated, for the purpose of assessment, as single units, but are divided into parts so small that even the poorer landowners may have more than the amount necessary to qualify them for citizen rights.

(2) Next best after the agricultural is a pastoral populace, living by its flocks and herds. They have many characteristics in common with the farmers; but their sturdy physique and their familiarity with camp life make them peculiarly adaptable to the conditions of warfare.

(3) The other kinds of populace (mechanics, shopkeepers, and day-labourers) which form the remaining types of democracy, are in almost every case much inferior to them. Their way of life is despicable, and there is no room for excellence in any occupation to which people of that sort put their hands. Revolving round the market-place and city centre, fellows of this class generally find it easy to attend the popular assembly, whereas the farmers, who are scattered about the countryside, neither attend nor have any wish to attend such meetings. Wherever you have the further advantage of a countryside lying at some distance from the capital, it is easy to frame a democracy or a polity. The masses are then obliged to settle on their lands; and so, even if there is still a city mob, no democracy should fail to prohibit meetings of the assembly which cannot be attended by the rural population.

In explaining how the first and best form of democracy should be constructed, I have made equally clear what pattern the other varieties should follow. They should deviate from it stage by stage, and the classes excluded at each stage should be of a progressively lower order.

[1319ᵇ] The last variety, in which *all* have equal rights, is one that cannot be borne by all states, and will not easily endure for long unless it is well constituted in respect of law and custom. The causes leading to the destruction of this and other forms of government have already been studied at considerable length.[2] Popular leaders who undertake to frame a democracy of this kind have a way of strengthening the masses by including in their number, and extending the franchise to, persons of illegitimate

---

[1] In Macedonia.   [2] Pages 135–50; 157–63.

as well as legitimate birth, and to those born of only one citizen parent—father or mother; for all these people are part and parcel of extreme democracy.   That is how demagogues set about their task; but it is unwise to increase the number of common people beyond a point at which they just exceed that of the upper classes and moderately well-to-do.   If there are too many of them they destroy the balance of the constitution and make it harder for men of higher social standing to tolerate democracy— an attitude which once led to revolution at Cyrene.[1]   A mote in the eye may well be overlooked; not so a beam.   Other measures which will be found useful in constructing an extreme demo- cracy are those employed at Athens by Cleisthenes [2] to intensify the democratic regime, and those adopted by the founders of popular government at Cyrene.[3]   The plan is to create a number of new tribes and clans, to reduce the private cults to a few public ones, and indeed to take every possible step that will cause the citizens to mingle with one another, and untie their former loyalties.   Certain measures characteristic of tyranny may likewise be regarded as democratic in spirit.   I mean such things as the licence permitted to slaves (which, up to a point, may even be advantageous), the indulgence shown towards women and children, and the right to live exactly as one pleases. This last feature, incidentally, cannot but enlist strong support for the constitution now under review; most men find more pleasure in living without restraint than subject to discipline.

The task confronting a legislator,[4] and indeed all who set out to erect a constitution of this type, is not only or even principally the work of construction; for any state, no matter what its form of government, may last for two or three days.   No, the real difficulty is to make it endure.   A legislator should therefore endeavour to construct stability in the light of our previous remarks [5] on the causes which underlie the destruction and preservation of constitutions.   He must avoid the destructive elements, and provide a body of [1320^a] written and unwritten law which will include, as far as possible, all the stabilizing factors.   He must also understand that the truly democratic or

---

[1] 401 B.C.
[2] 508 B.C.   Cf. *Ath. Con.* 21.
[3] *c.* 450 B.C.
[4] In the remainder of section (3) Aristotle leaves the subject of *construction* to complete that of *preservation*, with which he has only dealt in general terms (except in regard to monarchy) in Book V, pages 150–6.
[5] Book V.

oligarchical measure is not that which pushes either form of government to its utmost extreme, but that which enables it to last longest.   Modern demagogues curry favour with the people by confiscating large amounts of property through the medium of the law-courts.   Men who have the welfare of their constitution at heart should set their faces against methods of this kind. They should carry a law that all fines imposed by the courts, instead of becoming public property and being paid into the treasury, shall be devoted to religious uses.   Such a system will not encourage offenders, who will still have to pay the same fine; and the people, having nothing to gain, will be slower to convict every defendant.   Public prosecutions also should be reduced to a minimum, and heavy penalties should be introduced to prevent frivolous charges.   At present it is usually the notables who find themselves arraigned, not members of the popular party; but the wisest policy is to attach *all* citizens both to the constitution and to the government by whom it is administered, or at least to make sure that no citizen has cause to look upon the government as his enemy.

Extreme democracies are generally associated with large populations, the members of which find it hard to attend the popular assembly unless they are paid for doing so.   Now where there are no special revenues for this purpose a heavy burden falls on the notables, from whom the money has to be squeezed by means of property taxes, confiscations, and corrupt tribunals—all of which have at one time or another led to the overthrow of democracies.   In the absence of such revenues, therefore, the assembly should not meet too often; the courts, likewise, however numerous their membership, should confine their sessions to a few days in the year.   A system of this kind has two advantages: first, the rich will no longer fear the expense involved, even though they attend without payment while the poor are allowed fees; and secondly, justice will be better administered, because the wealthier classes (who dislike absenting themselves from business for days on end but have no objection to doing so for short periods) will be ready to attend the courts. Wherever special revenues *are* forthcoming, on the other hand, the modern demagogic scheme should be avoided.   It involves the distribution of surplus moneys among the people, who take it and at once ask for more.   Assistance on those lines is like pouring water into a leaky jug.   All the same, a true democrat should make it his business to see that there is no excessive poverty among the masses. Penury is the curse of democracy, and on that account steps should be taken to ensure a constant level of prosperity. This is in the interest of all classes, not excluding the rich, and surplus revenue should therefore be accumulated and distributed in block grants to the poor. If sufficient can be accumulated, the aim should be to grant in each case an amount large enough for the purchase of a plot of land, or at the very least to enable recipients to start a commercial [1320^b] or agricultural career. If such grants cannot be extended to all poor citizens at once, the money should be distributed in turn among the tribes or other groups; and meanwhile the rich should contribute the fees necessary to recompense the poor for their attendance at obligatory meetings of the assembly, and should be exempted in return from useless public services. It is by some such system that the Carthaginian government has won the favour of its subjects. From time to time it sends out a number of the rank and file to its provincial towns, thus enabling them to prosper. Gentlemen of feeling and good sense may also help the poor to make a start in some occupation, each of them adopting a group and allowing its members a grant for that purpose. The citizens of Tarentum have set a fine example in this matter of private assistance by sharing the use of their property with the poor and thereby earning their goodwill. They have also divided their magistracies into two groups, one of which is filled by election in order to ensure a high standard of administration, and the other by lot so as to allow the common people a share in office. Exactly the same result may be obtained by dividing each board of magistrates into two classes, one to be chosen by vote and the other by lot.

3. CONSTRUCTION OF OLIGARCHIES

I have now explained the proper method of constructing democracies, and in doing so have virtually made it clear how oligarchies should be constituted. Each variety of the latter should be framed on the principle of opposites; in other words, the structure of each ought to be calculated by that of the corresponding type of democracy.

The first and best-wrought form of oligarchy is akin to what we call 'polity.' Here there should be two distinct registers of property assessment, a higher and a lower. Inclusion in the lower should qualify its members for the least important offices that have to be filled; but the greater magistrates should be chosen exclusively from among those admitted to the higher register. At the same time, anyone who obtains enough property for enrolment in the lower register should be allowed constitutional rights; and in this way a sufficient number of the people will be admitted to make the civic body stronger than those who have no such rights. New citizens should always be drawn from the better.sections of the people.

The next variety of oligarchy should be constructed in the same way, but with a slight narrowing of the property qualification; and so on, until we reach that variety which corresponds to democracy in its extreme form. This is the type which most nearly resembles a family clique or a tyranny; it is the worst of all, and therefore requires the utmost vigilance. A body in good health, like a well-built and well-manned ship, can survive any number of risks; but the least mishap is fatal alike to a poor physique and to an unseaworthy or badly manned ship. The same is true of constitutions: the worst of them need the most careful nursing. [1321ª] In democracies the saving factor is generally the size of the population, which is the antithesis of distributive justice on the basis of desert. Oligarchies, on the other hand, must evidently rely for security on the opposite principle, viz. sound organization.

Just as the masses consist of four principal groups—farmers, mechanics, shopkeepers, and day-labourers—so too the armed strength of the state is fourfold, including cavalry, heavy infantry, light-armed troops, and the navy. Where the territory is suitable for cavalry manœuvres it will not be difficult to frame a strong type of oligarchy; the inhabitants rely upon this arm for their security, and only men with full pockets can afford to breed and keep horses. The next form of oligarchy is more natural in territory suitable for the employment of heavy infantry, because the wealthier classes are better equipped than are the poor to serve in this latter force. Light-armed troops and the navy are wholly democratic in character, and to-day, when their numbers are large, they can often overthrow an oligarchy in the event of civil war. A remedy for this state of affairs is suggested by the measure adopted by some military commanders, who combine an appropriate contingent of light-armed troops with the cavalry and heavy infantry. The masses can defeat the wealthier classes in civil war precisely because a light-armed force is so well equipped to deal with one consisting of heavy infantry and cavalry.   An oligarchy which raises a force of this kind *from the masses alone* is thus creating a challenge to itself.   Account should therefore be taken of different age groups: while they are in the younger of these groups, even the sons of oligarchs should be trained in light-infantry drill and weapons, so that when they are moved up into the older groups they will be fully qualified for service in that arm.

An oligarchy may admit the rank and file to office in one or other of the following ways.   (1) The right may be conferred, as I said above, on those who can satisfy a fixed property qualification.   (2) Following the example of Thebes,[1] it may be allowed to those who have not lived as traders for a stated number of years.   Or (3) it may be given, as at Massilia, to those whose names have been included in an official list as worthy of office, whether or not they are already members of the civic body.

The most important offices, which must invariably be held by men having full constitutional rights, should entail the performance of certain public services without pay. ..The people will not then begrudge their exclusion from such offices, and will bear no resentment against the magistrates who pay so heavy a price for their dignity.   It is also right and proper that these officials should be required to offer magnificent sacrifices on taking office, and to erect some public building before the end of their term.   The people, sharing in these entertainments and enjoying the spectacle of their city adorned with votive offerings and splendid buildings, will thus be quite content with the spectacle of a permanent oligarchy; while the notables, on their part, will find a reward in those memorials of their generosity. Such, however, is anything but the policy of oligarchs to-day; they court profit no less than honour, and thereby justify the saying [1321b] that oligarchy is a miniature of democracy.

4. Organization of Offices

The foregoing account of methods to be used in constructing democracies leads us back [2] to another subject, viz. the right distribution of offices, their number, their nature, and their proper functions.   No state can possibly exist without certain indispensable offices; and without those which ensure good organization and order you can have no well-governed state.

[1] Cf. page 75.   [2] Cf. pages 126–30.

Again, as I have already observed,[1] small states require fewer offices than large ones; and we must therefore devote some time to considering which offices can be conjoined, and which should be in separate hands.

(1) First among indispensable offices is that which supervises the market-place. Someone must be appointed to maintain order there and to exercise jurisdiction in the field of contract. For buying and selling are virtually essential to the life of every state; by their means men satisfy one another's wants, and they are the foundation of that self-sufficiency which is regarded as the *raison d'être* of a political community. (2) The second indispensable office is akin to the former: it controls public and private building schemes with a view to sound planning, undertakes the maintenance and repair of houses and streets, and intervenes in boundary disputes and other such matters. The holder of this office is usually known as the city superintendent; and in larger towns his duties are often shared by a number of officials—one, for instance, looking after the walls, another the fountains, a third the harbour. (3) Our third indispensable office is very similar to the last; it has the same kind of jurisdiction, but outside the city centre and in the country beyond. The magistrates in question are called rural inspectors and inspectors of forests. Besides these three, there is (4) the office for the receipt and disbursement of public funds; its holders are called receivers or stewards. (5) Another official keeps the registers of all private contracts, decisions of the courts, public and private indictments, and preliminary proceedings. His duties also are sometimes shared by several men; in that case the board is under a departmental head. These officials are known as sacred recorders, presidents, registrars, or some similar term. (6) Next comes an office of which the duties are absolutely necessary but thoroughly disagreeable: it is responsible for the execution of judicial sentences, the exaction of fines from those whose names [1322^a] have been officially posted, and the custody of prisoners. These duties are so disagreeable because of the odium attaching to them; no one will undertake them unless substantial profit is to be made therefrom, and anyone who does shoulder the burden still recoils from executing the law. All the same, this office is necessary. Judicial sentences are useless if they are not carried out; and the continuance of society demands their execution as it demands their

[1] Page 127, line 22–page 128, line 6.

imposition.   Hence it is better that this particular magistracy should not be held by a special group, but should consist of a board whose members are chosen from different courts.   An attempt should likewise be made to share out the duty of posting the names of those registered as public debtors.   It is also desirable that the magistrates, as distinct from the courts, should have authority to exact certain penalties, and that penalties due to outgoing magistrates should be exacted by their successors in office.   As regards penalties due to magistrates actually in office, when one magistracy has tried the case and condemned, another should exact the penalty.   The city superintendent, for example, should exact the fines imposed by the superintendent of the market-place, and others again those imposed by *him*. Penalties are more likely to be exacted when less odium attaches to the process; but the odium is multiplied twofold when those who have passed sentence carry it out as well, and if they carry out every sentence they will have every man's hand against them.

It is the custom in many states for one magistracy to execute sentences and for another to have custody of prisoners.   It is in fact a good thing to separate off this latter office too, and try by the same means as before to render it less unpopular.   The duty in question is every bit as necessary as that of executing sentences; but decent people do all they can to avoid it, and it cannot safely be entrusted to rogues who themselves need careful watching.   There ought not, therefore, to be a single or permanent board set apart for this duty; it should be entrusted to successive groups of young men, wherever they are organized into a police force or city guard, and different magistrates acting in turn should take charge of it.

These six offices must be ranked first, as being most indispensable.   Next in order come certain others which are equally necessary, but of greater importance and requiring considerable experience and the utmost trustworthiness.   Such are those concerned with the defence of the capital and other military duties.   In peace as well as in time of war, there must be persons to defend the gates and walls, and to inspect and drill the citizens. Some states have a number of such officers, others only a few, and small states are frequently content with one; they are called generals or commandants.   [1322^b] Where there are separate forces of cavalry, light infantry, archers, and marines, each of them is sometimes commanded by a separate officer known as admiral, general of horse, or general of light infantry.   Their subordinate officers are termed naval captains, captains of horse, and company commanders. Those commanding small sections have their appropriate titles, and the whole organization forms a single war department.

We pass now from military command to the financial system. Since many of the above-mentioned offices, if not all of them, handle large sums of public money, there must be a separate office concerned exclusively with the receipt of revenues and auditing of accounts. The holders of this office are known variously as auditors, accountants, examiners, and comptrollers.

There is yet another office which is supreme over all those so far mentioned. In many states it has the twofold power of introducing matters to the assembly and of bringing them to completion. Failing that, it presides in a democracy over the assembly; for there must be a body to convene the supreme authority of the constitution. The officials in question form what is known in some states as a preliminary council, because they initiate deliberation; but where there is a popular assembly they are called collectively the council.

This completes the list of political offices. But there is another sphere of duties, concerned with public worship. It requires priests and also custodians responsible for the upkeep of temples and other sacred property. Sometimes, e.g. in small states, the whole of this department is entrusted to a single office. Elsewhere it may be divided among several offices: besides priests there may be superintendents of sacrifices, guardians of shrines, and stewards of sacred property. Closely akin to the above there may also be a separate office charged with the management of all public sacrifices which have the distinction of being offered on the city's common hearth and are not entrusted to priests. Its holders are in some states called archons, in others kings, and in others prytaneis.

These, then, are the necessary offices, which may be classified as they are concerned with: (1) (a) public worship, (b) military affairs, (c) revenue and expenditure; (2) (a) the market-place, (b) the city centre, (c) the harbours, (d) the countryside; (3) (a) the law-courts, (b) registration of contracts, (c) execution of sentences, (d) custody of prisoners, (e) reviewing, scrutiny, and audit of official accounts; (4) matters connected with the deliberation of public affairs.

There are also magistracies peculiar to certain states which are more leisurely, more prosperous, and concerned with the preservation of good order.   Examples of this kind are those created to supervise women, to enforce obedience to the laws, to supervise [1323ª] children, and to direct physical training.   In this class too we may place the office which superintends athletic and dramatic contests.   In a democracy there is evidently no call for some of these offices, e.g. those for the supervision of women and children; for the poor, having no slaves, are obliged to use their wives and children as servants.

There are three offices responsible for conducting elections to the highest magistracies in certain states.   They are the Guardians of the Law, the preliminary council, and the council. The first is appropriate to an aristocracy, the second to an oligarchy, and the third to a democracy.

I have now given a rough sketch of almost every kind of office; but . . .   [*Unfinished.*]

Books VII and VIII

ARISTOTLE'S IDEAL STATE

A. POLITICAL AIMS AND EDUCATIONAL
PRINCIPLES (Book VII)

1. The Most Desirable Life

[1323ª14] No proper inquiry into the ideal constitution is possible unless we have first determined what is the most desirable way of life. The ideal constitution must remain uncertain so long as this question is unanswered; for it is only reasonable to expect that, in the normal course of events, those will lead the best life who live under the best form of government permitted by their circumstances.[1] First, therefore, we must ask, which is the most generally desirable life, and secondly, whether or not the same life is best both for states and for individuals.

(A) Enough has been said in discourses not peculiar to this school on the subject of the best life; and I will therefore content myself with repeating the substance of them here. No one will object to the division of goods into three classes—external, corporeal, and spiritual—or deny that the happy man must have all three. No one can maintain that he is happy who has no trace of fortitude, temperance, justice, or prudence: who is afraid of every passing fly; who will not hesitate to commit the worst crimes in order to satisfy his hunger or thirst; who will sacrifice his dearest friend for twopence-halfpenny; and who is as feeble and false in mind as a child or a madman. Propositions of this kind are almost universally acknowledged, but men differ as to the degree and relative superiority of particular goods. Some think that a minimum of virtue will suffice, but desire unbounded wealth, unlimited property, unrestricted power and glory, and so forth. We may answer them by an appeal to facts, which plainly show that virtue is neither acquired nor preserved by means of external goods, but vice versa; [1323ᵇ] and that felicity, whether it is held to consist in pleasure or virtue (or both), is rather the lot of those who are most highly cultivated

---

[1] It has been remarked that in these last four words Aristotle appears momentarily to forget the nature of his subject. He argues elsewhere, and also in this book, that the ideal constitution is *absolutely* the best, without any reference to circumstances other than ideal ones, which are presupposed.

in mind and character, and have only a moderate share of external goods, than of those who have a superfluity of external goods but lack higher qualities. Apart from experience, this fact will become clear from the theoretical standpoint. External goods, like all other instruments, have a limit. Everything useful, in fact, is such that an excess of it will inevitably prove harmful to its possessor, or at any rate fail to profit him. But with spiritual goods, the greater they are the more useful they prove to be.[1]   No proof is required to demonstrate that the best state of X is to that of Y as X itself is to Y itself; so that if the soul is more precious than property or the body, both absolutely and in relation to ourselves, it must be admitted that the best state of either has a similar ratio to that of the other. Again, external and corporeal goods are desirable at all only in so far as they benefit the soul, for whose sake every commonsensed man should desire them, and not vice versa.

Let us admit, then, that a man's felicity is in exact proportion to his moral and intellectual virtue, and to his virtuous and wise conduct.   God himself bears witness to this truth: He is happy and blessed, not by reason of any external good but in Himself and of His own nature.   And it is just because felicity does not spring from external goods that good fortune likewise differs from happiness; for external goods are the accidental result of fortune, but no one is just or temperate by or through chance. The same argument may be used to show that the happy state is that which is best and acts rightly; but in order to act rightly it must do right actions, which is impossible for individuals and states alike without virtue and wisdom.   Hence the fortitude, justice, and wisdom of a state have the same energy and character as those qualities which entitle us to call their possessors just, wise, and temperate.

So much by way of preface.   I could not but touch upon these matters, although it was out of the question to run through all the relevant arguments, which are the business of another science.

Let us assume, therefore, that the best life, both for individuals and for states, is the life of virtue along [1324^a] with such external goods as suffice for the performance of good deeds. Some may disagree with what I have said; but I will ignore them for the present and consider their objections another time.[2]

---

[1] Perhaps 'valuable' is a more appropriate word than 'useful' in this case. —(A.)

[2] This promise is not fulfilled in the *Politics*.

(B) It remains to inquire whether or not the felicity of the state is the same as that of the individual. Once again, the answer is clear: all would agree that they are the same. Those who maintain that the well-being of an individual consists in his wealth, hold likewise that the entire state is happy provided it is rich. Those who think most highly of a tyrant's life would deem that state the happiest which had the largest empire. Those who admire an individual according to his virtue will say that the happiness of a state is proportionate to its virtue. Two points here call for our notice: (1) Which is the more desirable life, that of a citizen who is a member of the state, or that of an alien free from political ties; and (2) Which is to be regarded as the best form of government and the best condition of the state, either on the supposition that membership of a state is desirable for all, or for a majority only? Since the welfare of the state and not that of the individual is the subject of political thought and speculation, upon which we are now engaged, the first of these questions is outside the scope of our inquiry, which will therefore be confined to the second.

Now that form of government is clearly the best which is so organized that it enables every man, no matter who he is, to act virtuously and live happily. But even those who admit that the life of virtue is the most desirable ask whether or not the life of politics and action is preferable to one which is wholly independent of external goods, i.e. than the contemplative life, which some say is the only one worthy of a philosopher.[1] It is of some importance to determine on which side the truth lies, because the life of a state, like that of a wise man, must always be directed to the higher end. Some think that, while a despotic rule over neighbouring states is the very limit of injustice, even constitutional government, if not actually unjust, gravely interferes with the ruling authority's personal well-being. Others hold the contrary opinion, believing that a practical and political life is the only life for a man. [1324^b] They maintain that statesmen and politicians have just the same opportunity of practising every virtue as have private individuals. Some of them go still further: they regard arbitrary and tyrannical rule alone as consistent with felicity; the constitution and laws of some states, indeed, are framed for the express purpose of conferring despotic

---

[1] Those who have shown themselves most keen in the pursuit of virtue, both in our own day and in earlier times, seem to have preferred one or other of these two ways of the life—that of philosopher or that of the statesman.—(A.)

power over neighbouring states. And therefore, although the laws in a majority of states are somewhat chaotic, if they have any object at all it is that of conquest. In Sparta and Crete, for instance, the educational system and most of the legal code have been drawn up with a view to war. And all nations which are able to gratify their ambitions hold military prowess in the highest esteem; e.g. the Scythians, the Persians, the Thracians, and the Celts. Some nations even have laws tending to encourage militarism. Carthage, for instance, is said to allow her troops the honour of wearing as many armlets as the campaigns in which they have served. There was at one time a law in Macedonia that anyone who had not killed an enemy should wear a halter in place of a belt; and in Scythia no one who had not slain his man might drink from the cup that was passed round at a certain feast. Among the Iberians, a warlike people, the number of enemies a man has slain is indicated by the number of pointed stones erected round his tomb. There are many similar practices among other peoples, some of them ordained by law and others established by custom. A reflective mind, however, must think it passing strange that a statesman should be for ever scheming to dominate and tyrannize over border states, with or without their consent. For how can that which is not even lawful be the business of a statesman or legislator? It is certainly unlawful to rule with indifference to the claims of justice. Conquest is not synonymous with right. Other professions afford no evidence to compare with statesmanship of this kind. It is no part of a doctor's duty to persuade or coerce his patients, nor of a pilot to browbeat his passengers. Yet most men appear to think that the science of despotic government is true statesmanship; and men have no hesitation in behaving towards others in ways which they would never recognize as expedient, let alone just, among themselves. While demanding just rule for themselves, they give it no thought where other men are concerned. Such conduct is altogether irrational, except where one party is naturally free and the other naturally servile. In this case the former may justly claim to rule, not indeed all and sundry, but only those intended by nature to obey; just as we have no right to hunt men for food or sacrifice, but only such animals as are intended for that purpose, i.e. those wild beasts which are edible. [1325ᵃ] It is possible to imagine a state happy on its own and in isolation. Let us assume the existence of such a state in some out-of-the-way

place, and living under a good legal system. It will clearly
have a sound constitution; but that constitution will not be
framed with any view to war or foreign conquest, for *ex hypothesi* the state will have no enemies.

Hence it is obvious that warlike pursuits are to be accounted
honourable, but only as means and not as the supreme end of all
things. The good lawgiver must ask himself how states, races
of men, and communities in general may lead a good life and
enjoy such felicity as they can thereby attain. His enactments,
however, will vary according to circumstances: if the frontiers of
the state march with those of other states, he will have to ask
himself whether his neighbours are so disposed as to call for
hostile or friendly relations, and how the measures appropriate
in each case are to be given effect. Discussion of the end at
which the ideal constitution should aim may be conveniently
postponed.[1]

We must now address ourselves to those who, while agreeing
that the virtuous life is most desirable, differ as to how it should
be led.[2] Some decline to accept political office, holding that the
life of the freeman is different from that of the politician, and
preferable to all others. But others hold that the politician's
life is best, on the grounds that one who does nothing cannot do
well, and that felicity is identical with virtuous activity. We
shall tell both sides that they are partly right and partly wrong.
The former are right in their view that the life of a man who
takes no part in public life is better than that of a despot; for
there is nothing particularly dignified or respectable in employing a slave *qua* slave, or in commanding the execution of menial
duties. On the other hand, it is wrong to suppose that every
kind of authority is equivalent to that of a master over his slaves;
for there is as great a difference between ruling freemen and
ruling slaves as there is between a natural slave and a natural
freeman, about whom I have said enough in the first treatise.[3]
It is equally wrong to value inactivity above action, for felicity is
activity, and the actions of just and temperate men are the
realization of much that is good.

It may be that someone will interpret these conclusions as

[1] Page 212, lines 2 sqq.
[2] The remainder of this section is really a discussion of the first question,
which Aristotle began by dismissing as outside the scope of his inquiry.
Second thoughts suggest that it is not altogether irrelevant.
[3] Pages 9–14.

meaning that supreme power is the highest good, because he who enjoys it is able to perform the greatest number of good deeds. On that theory, a man who is able to rule, so far from yielding to his neighbour, should deprive him of what power he has. A father should pay no regard to his child, nor a son to his father, nor a friend to his friend; they ought not so much as to think of one another in comparison with this all-important point: the best is the most desirable, and to do well is the best. There might be some truth in this view—[1325ᵇ] on the supposition that robbers and plunderers have achieved the most desirable form of existence. But assuredly this can never be; the hypothesis is false. A man's actions cannot be outstandingly good unless he is as far superior to others as is a husband to his wife, a father to his children, or a master to his slaves. No transgressor, therefore, can ever achieve a subsequent gain to offset the loss of virtue implied by his transgression. In a society of equals it is right and just that all should hold office in turn, as the notions of equality and parity require. But that equals should receive unequal shares, and likes be treated as unlikes, is contrary to nature; and nothing unnatural is right. And so, if there is anyone superior in virtue *and* in capacity for performing the best actions, it is only right that he should be followed and obeyed. Mere virtue is insufficient; he must also be capable of activity in doing good.

If this view is correct, and felicity is recognized as being virtuous *activity*, then the active life will be the best, both for every state collectively and for individuals. Such a life does not, as some imagine, entail relations to other men. Nor are those thoughts alone to be considered active which are directed to objects which cannot be attained except by action. Thoughts and speculations which are independent, i.e. whose end is in themselves, have a stronger claim to be described as active. Well-doing, i.e. action of some sort, is the end we have in view; but even in the case of external actions the directing mind can be truly said to act, in the strictest sense of the word. Again, it does not necessarily follow that states which are cut off from one another and choose to live in isolation are inactive. Activity, here as in other fields, may be achieved by sections; there are many ways in which the sections of such a state can interact. The same is equally true of every individual; otherwise God and the whole universe, who have no activity external to themselves over and above their own energies, would be imperfect. Hence it is clear that the same life which is best for individuals is also best for states and for mankind at large.

2. THE IDEAL STATE DESCRIBED

(A) *Population and Territory*

The foregoing remarks are by way of introduction. Other 'ideal' constitutions have been discussed elsewhere;[1] so we may now go on to complete our inquiry by asking what are the fundamental conditions of the ideal or perfect state. An ideal constitution is impossible without an adequate supply of the necessary equipment. We must therefore presuppose certain factors, which, though ideal, must be capable of realization. Among other things there must be (1) a certain number of citizens, and (2) a certain amount of territory. Just as a weaver [1326ᵃ] or shipwright, for example, requires material appropriate to his work,[2] so does the statesman or legislator.

(1) First among the materials required by the statesman is a body of human beings, whose quantity and quality he will have to consider, as well as the area and topographical features of the country they are to inhabit. Most people think that a state in order to be happy must be great; but even if they are right, they take no account of what is meant by 'great' and 'small' with reference to a state. They judge its size by the number of inhabitants instead of by the more truthful yardstick of capacity. A state, like an individual, has a function to fulfil; and that state which is best equipped to carry out its task must be reckoned the greatest, in the sense in which Hippocrates might be described as greater [3] than someone taller than himself. Even if it were right to judge by numbers, we should still have to exclude such people as slaves, alien residents, and foreign visitors, who abound in every city; we should count only those who were members of the state and formed an essential part of it. The numerical superiority of these latter is proof of the greatness of a state; but one which produces fewer soldiers than mechanics can never be great, for a great state is by no means the same thing as a populous one. Besides, we know from experience that it is difficult,

---

[1] Book II.
[2] The better this material is prepared the better will be the product.—(A.)
[3] i.e. as a physician, not as a man.—(A.)

if not quite impossible, for a very populous state to ensure general obedience to law; all those which are now reputed to be well governed have limited populations. The truth can also be demonstrated on philosophical grounds. Law is order, and general obedience thereto means a general system of good order. The unlimited, however, cannot be subject to order; that would require the intervention of divine power, of such a power as holds together the world in which we live. Beauty is realized within the boundaries of number and magnitude, and a state which combines magnitude with good order is necessarily the most beautiful. There is, in fact, a limit to the size of states as there is to that of all other things—animals, plants, and implements. None of these will be capable of its proper function if it is too small or too large: it will either lose its nature altogether or be defective. For example, a ship which is only nine inches long is not really a ship at all, any more than is one of four hundred yards; on the other hand, one might have a ship [1326^b] which, though perfectly genuine *as a ship*, is either too large or too small for purposes of navigation. Likewise, a state which is composed of too few members is not (as a state is by definition)[1] self-sufficing. One that is composed of too many is self-sufficing with regard to mere necessaries, as a barbarian tribe may be; but it is not a *state*, since it is incapable of true constitutional government. Who can be general of such an enormous multitude? Or who will give it orders, unless he has the voice of Stentor?

A state, then, comes into existence only when the population has grown large enough to live well as a political association. Should it exceed this limit, it may indeed be a greater state; but, as I was saying, there must be some point at which it stops increasing. What that point should be, it is not difficult to gather from experience. Governors and governed have each their appointed duties; and the special duties of a governor are to command and to judge. But in order to decide lawsuits and distribute offices according to merit, the citizens must know one another's characters; otherwise they will inevitably go astray in their elective and judicial functions. When the population is too large lawsuits will be determined and offices distributed haphazardly, which they clearly should not be. Besides, in an over-populated state foreigners and resident aliens will find it a simple matter to escape detection, and will therefore easily

[1] Page 7, lines 3–5.

acquire citizen rights.   Clearly, then, the best limit of population is the largest number requisite for self-sufficiency, and
which can be taken in at a single view.[1]   So much for the size
of the population.

(2) More or less the same principle will apply with regard to
territory.   If asked what kind is most desirable, all would agree
in recommending that which is most completely self-sufficing;
and because self-sufficiency consists in having everything
without exception, the territory in question must itself produce
all that it requires.   In size and extent it should be such as will
afford the inhabitants leisure and the means of living at once
liberally and temperately.   Whether we are right or wrong in
fixing this limit we shall discuss more exhaustively later on [2]
when we come to deal with the actual use of property and
wealth.   This matter is widely disputed, because men are
inclined to rush headlong into one of two extremes—meanness
or extravagance.   The requisite geographical characteristics of
the territory are easily determined: [3] it should be difficult of
access to an enemy, and easy of exit to the inhabitants.   [1327ª]
I said just now that the population should be such as can be
taken in at a single view; the same applies to the territory, for
country that is easily surveyed is easily protected.   The ideal
situation of the capital is one that makes it accessible both by
land and by sea.   Besides being a good military centre from
which the whole territory can be defended, it should be within
easy reach of the farms and market gardens as well as of the
sources of timber and other commodities which the surrounding
countryside may produce.

Whether or not communication with the sea is conducive to a
well-ordered state is a question that has been much debated.
It is said that the introduction of foreigners brought up under
other laws, as well as the increase of population,[4] will be adverse
to good order.   Apart from such contingencies, it is plainly
better that the capital, and indeed the whole territory, should
have ready access to the sea, both for purposes of defence and

---

[1] i.e. which will enable all the members to know one another's characters.
[2] He does not do so.   But cf. Books I and II.
[3] The advice of military experts should, however, be taken on some points.
—(A.)
[4] It is argued that an increase will result from the coming and going of a
crowd of seafaring merchants, and that this will interfere with good government.—(A.)

for the provision of necessaries. The defenders of a country, if they are to maintain themselves against an enemy, must be easily relieved both by land and by sea; and even though they are unable to harm their assailants on the two elements at once, they will find it less difficult to do so on one if they have the free use of both. Moreover, the state will have to import what its own territory does not supply, and export its surplus produce. This means that the capital should be a market, not indeed for others', but for the state's own benefit. States which turn themselves into marts for all and sundry do so merely for the sake of revenue; and since it is wrong for a state to indulge such greed, she must have no such emporium.

Nowadays we often find whole territories and individual cities provided with port-towns and harbours separate from the capital, but not so far away that they cannot be dominated by connecting walls and similar fortifications. In this way the capital will manifestly reap the benefit of communication with its port; and any harm which may result can be easily forestalled by legal measures which will determine once for all who may and who may not fraternize with one another.

Some degree of naval strength is an obvious advantage. Apart from the requirements of home defence, [1327^b] a state must be prepared to overawe or to assist her neighbours by sea as well as by land. As for the number and size of the fleet, that will depend on the character of the state. If she intends to play a leading part in relations with other states, her sea-power must be commensurate with her undertakings. This will entail no large increase of population. The oarsmen need not be citizens; and the marines, who administer the fleet and exercise command at sea, are freemen and also form part of the infantry. Besides, wherever you have a dense population of serfs and farm-workers, there will always be a virtually unlimited supply of oarsmen. Examples of this are not far to seek at the present day. Heraclea,[1] for instance, though small when compared with other states, is able to man a large fleet. So much, then, for the territory of the state, its harbours, its towns, its communication with the sea, and its naval strength.

(B) *Character and Classification of Citizens*

(1) Having dealt with the subject of population, we will now consider what sort of people the citizens should be. This matter

[1] Heraclea on the Black Sea.

will be clear enough to anyone who takes a glance at the most famous Hellenic states and the distribution of races in general. Those who live in cold regions, particularly in Europe, are full of spirit, but lacking in intelligence and skill; hence they remain comparatively free, but are backward as regards organization and are unable to govern others. Asiatics, on the other hand, are intelligent and inventive; but being without spirit, they are always in a state of subjection and slavery. The Hellenic race inhabits an area midway between the two, and shares likewise in the characteristics of both; it is at once high-spirited and intelligent. These circumstances enable it to remain free and make it the best governed of all nations; indeed, it might rule the world if only it could be welded into a single state. Similar differences are found among the Hellenic peoples themselves: some of these have one-sided natures, that is to say, they are *either* intelligent *or* high-spirited; others possess a happy combination of *both* qualities. It is evident that those whom a lawgiver will most easily lead to virtue are people endowed with both qualities—courage and intelligence. Plato [1] would have his Guardians friendly toward those whom they know, formidable toward those who are unknown to them. Now spirit is the faculty which begets friendship and enables us to love, [1328ª] as is clear from the fact that when a man feels himself slighted, he is more deeply roused against friends and acquaintances than against strangers. Thus Archilochus, complaining of his friends, addresses these words to his soul: 'For sure thy torments were from friends.' The power of command also, and the love of freedom, arise in all cases from this principle, for spirit domineers and will not be gainsaid. It is therefore quite wrong to say that the Guardians should be hostile to those whom they do not know: we should not be ill-disposed towards any man; a magnanimous spirit is not by nature stern, but only when roused against evildoers. Acrimony, as I said just now, is a feeling which men show principally towards friends at whose hands they believe themselves to have suffered injustice. Nor is this unreasonable; for beside the positive injury inflicted, they imagine themselves deprived of a benefit owed by those same friends. Hence the saying, 'Cruel is the strife of brethren,' [2] and again, 'They who love blindly, blindly hate.' [3]

That is about all there is to say on the number and character

---

[1] *Republic*, ii. 375 C. [2] Euripides, Frag. 975, Nauck⁴.
[3] The author of this saying is unknown.

of the citizens in an ideal state, as well as on the size and nature of their territory. I say 'about all,' because one must not look for the same minute accuracy in theory as in sensible perception.

(2) Just as among other natural compounds the necessary conditions of a composite whole are not all organic parts thereof, so in a state or in any other combination from which a unity results not every condition is a part. Members of an association, in order to be members, must have one particular thing in common, whether they share in it equally or unequally, e.g. food or land or some such item. But where you have two things, one of which is a means and the other an end, they have nothing in common, except that the latter receives what the former produces. Tools and workmen stand in this relation to their work; the house and its builder have nothing in common, except that the builder's art is a means to the house. Accordingly, if states need property, property (even though it consists largely of animate beings) is no part of the state; for a state is an association of *equals* aiming at the best life possible. Now the highest good is felicity, i.e. the realization and perfect exercise of virtue, which some can attain while others have little or no share in it. This explains why there are various kinds of state and many constitutions; [1328b] different groups of men pursue happiness along different paths and by different means, and so make for themselves different ways of life and forms of government.

We must next inquire what are the elements necessary for the existence of a state. Among them will be found what I call the 'parts' of the state as well as its conditions. Let us, then, enumerate the services which a state requires, and we shall easily discover the elements.

First, there must be food; second, arts and crafts; [1] third, arms; [2] fourth, a certain amount of revenue both for internal needs and for the purposes of war; fifth, but first in dignity, the maintenance of religion, i.e. of public worship; sixth in order, but most necessary of all, some power of deciding what is in the common interest and what is just as between one man and another.

These are the services which every state may be said to

[1] Because life needs many instruments.—(A.)

[2] Members of the community must be provided with arms *for their personal use* [as distinct from that of their allies and mercenaries], in order to coerce disobedient subjects, and also to defend themselves against attack from without.—(A.)

require. For a state, as we maintain, is no mere aggregate of individuals, but a self-sufficing unity; and if any of these services be lacking, it is impossible for the community to be absolutely self-sufficient. A state, therefore, should be constructed with a view to satisfying the above requirements: there must be farmers to procure food, craftsmen, a military force, a class of landowners, priests, and judges to decide day-to-day issues and to determine what the public interest demands.

We must now proceed to ask whether all should take part in the above occupations. Should all, I mean, be at once farmers, craftsmen, members of the deliberative body, and judges; or should we assume the existence of a separate class for each of the different services; or should some employments be assigned to individuals and others be common to all? The same arrangement is not found in every constitution: as I was saying, all may take part in all functions, or different persons may be entrusted with different functions. Hence arise constitutional differences: in democracies all take part in all, whilst in oligarchies the opposite is true. Now we are here concerned exclusively with the ideal constitution, i.e. that under which the state will enjoy perfect felicity.[1] It follows, therefore, (a) that in a state which has an ideal constitution and whose members are just in an absolute sense,[2] the citizens must not lead the life of mechanics or tradesmen, which is ignoble and far from conducive to virtue. Nor (b) must they be drawn from among the farming class, [1329^a] because leisure is necessary for the growth of virtue and for the fulfilment of political duties.

But (c) a military force and a body of men to deliberate on matters of public interest and to determine matters of law, are clearly essential, and may be described as members *par excellence* of the state. The question therefore arises, should they be kept distinct, or should the same persons be entrusted indiscriminately with both sets of functions? Once again, the answer is not far to seek: both sets will belong from one point of view to the same, and from another to a different group of persons. They will be assigned to different persons inasmuch as they are suited respectively to different primes of life;[3] for the deliberative-judicial require wisdom, and the military call for strength. On

---

[1] I have already explained [pages 191, 192, and 202, lines 19 sqq.] that felicity cannot exist without virtue.—(A.)

[2] i.e. not merely relatively to the principle of the constitution.—(A.)

[3] i.e. the physical and the mental.

the other hand, it is impossible to expect that those who are in a
position to employ and to repel force should remain in permanent
subjection; and from this point of view the same persons should
exercise both functions. Remember, those who bear arms can
uphold or overthrow the constitution as they please. The only
course left, therefore, is to assign military and deliberative-
judicial functions to the same persons; not, however, simultaneously, but in the order laid down by Nature, who has
endowed young men with strength and their elders with wisdom.
To confer powers in this way is not only expedient, but also just,
because rights will then be distributed according to merit.
Furthermore (d), those who exercise such powers should be the
owners of property; [1] for the citizens of an ideal state must have
property, and these persons alone are citizens. Mechanics,
however, and all those classes which do nothing to produce
virtue, have no share in the state. This follows from our first
principle, viz. that virtue is an essential condition of felicity, and
the felicity of a state is to be judged by reference to the whole
citizen body, and not to one part of it. That property should
be in the hands of citizens is likewise clear from the fact that the
farming community ought to consist of slaves or barbarian serfs.[2]

Of the classes enumerated there remain only (e) the priests,
and the source of their recruitment is quite plain. No farm-
worker or mechanic should be appointed to the priesthood, for
divine worship should be conducted by none but citizens. Now
(i) the citizen body is composed of two classes, military and
deliberative-judicial; and (ii) it is right and proper not only that
divine worship should be rendered, but also that those who have
retired from active life on account of age should be enabled to
relax in the service of the gods. Therefore priestly duties
should be assigned to the older men of the deliberative-judicial
class.[3]

(C) Distribution of Land

[1329[b]36] I have already stated that the land should be owned
by those who bear arms and by those who have a share in the
government, and that the farming class should be distinct from
them. I have also described the extent and nature of the territory. I must now proceed to discuss the distribution of land,

[1] Because only so will they have the necessary leisure.
[2] Cf. page 205, lines 29–40 infra.
[3] For 1329[a]40–[b]35 see Appendix VI, page 243.

explaining (1) how it is to be farmed and (2) the character of the farming class. I disagree with those who maintain [1330ᵃ] that property should be owned in common, although I am prepared to admit that there should be a friendly agreement for its common use, and that no citizen should lack subsistence.

(1) Common meals are generally recognized as advantageous to well-ordered states; personally, I agree, and will explain why later on.[1] All citizens should be entitled to a share in them; but it is not easy for the poor to contribute the regulation sum from their private means and at the same time to provide for their own housekeeping. The cost of religious worship should likewise be chargeable to public funds. For these reasons the land must be divided into two parts, public and private. Each of these parts must be subdivided as follows. One part of the public land shall be appropriated to the service of the gods, and the other used to defray the expenses of common meals. Again, part of the private land should be near the frontier, and another close to the city: in this way each citizen will have two plots, and all will have an interest in both areas. Such a division follows the principles of equality and justice, as well as inspiring unanimity among the people in border warfare. Without some such arrangement, part of the citizens will be too ready to provoke neighbouring states, while the rest will be pacific to the point of cowardice. This is why some states have a law barring those who dwell near the frontier from official debates on border warfare: private interest, it is feared, will obscure their judgment. So much, then, for the reasons why land should be distributed in the manner I have described.

(2) Under ideal conditions, those who farm the land should be slaves; they ought not, however, to be all of one race or of resolute character. This will prevent anything in the nature of a labour shortage, and will diminish the likelihood of rebellion. Failing slaves, they should be non-Hellenic serfs, who are likewise wanting in spirit. Some of them should be employed as tied workers on the estates of wealthy individuals; the remainder should belong to the state and cultivate the public land. I shall have something to say later on about the proper treatment of slaves, and when doing so I shall explain why liberty should always be held out to them as the reward of their services.[2]

[1] He does not return to this subject.
[2] He does not fulfil this promise.

(D) *The Capital: Choice of Site and Planning*

I have already explained that the capital should be accessible by land and sea, and should, as far as possible, be within easy reach of the whole countryside. Regarding the actual site, I like to think of it as having a fourfold advantage. (1) *Health* is an absolute necessity. The healthiest cities are those which lie toward the east and are open to the winds from that quarter; next best are those which are sheltered from the north wind and therefore enjoy a mild winter. The site should also [1330ᵇ] be convenient from the point of view of (2) *political administration* and (3) *strategic requirements*. With regard to (3), (a) it should allow the citizens ready egress, but an enemy should find it difficult of access and absolutely impregnable. (b) There should be numerous springs and/or an abundant supply of river-water in the town; in default of which large reservoirs may be constructed for the storage of rain-water, sufficient to last the inhabitants if they are cut off from the surrounding countryside in time of war. Public health demands careful consideration: it will depend chiefly on the healthy nature of the locality and of the quarter to which it is exposed, and secondly on the use of pure water. This last is of no small importance; for those elements (among them water and air) which we use most often and in the largest quantity for the nourishment of our bodies are most conducive to health. And so, in the absence of pure water, or if the supplies are not of uniform standard, it will be as well to isolate the drinking water from that which is destined for other uses. (c) As to defences, they will vary with the needs of different constitutions. Thus an acropolis is suited to an oligarchy or a monarchy, but a level site to a democracy. Neither is suited to an aristocracy, which is better provided with a number of strongpoints. (d) The arrangement of private houses is considered more pleasant and generally more convenient if it follows the modern and regular lay-out introduced by Hippodamus.[1] But for security in time of war I prefer the old-fashioned plan, which made it difficult for a foreign garrison to escape from the town, while an assailant could not easily find his way in. Both systems therefore should be adopted: it is possible to arrange the houses in the same way as farmers plant their vines in what are called 'clumps.'[2] The whole town

[1] See page 46.
[2] Vines were planted in the form of a quincunx; i.e. they were set out in the same way as the five spots on a dice.

should not be laid out in straight lines, but only certain quarters or regions; thus security will be combined with (4) *beauty*.   (5) As to *walls*, those who maintain that cities with any pretension to military strength should do away with them, take a very old-fashioned view; states which prided themselves on this scheme afford ample proof to the contrary.   True, it is unmanly to look for safety behind a rampart when the enemy differs little from oneself either in character or numbers.   But the superiority of a besieging force may be, and often is, too much even for extra-ordinary valour, let alone for the courage of ordinary men.   And so, if the defenders are to survive and to escape defeat and humiliation, the strongest wall possible must be considered the most effective, [1331ᵃ] especially in these days of powerful artillery and other siege weapons.   If you are going to build a city without walls, you might as well choose an exposed site and level the high ground; you might as well build your own house without walls, for fear the family will become cowards.   It must also be borne in mind that the inhabitants of a walled city may take advantage of them or not, as circumstances require, whereas unwalled cities have no choice.   If my argument is sound, i.e. if cities *should* have walls, care should be taken to make them not only ornamental, but serviceable from the military point of view: they must be capable of resisting even the most up-to-date methods of assault.   Just as a besieger does all in his power to gain an advantage, so also it is up to the besieged to employ all the known means of defence and any others which they can devise; for no one dreams of attacking those who are well prepared.

There will, of course, be guard-houses situated in towers built at convenient intervals along the walls; and because the whole citizen body is to be distributed in messes for common meals, it will be natural to think of locating some of these tables in the guard-houses—a perfectly satisfactory arrangement. The principal common tables of the magistrates may occupy a convenient site close to the buildings set aside for religious worship.   In these latter I do not, of course, include such temples as are required by law or by the Delphic oracle to be kept distinct.   The site in question should be visible over a wide area, towering over the neighbourhood, as it were a throne of virtue.   Below this site should lie a public square, similar to what is called in Thessaly the Free Square.   All trade must be

excluded therefrom; and no mechanic, farmer, or any such
person must be admitted unless he is summoned by the magistrates. This indeed would be an admirable place for use as a
gymnasium by older men. Recreation should be organized
according to age groups; in which case some of the magistrates
should remain with the younger men, and the older men with
the rest of the magistrates. The visible presence of the magistrates is the surest means of inculcating true modesty and a
sense of shame. [1331^b] There should also be a separate
market-square for tradesmen, so situated as to form a convenient *entrepôt* for all kinds of merchandise arriving by land or
sea.

Besides the magistrates, we have another class of citizen, viz.
the priests, for whom common meals should also be provided
near the temples. The magistrates who deal with contracts,
indictments, summonses, and the like, as well as those who have
charge of the market-square and of the city, should be established near a square or other public resort. The market-square
itself will be found most convenient for this purpose. We
intend the upper or public square for leisurely pursuits; the
market-square is meant for the necessities of trade.

Similar arrangements will be required in the surrounding
country, where the magistrates known variously as Inspectors of
Forests and Rural Wardens should have guard-houses and
common tables while they are on duty. There should also be
temples up and down the countryside, some of them dedicated
to gods and others to heroes.

However, it is a waste of time to dwell on particulars of this
kind. The difficulty lies not so much in planning them as in
giving them effect. We may talk about them to our heart's
content, but their execution is the work of Fortune; so let us
leave this subject for the present.

3. EDUCATIONAL SYSTEM OF THE IDEAL STATE

(A) *The Purpose of Education*

We have now discussed the constitution itself, in order to
identify and describe the elements which will compose a happy
and well-governed state. There are two things in which well-
being always and everywhere consists: choice of a right aim and
end of action, and discovery of the proper means thereto.

End and means may or may not be in harmony. In some cases men have the right end before them, but fail to accomplish it in practice; in other cases they are successful in attaining all the means but look to a wrong end. In others again they are mistaken as to both. Take, for example, the art of medicine: a doctor may not only misunderstand the nature of health, but he may also fail to discover the means to his self-appointed end. In all the arts and sciences one should have a clear understanding both of the end and of what leads thereto.

It cannot be disputed that all men seek felicity, or well-being. Some manage to attain it; but it is beyond the reach of others, owing to a natural deficiency in themselves or to lack of opportunity.[1] There are also persons who, though not debarred from felicity in either of these ways, err in their pursuit of it from the very start. Now, our purpose is to discover the best constitution—that, namely, under which a state will be best governed; and the state which is best governed is the one which has the greatest opportunity of attaining felicity. We must therefore begin by asking: What is the exact nature of felicity?

It may not be out of place to recall what I said in the *Ethics*,[2] viz. that felicity is the realization and perfect practice (*not relative, but absolute*) of goodness. I use the word 'relative' to describe that which is necessitated from without, and 'absolute' to denote that which is good *in itself*. In the case of just actions, for example, the infliction of just penalties or punishments is undoubtedly an act of goodness; but at the same time it has no value except as a necessity imposed from without. Better far if no state or individual needed to adopt penal measures. Those actions, on the other hand, which aim at conferring honours and wealth upon one's fellow men are of the greatest intrinsic value. A punitive act is a choice of what is in itself evil; acts of the other sort are foundations and creations of good. A good man may turn even poverty, disease, and other such misfortunes to good uses; felicity, however, is not to be found in them but in their opposites. As I had occasion to note in a lecture on ethics,[3] the truly good man is one who by virtue of his absolute goodness enjoys absolute advantages; and it is clear that his use of them must be absolutely good and possess an

---

[1] The good life needs equipment [1332ᵃ] to an extent proportionate with one's natural endowments.—(A.)
[2] *Nic. Eth.* 1098ᵃ16; 1176ᵇ4.
[3] *Eudemian Ethics* 1248ᵃ26. Cf. *Nic. Eth.* 113ᵃ22–ᵇ1.

absolute virtue. But his enjoyment of absolute advantages has
led men to imagine that external goods are the *causes* of felicity.
You might as well attribute a brilliant performance on the lyre
to the instrument rather than to the player's skill.

It follows, then, from what I have said, that whilst a legislator
may expect to find some elements of the state ready to hand, he
must himself supply the rest. And so, acknowledging the power
of Fortune, we can only pray that our state may be fully equipped
with those advantages of which she disposes. A good state,
however, is not the work of Fortune, but of knowledge and purpose. A state is good only when those citizens who have a
share in the government are themselves good. Now *all* the
citizens of our ideal state have such a share; and we must therefore explain how a man becomes good. It may be possible for
the citizen body as a whole to be virtuous without every individual being so; but it is preferable that every individual citizen
should be good, for the goodness of all depends on that of each.

Three things make men good and virtuous: (1) nature, (2)
habit, and (3) rationality. (1) Everyone must be born a man as
distinct from the brute beasts; and he must have certain qualities both of body and soul. But there are some qualities with
which it is useless to be born, because (2) habit alters them:
[1332ᵇ] nature implants them in a form which is susceptible of
change, under the impulse of habit, towards good or bad.
Brute beasts live mostly under the guidance of nature, though
some are to a small extent influenced by habit as well. Man
alone lives by (3) reason, for he alone possesses rationality. In
his case, therefore, nature, habit, and the rational principle must
be brought into harmony with one another; for man is often led
by reason to act contrary to habit and nature, if reason persuades
him that he ought to do so. We have already determined [1]
what natures will be most pliable in the legislator's hand. All
else is the work of education; some things are learned by habit
and others by instruction.

Since every political association consists of governors and
governed, we must determine whether each of these two classes
should be permanently distinct or merged into one body; for
upon the answer to this question will necessarily depend the education of our citizens. Well, if some members of the state (i.e.
the ruling stock) were to surpass all others in the same degree as

[1] Page 201, lines 17–19.

gods and heroes are believed to surpass mankind, their unquestionable superiority would be manifest to their subjects.
In those circumstances it will of course be better to draw a
permanent distinction once and for all between governors and
governed. But the circumstances in question are unlikely to be
realized; nor can we find any example of a king enjoying that
marked superiority over their subjects which Scylax [1] attributes
to the monarchs of India. It is therefore permissible to argue,
and on many grounds, that all the citizens alike should take their
turn of ruling and being ruled. Equality means that persons of
the same standing enjoy the same rights; and no constitution
can last which is not founded upon justice. Otherwise every
serf in the neighbouring countryside will combine with the
subject citizens to effect a revolution, and it is too much to
expect that the civic body will be so numerous as to prevail
against the whole mass of their opponents. On the other hand,
it cannot be denied that rulers should differ from the ruled.
The legislator, therefore, must devise some scheme to make such
difference compatible with the right of every citizen to take his
turn of government—a topic about which I have already spoken.[2]
Nature herself has provided the solution by distinguishing old
and young within the same species, of whom the former are
meant to rule and the latter to obey. No one objects to being
governed or thinks himself superior to his rulers while he is
young, especially as he will enjoy the same privilege when he
comes of age.

And so we conclude that in one sense governors and governed
are the same sort of persons, but in another different. [1333ª]
Therefore their education must be likewise; for it is commonly
recognized that a man who would rule well must first learn how
to obey. As I remarked in the introductory treatise on constitutions,[3] government may be carried on either in the interest of the
ruler or in that of the ruled. In the former case it is 'despotic,'
and in the latter 'free.' Some of the duties imposed on free men
differ from servile tasks not in the work ordered, but in the
purpose for which that work is to be done. And therefore
many duties, however menial they may appear, can be undertaken without disgrace by freeborn youths; for actions differ as

[1] Scylax of Caryanda in Caria was sent by Darius Hystaspis (521–485
B.C.) to explore the coast of Asia. Aristotle is no doubt referring to the still
extant *Periplus* wrongly attributed to him.
[2] Page 203, lines 28–35.
[3] Page 76, lines 29–77, line 16.

honourable from dishonourable not in themselves but in their
end or object.   Now we maintain [1] that the virtue of a citizen
ruler is the same as that of a good man, and that every subject
must one day take his turn of government.   The legislator,
therefore, looking to the end or aim of the good life, must
devise adequate means to ensure that his citizens become good
men.

Now the human soul consists of two distinct parts.   One of
these has a rational principle of its very nature; the other has
not, but it is capable of obeying that principle.   When we call a
man good we do so because he has the virtues of these two parts.
But those who accept our twofold division, as above, will recognize immediately in which part the end of human life is more
particularly to be found.   In nature, as well as in the arts, the
inferior always exists for the sake of the superior, and the
superior part of the soul is that which has the rational principle.
According to our usual method of analysis, however, the
rational principle is itself twofold—practical and speculative; so
that the part endowed therewith must be divided similarly.   We
must also acknowledge a corresponding division of actions; and
therefore those who can attain all three activities,[2] or two of
them, will inevitably prefer that which belongs to the naturally
superior part; for that is always and in every case the most
desirable which is the highest attainable.

Again, life as a whole is capable of divisions: activity and
leisure, war and peace; and while some actions are no more than
necessary or useful, others are good in themselves.   And the
same preference must be accorded to the parts of life and their
respective activities as is accorded to the parts of the soul and
their activities.   War must be looked upon simply as a means to
peace, action as a means to leisure, acts merely necessary or useful as a means to those which are good in themselves.   The
statesman should bear all this in mind when he drafts his laws.
He should consider the parts of the soul and their activities,
aiming at the superior rather than the inferior, at the end rather
than the means.   He should likewise remember the diversity of
human life and activity.   For although men must be able to do
business and to fight, [1333^b] peace and leisure are preferable;
they must do what is necessary and useful, but good actions are

[1] Pages 71–5.
[2] i.e. rational-speculative, rational-practical, and obedience to the rational
principle.

more important. It is with these ends in view that children,
and indeed adolescents [1] at every stage of education, should be
trained. As things now are, the legislators to whom even the
reputedly best governed of Greek states are indebted for their
constitutions do not appear to have worked with an eye to this
ideal. So far from providing them with such laws and educational systems as tend to breed all the virtues, they have fallen
back in vulgar fashion upon those which are supposed to be
useful and more profitable. A number of contemporary
writers have taken a similar view, commending the Spartan constitution, and praising its author for having made war and
conquest his sole aim—a doctrine which may be refuted upon
grounds of reason and was long ago disproved by facts. The
great majority of men covet empire as a means to prosperity; and
Thibron, with other writers on the constitution of Sparta, evidently admires its legislator for having trained that people to
meet danger and thereby to build an empire. But look at what
has happened: the Spartans have never been a happy people
since their empire vanished; so their lawgiver cannot have been
right. It is indeed a strange commentary upon his system that
a people who observed his laws uninterruptedly should have lost
all that makes life worth while. Thibron and the others are also
mistaken about the kind of government which the legislator
should prefer; the government of freemen is nobler and implies
more virtue than despotic rule. Further, no state is to be considered happy, and no legislator is to be admired, when the
citizens are trained for conquest with a view to empire. This is
a most dangerous precedent; for it implies that any citizen who
can do so should try to seize power in the state to which he himself belongs—a crime of which the Spartans accuse King
Pausanias, notwithstanding the high office he already held. No
such principle and no law with such an end in view is either
statesmanlike or useful or right. For the good is the same for
states as for individuals; and it is the good which a lawgiver
should try to instil into the minds of those for whom he legis-
lates. Men should not be trained for war with the idea of
enslaving those who deserve no such fate. The purpose of such
training should be (1) to prevent their own enslavement; (2) to
fit them for a hegemony which will benefit those whom they
intend to lead, [1334ᵃ] not for the exercise of universal despotism; and (3) to qualify them for the mastery of those who

[1] Cf. Plato, *Laws*, 628, 638.

deserve to be slaves.   There is cogent evidence that a lawgiver
should direct his legislation—especially those parts of it which
are concerned with war—to securing leisure and the reign of
peace.   For most militaristic states endure only so long as they
are at war, and do not long survive their victories.   Like unused
iron, they lose their edge in time of peace; and because the
legislator has not taught them how to employ their leisure, he
must be held to blame.

Since the end of a state is the same as that of an individual, the
distinctive aim of the ideal constitution must be identical with
that of the best man.   It is therefore evident that both of them
should possess the qualities required for the use of leisure; for
peace, as I have more than once remarked, is the end of war,
leisure the end of occupation.   The qualities required for the
use of leisure and intellectual cultivation fall under two headings: those which operate in and during leisure itself, and those
which operate in and during the activities of occupation.   These
latter qualities are necessitated by the fact that many indispensable conditions have to be fulfilled before there can be any
use of leisure.   Therefore a state must have the quality of
temperance, as also that of courage and endurance; for, as the
proverb says: 'There is no leisure for slaves.'   The activities
of occupation, then, require courage and endurance; those of
leisure, wisdom.   Both sets of activities, especially those of peace
and leisure, require temperance and justice.   For whereas war
obliges men to be temperate and just, the enjoyment of prosperity rouses them to insolence.   Those, therefore, who appear
to ride the flood-tide of good fortune with all its advantages—
like those whom the poets describe as dwelling in the Islands of
the Blest—have particular need of temperance and justice in
proportion to their leisure and abundance.   It is now quite
clear why states that would achieve felicity and goodness must
possess these virtues; for while it is always shameful to err in
one's use of the goods of life, it is even more so thus to err in
times of leisure—to prove one's merit in times of occupation and
in war, but to behave no better than a slave in times of peace and
leisure.   We must not, therefore, seek general excellence from
the Spartan type of training.   The Spartans agree with other
men [1334b] in their notion of the highest goods,[1] but differ
from the rest of mankind in thinking that those goods are to be

[1] Identifying them with mere external goods.

obtained by fostering a single virtue.[1] Believing external goods
to be better than any others, and the enjoyment thereof greater
than that derived from the cultivation of all-round excellence,
they practise only that virtue which is thought to be useful as a
means to external goods. But it should be clear from what I
have said that the whole of excellence ought to be cultivated, and
cultivated for its own sake alone; and our next task is to consider how and by what means it can be attained.

I have already observed [2] that virtue depends on nature, habit,
and the rational principle. I have also determined [3] what sort
of people the citizens of an ideal state should be. It remains,
therefore, to inquire whether their early training should concentrate on habit or the rational principle. These two must be
as near as possible in perfect harmony; otherwise the rational
principle may fail to achieve the highest ideal of life, and the
same misfortune may result from habit. In the first place it is
clear that, according to a universal principle, birth implies an
antecedent beginning,[4] and that the ends of such beginnings are
stages on the road to further ends. Now the functioning of the
rational principle and thought is the end of man's natural
development, so that birth and moral training should be regulated with that end in view. In the second place, just as the
body and soul are two, we see that the soul has two parts
(rational and irrational) and two corresponding states (that of
pure thought and that of appetite). And as the body is prior to
the soul in order of generation, so the irrational part of the soul
is prior to the rational. This is proved by the fact that anger,
obstinacy, and desire are apparent in a child from his very birth,
whereas reasoning and thought develop gradually as he grows
older. It follows that care of the soul should be preceded by
that of the body, which must be followed immediately by training of the appetites. This training, however, should be directed
to the benefit of the mind, and care of the body to that of the soul.

(B) *Prenatal Care and Infant Training*

Firstly, the legislator must start by endeavouring to make sure
that the infant population shall enjoy the highest possible state
of physical health. In the first place, therefore, he must concern
himself with the union of man and wife, i.e. with their ages and
condition at the time of marriage.

[1] i.e. physical courage.   [2] Page 210.   [3] Pages 200–2.
[4] i.e. a union of male and female.

In legislating for matrimony he must take account of the probable length of time during which the parties will live together. It is best that the procreative period of each should terminate simultaneously. In other words, their physical powers should not differ to such an extent that the man is still capable of begetting children while the woman is unable to bear them, or vice versa; for a situation of that kind results in open quarrels or at least in differences between the spouses.

Secondly, he must look forward to the day when the children will succeed their parents; there should not be too great an interval between the ages of father and son, otherwise the father will be too old to profit by his son's affection, or to be of any use to him. [1335ᵃ] Nor, on the other hand, should they be too nearly of an age. There is a grave objection to early marriages; for the children, looking on their parents as contemporaries, will fail in respect towards them, and disputes will arise over management of the household.

Thirdly, returning to the point from which I digressed, the legislator must decide how best to mould the infant body to his will.

All these objects, I think, may be achieved by attention to one point. Since the period of procreation is ordinarily terminated at the age of seventy in the case of men and of fifty in that of women, there should be a proportionate difference between their ages at the time of marriage. The coitus of male and female when too young is bad for procreation. In the animal kingdom as a whole the offspring of very young parents are undersized, ill-developed, and with a tendency to produce female children. The same, therefore, is true of man, as witness the fact that in states where men and women habitually marry young, the inhabitants are small and physically imperfect. Childbirth, too, involves more pain and a higher death-rate among young women.[1] Besides, apart from procreation, to abstain from early marriage conduces to self-control; for women who have sexual intercourse too soon are apt to be wanton, and a man's body also is stunted if he exercises the reproductive faculty before the semen is full grown.[2] Women should marry

---

[1] Some hold that this was the meaning of a response ['Plough not the young field'] once delivered to the Troezenians; they say that the oracle was referring not to arable farming, but to the fact that many girls die as a result of marrying too early.—(A.)

[2] The growth of the semen, as well as of the body, is subject to a time limit which it does not exceed, unless very slightly.—(A.)

at the age of about eighteen years, and men at about thirty-seven; for then the coitus will begin when their bodies are in the prime of life, and their respective powers of procreation will decline simultaneously. Moreover, if reproduction begins soon after marriage, as may reasonably be expected, children will succeed their parents in their own early prime, just when the father has reached the age of seventy and lost his vigour.

So much for the age at which men and women should enter into wedlock. As regards the time of year, most people to-day limit marriage to the winter season; they are quite right, and their example should be followed. The parents themselves should study what physicians and scientists have to say on the subject of generation; the physicians offer good advice about bodily conditions, [1335^b] while the scientists tell them about favourable winds, preferring the north to the south.

When we come to discuss the management of children I shall go more deeply into the question of the parent's physical condition as it affects the offspring's welfare.[1] For the present, however, I must content myself with a few general remarks which apply equally to both father and mother. The condition of an athlete is not appropriate to civic life, or to the procreation of children, any more than is the condition of a valetudinarian or congenital weakling. What we need is something between the two: it must be attained by exertion, but not by violent or specialized exertion such as an athlete undertakes; it must, in fact, be adapted to all the duties of a freeman.

Pregnant women also must take care of their bodies; they should take exercise and eat nourishing food. The legislator will have no difficulty in carrying out the first of these prescriptions: he need only require that they take a walk each day to some temple, where they can worship the deities who preside over childbirth.[2] Expectant mothers should, on the other hand, keep their minds as tranquil as possible; for it seems that embryo children derive their nature from the mother as plants do from the soil in which they grow.

As to the question whether children must in every case be reared or whether exposure is sometimes permissible, there should be a law that no deformed child shall live. But if established custom is opposed (as it will be in our state) to an un-restricted birth-rate, no child must ever be exposed merely with

[1] He does not do so.
[2] e.g. Eileithyia, who was often identified with Artemis or Hera.

a view to limiting the population. If couples beget too many children, abortion must be procured before the embryo has reached the stage of sensitive life, upon which will depend what may and may not be done in these cases.

Now that we have determined the respective ages at which men and women are to enter upon wedlock, we must decide for how long they should devote themselves to this task of providing children for the state. The offspring of men who are too old, no less than of those who are too young, come into the world defective both physically and mentally; the children of very old men are weaklings. The limit, therefore, should be marked by the husband's mental prime, which in most cases, according to some poets who measure life by periods of seven years, is reached at about the age of fifty; four or five years after this they should cease from having families, and cohabit thenceforward only in the interests of health or for some such reason.

Disgrace must invariably attach to the intercourse of a husband with a woman other than his wife, and vice versa. [1336a] If any such thing occurs during the time of bearing children, the guilty person must suffer loss of privileges in proportion to the offence.

Once the children have been born, their physical development must be recognized as depending in large measure on their diet. It appears from the habits of other animals and of militaristic nations that food with the highest milk content is best for human beings; the less wine the better—it causes disease.

Again, much benefit is derived from all the movements of which the infant body is capable; but in order to preserve their fragile limbs from distortion, some nations even to-day use mechanical appliances which keep their bodies straight.

To accustom children to the cold from their earliest years is also a most useful practice; it makes them healthy and toughens them for military service later on. Hence many barbarian peoples have a custom of plunging their children at birth into a cold stream; others, like the Celts, clothe them in the flimsiest of wrappers. All creatures susceptible of habituation should be inured to hardship from the very beginning, but the process must be gradual. The natural warmth of children makes them fit subjects for training to bear cold. Such, then, is the care which infants should enjoy during their first few years.

The next period lasts until the age of five, and during that time the child should not be required to study or to labour, lest its growth be hindered. There should, however, be sufficient movement to prevent atrophy of the limbs. Games are one way of ensuring movement of this kind, but they must not be vulgar or exhausting or effeminate.[1] For all such things are intended to prepare children for the tasks of later life, and therefore games should be for the most part imitations of those pursuits to which they will hereafter devote themselves in earnest. Plato is quite wrong in that passage of the *Laws* [2] where he would check the screaming and yelling of babies, for these are a kind of physical exercise and help on their growth. The effort involved has a strengthening effect not unlike that produced by holding the breath during periods of violent exertion. Educational directors should keep an eye on the way in which children pass their time, and in particular make sure that they spend as little time as possible with slaves; [1336b] for until they are seven years old they must live at home, and even at this early age they are likely to contract the servile spirit from what they see and hear. There is indeed nothing which a legislator should so strictly exclude as indecency of speech; for the casual utterance of any shameful word soon leads to shameful deeds. The young especially must be prevented from repeating or even hearing anything of the kind. A freeman caught saying or doing what is forbidden, if he is still too young to enjoy the privilege of reclining at common meals,[3] should be disgraced and flogged; an older man should be degraded in keeping with his slavish conduct. Having pro-hibited indecent language, we must obviously do the same with undesirable pictures and speeches from the stage. The govern-ment must take steps to see that no statue or picture representing improper actions is exhibited anywhere but in the temples of those gods at whose festivals scurrility is authorized by law, and to whom sacrifice may legally be offered by persons of mature years on behalf of themselves, their children, and their wives. The legislator should not allow young people to be spectators of mimes or comedies until they reach the age when they may recline at the common tables and drink undiluted wine. By then their education will have made them proof against the evil influence of such performances.

[1] Educational directors, as they are called, should be careful what tales (fact or fiction) children hear.—(A.)

[2] 792 A.

[3] Up to a certain age young freemen *sat* at the dinner table. Older men reclined on couches.

The foregoing remarks, though cursory, are sufficient for the time being. Later on I shall deal with the subject at greater length, when we have discussed the pros and cons of legal restriction and the methods it should employ. Theodorus, the tragic actor, used to say (and I think rightly) that he would never allow another performer, however second rate, to enter before himself, because audiences were won over by the voices they first heard. The same principle holds good in our relation with things as with persons: we like best whatever comes first. Children, therefore, must not become familiar with anything bad, especially with those things which may give rise to depravity or hate. Between the ages of five and seven they must be spectators of the lessons they will afterwards learn. Education must be divided with reference to two periods of life—from seven until the age of puberty, and thence to the age of twenty-one. The poets who reckon age in groups of seven years are mainly right; [1337ᵃ] but we should follow the divisions marked out by Nature, for it is precisely her deficiencies which art and education seek to make good.

Let us then inquire (A) whether any regulations are required for the education of children; (B) whether the education of children should be entrusted to the state or, as in most cases nowadays, to private individuals; and (C) what such regulations ought to be.

B. YOUTH TRAINING (Book VIII)

1. General System

[1337ª11] (A) No one can doubt that it is the legislator's very special duty to regulate the education of youth, otherwise (1) the constitution of the state will suffer harm. The citizen should be trained in accordance with the particular form of government under which he is to live; for each type of constitution has a distinctive character which originally formed it and makes possible its continued existence. Thus the democratic character is responsible for democracy, the oligarchical for oligarchy; and you will invariably find the excellence of a constitution proportionate to that of its character. Again (2) some preliminary training and habituation are required for the exercise of any faculty or art; and the same, therefore, obviously applies to the practice of virtue.

(B) Since the whole state has a single end, it is clear that education must be one and the same for all, and that it must be in public rather than, as to-day, in private hands, when every father has authority to provide for the instruction of his children just as he thinks fit. No, the training in matters which are of public concern must be carried out by the state. It is indeed quite false to imagine that any citizen belongs to himself. The correct view is that all belong to the state because each is a part thereof; and care of the whole follows inevitably from that of the parts. In this respect, as in much else, the Spartans deserve our admiration; their educational system has been planned with the utmost care, and is conducted by the state. We conclude, therefore, (A) that education must be regulated by law, and (B) that it must be controlled by the state.

We must now deal with (C) the nature and methods of public education. At present there is some difference of opinion about the subjects to be taught. There is no general agreement as to what young people should learn that is conducive either to simple goodness or to the best life; neither is it clear whether education should be more concerned with intellectual or with moral character. No satisfactory conclusion can be drawn from modern practice; there is no certainty as to whether our training should be directed mainly to practical ability, to the acquisition of virtue, or to an increase of knowledge. All three opinions have been held, but none of them is conclusive. [1337^b] There is no agreement, for example, about the means to virtue, the various definitions of which have understandably led to different views about its practice.

Children should undoubtedly be instructed in such useful acquirements as are *really necessary*. Occupations are divided into liberal and illiberal, and young people should be admitted only to such kinds of knowledge as will prove useful without giving them a 'working-class' outlook—an outlook which is bred by those occupations, arts, and sciences which unfit the body, soul, or mind of a freeman for the pursuit and practice of virtue. The 'working-class' mentality may accordingly be said to arise from any art or craft which tends to undermine physical fitness, as well as from any employment which is undertaken solely for gain and therefore absorbs and impoverishes the mind. There are also some liberal studies to which a freeman may devote himself only *up to a certain point*; if he goes too far, hoping to reach perfection, the same disastrous consequences will ensue. Much, however, depends upon the object with which a man sets to work. If he does so for his own needs, to help his friends, or with a view to goodness, his action will not be regarded as illiberal; but the same work repeatedly undertaken in obedience to others must be set down as menial and servile.

The studies nowadays prescribed, as I said above, point in two directions.[1] There are four recognized branches of education: (1) reading and writing, (2) physical training, (3) music, to which some add (4) drawing. Reading, writing, and drawing are looked upon as useful for the purposes of life in several ways, and physical training is believed to instil courage. With regard to music, there is some room for doubt. Nowadays most people cultivate it merely for pleasure, but it was originally made part of education because Nature herself, as I have frequently remarked,[2] demands not only that we should be able to *work* well, but also to make right use of *leisure*; indeed (repeating myself once again), this latter power is the basis of all human activity. Occupation and leisure are both necessary; but leisure

---

[1] i.e. they may be invoked in favour of studying useful subjects, and also in favour of those studies which promote virtue.

[2] Page 214, lines 1–24.

is preferable to and the end of occupation; and the question therefore arises, how are we to employ our leisure? Clearly not just in amusing ourselves, for then amusement would be the sum total of life. That is inconceivable. We should have recourse to amusement during the intervals of more serious occupation rather than at other times.[1] We should also be sparing in its use, treating it as a medicine. Its spiritual effects are a relaxation from strain, and the pleasure it affords allows us rest. [1338ᵃ] Pleasure, on the other hand, happiness, and enjoyment of life are to be found in leisure itself without the accompaniment of play. They are the privilege not of men engaged in occupation, but of those who have leisure. The former have their eyes upon some distant goal; but felicity is a present end inasmuch as all men think of it as conjoined with pleasure and not with pain. Still, this pleasure is regarded differently by different persons, and varies according to their personality and outlook; the pleasure of the best man is the best and springs from the noblest sources.

It is clear then, that there are branches of learning and education which must be studied simply with a view to leisure spent in cultivating the mind. It is likewise clear that these studies are to be valued for their own sake, while those pursued for the sake of an occupation must be looked upon as no more than necessary means to other ends. This is why our ancestors made music a part of education: not because it is necessary (which it most certainly is not); nor because it is useful in the same way as reading and writing are useful in money-making, in household management, in learning, and in many political affairs; nor because it helps, like drawing, to a more refined judgment of artistic works; nor again because it develops health and strength as physical training does, for there is no evidence that music produces either. We are left, therefore, with music as a source of intellectual culture in leisure hours. And this is manifestly the purpose of its introduction; it forms part of that culture to which men think a freeman should devote himself. Thus Homer says: 'Such alone should be called to the bountiful feast,'[2] and goes on to mention several guests, of whom he speaks as inviting 'the bard who would delight them all.'[3]

---

[1] A hard-working man has need of relaxation, which is afforded by amusement, whereas occupation always involves effort and exertion.—(A.)

[2] This line is not found in our text. It may have supplanted or followed *Odyssey*, XVII. 383.

[3] *Odyssey*, XVII. 385.

Elsewhere [1] Odysseus says there is no better way of passing the time than when men's hearts are cheerful and 'The diners in hall, sitting in order, hear the minstrel's voice.'

Clearly, then, there is a course of training which boys should undergo not because it is useful, let alone necessary, but because it is liberal and noble. Whether it should include more than one subject, and if so *what* subjects, and how they should be taught, we must discuss later on.[2] At all events, we are now in a position to rest our claim on the testimony of ancient writers, who bear witness to the fact that music is one of the recognized and traditional branches of education. It is likewise plain that children should be taught some useful things (e.g. reading and writing) not only for their utility, but also because they are the gateway to many other kinds of knowledge. The same applies to drawing, which they should learn not as a precaution against error in making their own purchases, or as a protection against dishonest dealers, [1338^b] but rather as a means to aesthetic appreciation of the human body. To be for ever hankering after what is useful ill becomes high-minded and liberal souls.

2. PHYSICAL TRAINING

It is clear that the practical side of education must precede the theoretical, i.e. that the body must be trained before the mind. Young men should therefore be handed over to physical instructors who will give them a proper habit of body, and to games masters who will teach them all they need in the way of accomplishments.

Among modern states which are commonly recognized as expert in youth training, some concentrate upon developing the athletic type, thereby damaging the youthful figure and impeding growth. The Spartans, it is true, are not guilty of this error, yet they brutalize their children by abnormal exertion which is supposed to endow them with courage. In point of fact, however, as I have several times remarked,[3] courage should not be the sole or even the principal end of youth training; and even though we allow it to be so, the Spartans go to work in quite the wrong way. Among barbarians, as among the brute beasts, we find that courage goes hand in hand not with extreme ferocity, but with a gentle and more leonine disposition. There are indeed many

---

[1] *Odyssey*, ix. 7.   [2] He does not fulfil this promise.
[3] Pages 55, last line; 56, line 10; 217, lines 20 sqq.

peoples, e.g. the Achaei and Heniochi on the Black Sea, who are prone to cannibalism; and there are other mainland tribes, as bad if not worse, who live by plunder. But they all lack true courage. We know, too, that the Spartans were invincible so long as they were the only people who devoted themselves to rigorous training; but now they are beaten in war—yes, and even on the playing-field. Why? Because their former superiority was due not to their methods of training, but merely to the fact that their young men had discipline at a time when their opponents had none. From all this it follows that what is noble, in contrast to what is brutal, should take the first place. No wolf or other wild beast will ever face danger in circumstances that demand a noble spirit; only a brave man will do that. Those who compel youth to undergo this hard physical training to the exclusion of more necessary instruction, are in fact degrading them. They prepare them for the statesman's purpose in one respect only; and even here, as I have just shown, those same young men are inferior to others. The Spartans must be judged not from their past achievements, but from their present situation: now they have rivals in the sphere of education, whereas formerly they had none.

All agree that physical training should form part of education, and that until the age of puberty it should be less exacting, avoiding too strict a diet and overmuch work, so as not to hinder growth. [1339a] The disadvantages of excessive training in early years are amply proved by the list of Olympic victors, not more than two or three of whom won a prize both as boys and as men; the discipline to which they were subjected in childhood undermined their powers of endurance. Having reached the age of puberty, they ought to spend the next three years in other studies, after which they may be subjected to hard exercise and a strict diet. One should not labour simultaneously with mind and body; for the two kinds of work impede one another, and to that extent are incompatible.

3. MUSIC

I have already raised a number of questions about music; it will be as well now to resume them and carry the matter a stage further. My remarks will serve as a prelude to any full-dress review of the subject. It is not easy to determine the exact effects of music, or to say exactly why it should be studied.

Ought we to treat it (A) as a source of amusement and relaxation,[1] or (B) as conducive to moral virtue,[2] or (a third possibility) as (C) contributing to the enjoyment of leisure and to the cultivation of our minds?

Well, (A) no one can maintain that young men should be educated with a view to their amusement; learning is no amusement, it goes hand in hand with pain. Nor indeed is cultivation of the mind suitable for children and adolescents; the end is not for the imperfect. It might be argued, on the other hand, that lads study music for the sake of the amusement it will afford them as grown-up men. But if that is so, why should they themselves learn to play, and not, like the Persian and Median kings, enjoy the pleasure and edification derived from listening to others? After all, those who have adopted music as their profession must be far more accomplished performers than men who have devoted themselves to the art for no longer than it takes to learn. If music is to be a compulsory part of education, a course of cookery should likewise be included—which is absurd. Even on the assumption (B) that music can build character, there is the same objection: Why study it ourselves? [1339ᵇ] Why not learn the right way of enjoying and appreciating it from listening to others. The Spartans, for example, never learn to play; nevertheless it is said that they can accurately distinguish a good from a bad melody. Again (C), if music is held to promote felicity and intellectual refinement, the same argument holds good: why should we ourselves learn it instead of enjoying the performances of others? Look, for instance, at the gods: Zeus is never represented by the poets as singing or playing the lyre. Indeed no, we speak of professional musicians as mere mechanics; a freeman would never play or sing unless he were either drunk or jesting. But further discussion of these matters may be postponed.[3] Our first question is whether or not music should form part of education.

There are grounds for reckoning music under each of the three headings mentioned above—character-building, amusement, or cultivation of the mind—with all of which it appears to

---

[1] Sleep and drink, though not virtuous in themselves, are pleasant and at the same time 'put an end to care' as Euripides says [cf. Bacchae, 381]. For the same reason music (and even dancing) is prescribed as an accompaniment of the other two.—(A.)

[2] On the ground that it can form our minds and habituate us to true pleasure as physical training affects our bodies.—(A.)

[3] Pages 229–31.

be connected. Which of these does it in fact produce? The end of amusement is relaxation; and relaxation must be pleasurable because it is the remedy for discomfort resulting from toil. Again, cultivation of the mind is universally acknowledged to contain an element not only of nobility, but also of pleasure, because felicity is compounded of both. Now all men agree that music, with or without song, is one of the greatest pleasures, as Musaeus says: 'Song is to mortals of all things the sweetest.' Hence, and with good reason, it is an accepted item in social gatherings and entertainments, because it makes the company cheerful; so on this ground alone we may conclude that the young should be trained therein. For harmless pleasures are not only conducive to felicity, which is the end of life, but they also provide relaxation. We seldom attain our end. But we frequently pause and amuse ourselves, not so much with a view to a further end as for the sake of pleasure here and now; and it may therefore be well at times to let the young rest awhile in the delights of music.

Men do, of course, tend to treat amusement as the goal of life, because that goal would seem to contain an element of pleasure. The pleasure which it does contain is not the ordinary kind; but men often mistake the lower for the higher, because every pleasure bears some resemblance to the ultimate end of action. The end is not desirable as a means to any future good; nor are the pleasures of amusement, which are desired rather because of some past event, namely the exertion and pain already suffered. This, it may be reasonably supposed, is the reason why men seek happiness from such pleasures. But we have recourse to music not only as an alleviation of past toil, but also as recreation; [1340^a] and this being so, we may well ask whether it has not another and nobler use. Beside this common pleasure, which all men experience and in which all share,[1] may it not have some bearing upon our characters and souls? That it does so will be clear if we can establish that our characters are actually affected by it. And that they are so affected is clear from the influence exerted by many tunes, and in particular by those of Olympus whose music is recognized as having an inspiring effect on the soul; and a feeling of inspiration is an affection of the soul's character. Moreover, even mere imitative sounds, without the aid of melody or rhythm, call forth in everyone the feelings which they imitate.

[1] Music is of its nature pleasant and therefore its use is adapted to all ages and characters.—(A.)

Since music is to be classed as a pleasure, and since goodness consists in rejoicing and loving and hating aright, we may draw the following conclusions. (1) There is nothing we should be so anxious to acquire and cultivate as the power of forming right judgments upon, and of taking delight in, noble characters and noble deeds. (2) Rhythm and melody above all else provide imitations of anger and calm, of courage and temperance and their contraries, as well as of other spiritual affections, which come very near to the affections themselves. This is proved by experience; for as we listen to rhythm and melody our souls experience a real change. Now the habit of feeling pleasure or pain at mere representations is not far removed from the same feeling about realities; for if someone looking at a statue derives pleasure from *its* beauty, he will necessarily experience the same emotion in presence of the original. The objects of other senses, e.g. taste and touch, bear no resemblance to moral qualities. In visible objects the resemblance is there, but it is only slight. There are figures, I mean, which have the power of imitating emotions and ethical states, but only to a slight extent, and all do not share the same feelings about them. Besides, shapes and colours are indications rather than representations of ethical states, indications of character which are given only by depicting the body under the influence of emotion. Their connection with morals is slight; but in so far as it exists, young people should be encouraged to look not at the works of Pauson,[1] but at those of Polygnotus [2] and any other painter or sculptor who depicts moral character.

In musical compositions, on the other hand, there are clearly imitations of character; for, to begin with, the musical modes differ essentially from one another, and those who hear them are differently affected by each. Some of them, [1340^b] e.g. the so-called Mixolydian, make us sad and solemn; others, i.e. the softer varieties,[3] enervate the mind; another, viz. the Dorian, gives rise to a moderate and settled state of mind; while the Phrygian inspires enthusiasm. The effects of these various modes have been well described by specialists in this branch of education, who derive their arguments from actual experiment. The same principles apply to rhythm: some induce restfulness, others excitement; and these latter may be distinguished again, according to their vulgarity or otherwise.

[1] A trick-painter, *c*. 360–330 B.C. Cf. *Metaphysics*, 1050^{a}20.
[2] Fl. 463 B.C., a native of Thasos. See Pausanias, x. 25–31.
[3] Probably the Ionian and Lydian.

It is evident from the foregoing remarks that music can build character, and should therefore be in the curriculum of early education. The subject is well adapted to young minds; for music has a natural sweetness, and youth is intolerant of anything unsweetened. The human soul appears to have a kind of affinity to musical modes and rhythms, whence some philosophers maintain that the soul *is* a harmony, others that it *possesses* harmony.

Some way back I asked the question whether children should be taught actually to sing and play; [1] this must now be answered. Practice of the art certainly has an important influence upon character-building. It is difficult, if not impossible, for those who do not themselves perform to become good judges of others. Besides, children should have something to while away the time, and the rattle of Archytas must be considered an admirable invention; it is given to children both for their amusement and to prevent them getting up to mischief in the home. Small people can never keep still! This rattle is well suited to the infant mind, and training in music is a rattle in the hands of older children. It is clear then that children should be taught music in such a way that they become not only critics but performers.

It is not hard to distinguish what is from what is not suitable for different ages; and it is easy to refute those who say that the study of music is degrading. (1) We prescribe instrumental playing simply in order to form musical judgment. It should therefore be practised by children, who may abandon it when they grow older, being then qualified by their early training to appreciate and delight in what is good. (2) As to the degrading effect which music is supposed to have, this is a matter of which we shall easily dispose when we have considered (*a*) how far those who are being trained in civic virtue should practise the art, [1341ᵃ] (*b*) what kinds of melodies and rhythms they should use, and (*c*) the important question of what instruments should be employed in teaching them to play. [2] Our answer to the objection turns upon these three points; for certain methods of teaching and learning music may well have a degrading effect.

Clearly then (*a*) the learning of music should neither impede the activities of more advanced years, nor harm the body by

---

[1] Page 226.
[2] Aristotle deals with these three questions in the order (*a*), (*c*), (*b*); and they are labelled accordingly here.

rendering it unfit for military and civic training, either in the purely physical way or as an assistant for the mind in later studies. Students of music will not exceed the proper limit if they stop short of the sort of performances which belong to professional competitions, and do not seek to acquire those extravagant feats of execution now fashionable in such contests, from which they have passed into education. Even then students should practise music only until they can appreciate good melodies and rhythms, and not merely that commonplace element of music in which every slave and child, and even some of the animals, find pleasure.

(c) These observations give us the clue to what instruments should be employed. Neither the flute nor any other instrument requiring abnormal skill, e.g. the harp, should be made part of the curriculum, but only such as will turn the child into an intelligent student whether in the field of music or in other branches of education. There is another objection to the flute: it is an instrument expressive not of moral character, but rather of orgiastic states; it is best used on those occasions when the performance is intended not so much to instruct as to release emotion. There is yet another objection to the flute as a means of education: you cannot sing or recite while you are playing it. Though used by the ancients, it was rightly forbidden to youths and freemen by our more immediate ancestors.[1]

Accordingly we reject the professional instruments; and we reject also the professional mode of education,[2] in which the performer practises his art not for the sake of improving himself,

---

[1] The introduction of flute-playing into education was due to three causes: (a) increase of wealth giving rise to greater leisure; (b) more refined taste; (c) pride in material achievements (both before and after the Persian war), which led the Greeks to cultivate every branch of science with more zeal than discrimination. At Sparta there was a choragus who led the chorus in person with a flute. At Athens the flute became so popular that almost every freeman could play it; and this popularity is likewise evident from the tablet dedicated by Thrasippus when he supplied a chorus to Ecphantides. Later, when experience had taught men to understand more clearly what was or was not conducive to virtue, they rejected the flute, together with such old-fashioned instruments as the Lydian harp and multi-stringed lyre. They also discarded a number of instruments which were intended only to please the ear, and required extraordinary skill, e.g. the heptagonal and triangular harps and the sambuca. The ancients, moreover, used to tell a story about Athena, which is not without significance. It was said that she discovered the flute, and then threw it away because it distorted the player's face. Maybe, but considering her association with knowledge and art, we may hold with more probability that she rejected it because flute-playing contributes nothing to intellectual development.—(A.)

[2] By 'professional' I mean such as is employed in musical contests.—(A.)

but in order to provide his audience with entertainment—and vulgar entertainment at that. For this reason we consider that the performance of such music is beneath the dignity of a freeman; it belongs rather to hired instrumentalists, who are degraded thereby because the end they have in view is bad. The vulgarity of the audience tends to affect the music and consequently of the performer: intent upon them, he is affected by it, and distorts even his body by the movements to which their requirements drive him.

As regards (b) modes and rhythms, we must ask whether they should all be used indiscriminately; and whether, if some selection is required, the same one should be adopted by those who practise music with a view to education as by other practitioners. Seeing that music is produced by melody and rhythm, we ought to know what influence each of these has upon education, and whether we should prefer excellence in melody or in rhythm.

But there are several good treatises on the subject by present-day musicians, as well as by those philosophers who have had experience of musical education; and to them I will refer those of you who seek more detailed information. Here I shall content myself with a mere outline, stating general principles in the manner of a legislator.

Certain philosophers distinguish melodies as (i) those which express character, (ii) those which rouse to action, and (iii) those which produce inspiration. Each, they say, has a corresponding mode. While accepting this classification, I hold, as already stated, that more than one advantage is to be looked for in the study of music. These advantages are education, release of emotion;[1] cultivation of the mind, together with recreation and relief from the pressure of work. [1342ᵃ] It is clear, then, that all the modes should be employed, but not all of them in the same way. Those which best express character are the best for education. But those included under (ii) and (iii) above are also admissible when performed before an audience; for emotions such as pity and fear, and even inspiration, while predominant in some souls, are found to a greater or less extent in all. Certain persons are particularly liable to feel themselves

[1] I use the phrase here in a general sort of way, but shall do so with greater precision when we come to deal with poetry [probably in a lost part of the *Poetics*].—(A.)

possessed by some kind of inspiration. We find that such persons are affected by religious melodies: when they hear those which fill the soul with religious excitement they are brought back to normal as if they had received medical treatment and catharsis. Men who are subject to pity or fear, and indeed all emotional people, experience the same kind of effects; [1] and so, indeed, do we all in proportion as we are susceptible of feeling. All, therefore, will be in some way purged and restored to the delights of tranquillity. Cathartic melodies, incidentally, are likewise a source of harmless enjoyment to mankind.

Such are the modes and melodies which should be prescribed for those taking part in musical contests. [2] But for the purposes of education, as I remarked above, we should employ those modes and melodies which express character, e.g. the aforementioned Dorian; but we shall not exclude others which may be approved by philosophers who are experts on the subject of musical education. Socrates in the *Republic* [3] is quite wrong when he retains only the Phrygian along with the Dorian mode, especially in view of the fact that he rejects the flute; [1342^b] for the Phrygian occupies a place among the modes exactly corresponding to that of the flute among musical instruments. Poetry makes this clear; for Bacchic frenzy and all such emotions are expressed more adequately by the flute than by any other instrument, and are better set to the Phrygian than to any other mode. The dithyramb, for example, is universally recognized as a Phrygian melody. Many proofs of this are advanced by musical authorities. They assure us, among other things, that Philoxenus, [4] having tried but failed to write a dithyramb, entitled *The Mysians*, in the Dorian mode, was inevitably forced back into the more suitable Phrygian. As regards the Dorian, all agree that it is the most solemn and sturdiest of modes; and so long as we hold that extremes should be avoided in favour of the mean, there can be no doubt but that our youth should be

[1] Produced, that is to say, by the appropriate melodies.

[2] Audiences, however, fall into two classes—one of educated freemen, the other a common herd of mechanics, labourers, and so forth. Contests and displays should therefore be arranged for the entertainment of this second group also. The music on such occasions will be adapted to their minds; for as the latter are perverted from their natural state, so there are perverted modes and tense or unnaturally coloured melodies. Every man derives pleasure from what is natural to himself, and therefore contestants must be allowed to perform this inferior kind of music before a corresponding type of audience.—(A.)

[3] 399 A.

[4] Philoxenus of Cythera (436–380 B.C.).

taught the Dorian melodies, for the Dorian stands midway between the other modes.

There are two other things which should always be kept in view—the possible and the proper; and at these also every man should aim. He should do so, however, with reference to his age. Old men, who are no longer vigorous, cannot easily sing in the high-pitched modes; indeed, nature herself appears to suggest the lower and softer modes for their use. There is accordingly some excuse for the censure passed by some musicians upon Plato [1] for excluding the lower and softer modes from the educational curriculum, on the ground that they are connected with drinking. He does not base his argument on the proximate effects of drink (i.e. the frenzy of intoxication), but on the exhausting nature of a hangover. With a view, therefore, to old age and its needs, youth should practise the lower and softer modes and melodies as well as others. The curriculum should also include any mode (e.g. the Lydian in particular) which is suited to a man's early years inasmuch as it combines the elements of beauty and instructiveness. Clearly, then, there are three standards to which musical education should conform. They are the mean, the possible, and the proper. . . . [*Unfinished.*]

Republic, 398 E sqq.

APPENDICES

APPENDIX I

(SEE INTRODUCTION, PAGE xiii)

[1274b9–15] The equal distribution of property is characteristic of Phaleas. In the legislation proposed by Plato the following points are worthy of special notice: community of wives, children, and property; common meals for women, and the law about drinking, which lays down that the sober shall be masters of the feast; and the requirement that soldiers shall be trained to use both hands with equal skill.

APPENDIX II

(SEE INTRODUCTION, PAGE xiii)

[1288a6–15] First we have to distinguish the kinds of society to which kingship, aristocracy, and 'polity' are respectively appropriate.

Kingship is appropriate to a society which tends naturally to produce a family of outstanding brilliance in the field of political leadership. Aristocracy is appropriate to a society which tends naturally to produce a body of persons capable of being ruled, as free men, by others of exceptional capacity for government. 'Polity' is best suited to one in which there naturally exists a body of persons endowed with soldierly qualities, capable of ruling and being ruled alternately under a legal system which distributes offices among those wealthy enough to provide themselves with military equipment.

APPENDIX III

(See Introduction, page xiii)

[1288ª34–ᵇ5] We maintain that there are three right forms of constitution, and that the best must be that which is administered by the best man.[1]   Evidently therefore a man will frame a state, whether it is to be ruled by an aristocracy or by a king, in the same way and by the same means that lead him to true goodness; and the same education and habits will go to the making of a good man as fit him to be a statesman or a king.

Having reached these conclusions, we must go on to discuss the perfect state, and describe how it comes into being and is established.   Before inquiring into this subject we must . . .[2]

[1] i.e. that in which (a) there happens to be one man or one family, or a number of persons excelling all the rest in virtue, and in which (b) both rulers and subjects are fitted respectively to rule and to be ruled in such a manner as to attain the most desirable life.   Earlier in this book [pages 71–5] it was shown that the virtue of the good man is necessarily identical with that of a citizen of the perfect state.—(A.)

[2] The original breaks off here.

APPENDIX IV

(See Introduction, page xiii)

[1290^b21–1291^b13] I have stated that there are various types of constitution, and have established the cause of that variety. I must now explain why there are more constitutions than the two previously mentioned (democracy and oligarchy); what they are; and the reasons for their existence. We start from the principle, already admitted, that every state consists, not of one, but of many parts.

If we were going to classify the animal kingdom, we should begin by listing the organs which are indispensable to every animal. These will include certain sensory organs, the organs for taking in and digesting food (e.g. mouth and stomach), and the organs of locomotion. Assuming that our list of organs is full and complete, we shall go on to assume also that there are varieties of each—different kinds of mouths, stomachs, sensory and locomotive organs. This will lead us to infer that the possible combinations of the several varieties will necessarily produce as many kinds of animals; for the same kind of animal cannot have different kinds of mouths or of ears. Thus, when all the possible combinations have been exhausted, their total number will be that of the kinds of animals.

The same is true of the constitutions I have mentioned. States too, as I have repeatedly said, are composed, not of one, but of many parts or elements. One of these is the food-producing class, i.e. the farmers. Another is that of mechanics, [1291^a] who practise the arts and crafts required by the state, some of them absolutely necessary and others contributing to luxury or to the good life. A third element consists of tradesmen, engaged either in commerce or in retail trade. Serfs, i.e. farm-labourers, constitute a fourth element, and the military a fifth. This last is as necessary as the other four if the state is to avoid enslavement by invaders. It is surely wrong to describe a naturally servile community as a 'state.' A state is of its very nature independent and self-sufficing, whereas a slave is the reverse of independent.

By the way, this accounts for the unsatisfactory list of the
239

parts of a state as given by Plato in the *Republic* [369].   Socrates is made to say that the state is made up of four *necessary* elements—weavers, farmers, shoemakers, and builders.   Then, realizing that these are not sufficient, he adds smiths, herdsmen to look after the necessary cattle, merchants, and retail traders. These eight together form the complement of his 'first state'— as though a state existed merely to supply the necessities of life rather than in order to achieve the good, and as though it needed the shoemaker as much as the farmer.   He makes no allowance for the military element until such time as the growth of the city's territory and its encroachment on that of its neighbours' lead it into war.   Besides, the four original elements—or whatever number he includes in his association—will need someone to administer justice and to determine what is just.   Even as the mind can be reckoned more truly a part of a living being than the body, so there must be elements in the state corresponding to the mind and more necessary to the state than those elements which supply its material needs.   These 'corresponding elements' are (1) the military, (2) the judicial, and (3) the deliberative bodies, the duties of which last require political insight. Whether the functions of these three bodies belong to different groups or to a single group is immaterial to my argument.   It often happens that the same persons are at once soldiers and farmers; and the same may be true of the duties in question. We see, then, that since (1), (2), and (3) above are just as much elements of the state as those which serve its material needs, they—or at the very least (1)—are *necessary* parts. . . .[1]

Anyway, returning to our main subject, a seventh element consists of the well-to-do, who minister to the state with their property.   The eighth is formed by the magistrates who serve the state in its various official departments.   No state can exist without a government; so there must be persons capable of taking office and thereby serving the state, either permanently or according to a system of rotation.

That leaves us with the two elements to which I made a brief reference above—the deliberative and judicial elements.   All states require them, and require that they be well and fairly organized; they must therefore be in the hands of [1291b] those with political ability.   Now different functions are often found combined in a single individual.   For example, the soldier may

[1] At this point there appears to be a lacuna.   The missing part presumably dealt with a sixth element.

also be a farmer and a craftsman; and again, members of the deliberative body may also sit in the law-courts.   Furthermore, everyone believes himself endowed with political ability, and competent to hold most offices.   Yes, but *the same persons cannot be at once rich and poor*.   This explains why rich and poor are looked upon as members *par excellence* of the state. And then again, the rich generally form a small class, the poor a large one; and therefore they appear to belong to opposite elements, which explains why each will establish a constitution to suit its own interests, and why so many people think that democracy and oligarchy are the only two forms of government.

APPENDIX V

(See Introduction, page xiii)

[1315^b11–39] No constitutions are so transient as oligarchies and tyrannies. The tyranny which lasted longest was that of Orthagoras and his descendants at Sicyon. It continued for one hundred years, owing to the fact that they treated their subjects with moderation, ruled according to law, and generally looked after the people in such a way as to earn their goodwill. Cleisthenes, in particular, was admired for his soldierly qualities. It is said that on one occasion he placed a wreath on the head of a judge who had decided against him in the games; [1] and some authorities hold that the sitting statue in the public square at Sicyon represents the said judge.

Next in order of duration was the Cypselid tyranny at Corinth, which lasted for seventy-three years and six months. Cypselus himself ruled for thirty years, Periander for forty and a half, and Psammetichus, the son of Gorgdias, for three. Their survival may be attributed to similar causes. Cypselus was extremely popular; during the whole of his reign he never had a bodyguard. Periander, tyrant though he was, proved himself a brilliant soldier.

Next comes the tyranny of Peisistratus and his sons at Athens. It was, however, a period of interrupted rule. Peisistratus was twice expelled, so that he actually reigned for only seventeen out of thirty-three years. His sons reigned for eighteen years, making a total of thirty-five years.

Of other tyrannies, that of Hieron and Gelon at Syracuse lasted longest. In terms of years, however, it was comparatively short: Gelon died in the eighth year of his reign; Hieron ruled for ten years; and Thrasybulus was expelled before the expiry of his eleventh month. Tyrannies, in fact, have usually been of quite short duration. [2]

---

[1] After the manner of Peisistratus, who is related once to have answered a summons and stood his trial before the court of Areopagus.—(A.)

[2] There are errors both of fact and of chronology in the foregoing account.

APPENDIX VI

(SEE INTRODUCTION, PAGE xiii)

[1329ª40–ᵇ35] It is no new or even recent discovery of political science that the state should be divided into classes, [1329ᵇ] and that the military and farming classes should be kept separate from one another. To this day it is the case in Egypt, and also in Crete: in Egypt the system is believed to have been introduced by the legislation of Sesostris, and in Crete with that of Minos. The institution of common tables also appears to be of great antiquity: in Crete it can be traced to Minos, and in Italy to a still earlier date. According to the historians of Italy, the Oenotrians received the appellation 'Italians' from one of their kings whose name was Italus, who likewise gave his name to the European peninsula between the Scylacic and Lametic Gulfs [1] and the Straits of Messina. These historians go on to say that Italus made farmers of his shepherd subjects, and that his legislation included a provision for common meals, which have been retained in some parts of Italy, together with other institutions of his, down to our own times. The west coast of Italy is inhabited by the Ausones (formerly known as the Opici). The Chones, who are also of Oenotrian descent, dwell in the eastern half of the peninsula, in a region known as Siritis. It was in this part of the world that common tables originated. The division into classes originated in Egypt; for the reign of Sesostris was far earlier than that of Minos. These and many other institutions have been invented in course of time on countless different occasions. Necessity, it may be fairly supposed, has always been the mother of invention. Once the indispensable discoveries had been made, it was only natural that others should gradually appear, ministering now to the adornment and graces of life; and the same process may be held to have taken place in politics and other spheres of activity. Egypt bears witness to the antiquity of political institutions. Her people are recognized as the most ancient of all races; and from time out of mind they have had a legal code and a regular system of government. We ought, therefore, to make good use of what has come down to us from the past, and merely try to supplement its defects.

[1] They are only half a day's journey from one another.—(A.)

THE ATHENIAN CONSTITUTION

PART I

CONSTITUTIONAL HISTORY TO 403 B.C.

I. FROM THE EARLIEST TIMES TO 594 B.C.

(CHAPTERS 1–4)

[1] . . .[1] [The Alcmaeonidae] were tried before a jury consisting of noblemen who had taken an oath upon the sacrifices, and with Myron acting as prosecutor.[2] They were convicted of sacrilege; their bodies were exhumed; and the whole family was condemned to perpetual banishment from Athens. In view of these expiatory measures Epimenides of Crete purified the city.[3]

[2] There followed a long struggle between the notables and the populace. At that date the constitution of Athens was an extreme form of oligarchy, under which the poor of both sexes and of all ages were serfs of the rich. They were called Pelatae or Hectemori, the latter term signifying that they cultivated their masters' lands at one-sixth rental. The whole territory was owned by a few landlords; and those tenants who fell into arrears of rent were reduced to slavery, together with their children. All loans were secured upon the debtor's person, an arrangement which continued down to the time of the people's first champion, Solon; but the masses, notwithstanding their general discontent with a form of government which denied them constitutional rights of any sort or kind, found their main grievance in the fact that they were serfs.

[1] The first pages of the manuscript have not survived. They dealt with the 'original constitution' in the time of Ion, son of Apollo, with the modifications effected under Theseus, and with the events summarized in the following note.
[2] In 632 B.C. Cylon led an armed insurrection, hoping to make himself tyrant of Athens; but he and his adherents were driven to take sanctuary. The archon Megacles, an Alcmaeonid, induced them to leave their refuge by promising to spare their lives. In the event, however, they were all put to death, excepting Cylon, who escaped. Years later, in consequence of misfortunes which were believed to have resulted from this sacrilege, the Alcmaeonid family were brought to trial with the consequences mentioned by Aristotle.
[3] c. 596 B.C.

[3] The following is an outline of the constitution as it existed before the time of Draco.[1] The magistrates were chosen on a basis of birth and wealth. Originally they held office for life, but afterwards [2] for periods of ten years. The first magistrates, both in date and dignity, were the King, the Polemarch,[3] and the Archon. The earliest of these magistracies was the kingship which had existed from time immemorial. The office of Polemarch was added because some of the kings proved inefficient on active service; and it was for this reason that Ion accepted the post in a grave emergency.[4] The third magistracy, and the one latest in time, was the archonship; it is believed by most authorities to have been created in the reign of Medon.[5] Others attribute it to that of Acastus,[6] arguing from the oath still taken by the archons to execute their duties 'as in the days of Acastus'; and this fact does, of course, suggest it was in his time that the descendants of Codrus laid down the prerogatives of absolute monarchy, corresponding privileges being at the same time allowed to the Archon. Whichever is the correct view, there is little difference as regards date. But the archonship was the last of these three magistracies in point of time: that is abundantly clear from the fact that its holders have no part in ancestral sacrifices, as have the King-Archon and the Polemarch, but only in those of later institution. The importance of the archonship, therefore, is of comparatively recent origin, and is due to the dignity conferred by these subsequent additions. The appointment of Thesmothetae [7] dates from many years later,[8] when the offices abovementioned had already become annual. Their duty was to keep an official record of all legal decisions, which was intended for use as a body of case-law in future litigation. This office alone, then, of those so far mentioned, was never of more than annual tenure.

So much for the chronological order in which these magistracies were created. The nine archons did not at first share one official residence. The King-Archon lived in a building now called the Boucolium, near the Prytaneum; [9] the Archon in

---

[1] His date is usually given as 621 B.C. Aristotle here returns to a period long before the exile of the Alcmaeonidae.
[2] From 752 unto some date before 682 B.C.
[3] Military commander-in-chief.
[4] When his grandfather Erechtheus II was at war with Eleusisa.
[5] He was successor of Codrus, whose traditional date is 1066 B.C.
[6] Successor of Medon.   [7] See pages 299–300.   [8] 683 B.C.
[9] As evidence, note that the Boucolium is still the scene of a 'marriage' between the King-Archon's wife and the god Dionysus.—(A.)

the Prytaneum itself; the Polemarch in the Epilyceum; [1] and the Thesmothetae in the Thesmotheteum, where the whole nine resided as from the time of Solon. They had the right of deciding cases finally on their own authority; in other words, their jurisdiction was not limited as at present to preliminary hearings.

Besides the magisterial organization, there was the Council of Areopagus. In the theory of the constitution it was no more than protector of the laws. However, as well as summarily inflicting personal chastisement or fines on all transgressors, it was in point of fact the main organ of government. This was more or less inevitable, seeing that, whereas the archons were chosen on a basis of birth and wealth, the Areopagus consisted of men who were qualified by service in that capacity—which also accounts for the fact that to-day membership of the Areopagus is the one single office held for life. [4] The foregoing is a sketch of the earliest Athenian constitution. Not long afterwards, in the archonship of Aristaichmus, Draco enacted his ordinances. [2] The Council of Areopagus acted as watchdog of the laws and saw to it that the magistrates governed in accordance therewith. Anyone having a grievance might lay an information before the Council of Areopagus, but he had to state what law had been violated by the wrong he claimed to have suffered. As already noted, loans were still secured on the debtor's person and the land continued to be owned by a mere handful of men.

II. THE CONSTITUTION OF SOLON

(CHAPTERS 5–13)

[5] In consequence of a governmental system which left the many as virtual slaves of the few, the masses rose against the notables. There was keen and prolonged strife between the two parties, until at length both agreed to the appointment of Solon as mediator in the capacity of Archon [3] with extraordinary powers over the whole constitutional field. This

---

[1] This was formerly known as the Polemarcheum, but was renamed after Epilycus, who rebuilt and furnished it during his term of office.—(A.)
[2] This was the first reduction of the laws to a written code. For what follows between this and the next sentence see Appendix, page 308.
[3] Traditionally 594 B.C.

measure was prompted by a poem of Solon's which began as follows:

> Lo, my heart is the seat of sadness
> As I watch the ancestral Ionian house
> Put to the sword. . . .

In this poem he does battle for each side in turn against the other, concluding with some advice to make terms and end their quarrel.

By descent and reputation Solon was among the leading figures of his age. Judged, however, by wealth and position, he is recognized as having belonged to the middle class; and that he did so belong is clear from those lines in which he begs the wealthy not to be avaricious:

> Now you whose coffers are full, pressed down, and overflowing,
> Put a curb on your greedy soul; keep it at rest in subjection.
> Train the proud among you to follow a humbler path;
> You shall not have for ever your will, nor we for ever obey.

Solon, in fact, repeatedly blames the rich for having caused civil strife. Earlier in the same poem he expresses his fear of 'avarice and an overweening spirit,' evidently suggesting that they were responsible for the conflict.

[6] Immediately he had taken office, Solon set the people free once and for all by forbidding loans on the security of the debtor's person, and by enacting laws to cancel all debts, public and private. These measures are known as the Seisachtheia [1] because the people were thereby relieved of their burdens. Now the Seisachtheia has been used to denigrate the character of Solon. The fact is that when he was on the point of enacting it, he told some members of the notables what he had in mind. These persons took advantage of their information to borrow money and buy up land. Very soon afterwards all debts were cancelled, and they, of course, were rich men. Advocates of the popular party say that in this matter Solon's friends stole a march on him; but his detractors maintain that he himself profited by the fraud. The former view is much the more likely. Here you have a man who could easily have ridden roughshod over his fellow citizens and made himself tyrant.[2]

---

[1] The word means 'removal of loads.'
[2] That he had such power is universally admitted: it is clear from the well-nigh hopeless state of the country, as well as by numerous references in Solon's own poems.—(A.)

Yet he was in other respects so moderate and upright that he was prepared to incur the enmity of both parties by setting his honour and the public weal above his personal advantage. Surely such a man would not have consented to disgrace himself by a piece of low-down jobbery that could deceive no one. The accusation must therefore be considered false.

[7] Solon's next step was to draw up a new constitution, and enact new laws which replaced the ordinances of Draco, excepting those concerned with homicide. His laws (which he ratified for 100 years) were inscribed on wooden pillars erected in the royal porch; all took an oath to obey them, and the nine archons swore on the stone to dedicate a golden statue if they should be found to have violated any of them.[1]

Here now is the framework of Solon's constitution. (A) The population was divided, as before, on a basis of property into four classes: (1) Pentacosiomedimni, (2) Knights, (3) Zeugitae, and (4) Thetes.[2] The various magistrates—archons, treasurers, commissioners for public contracts, the Eleven,[3] and clerks of the exchequer—were drawn from the first three of these classes in accordance with the value of their rateable property. The Thetes were allowed no more than membership of the popular Assembly and of the law-courts. All were reckoned as Pentacosiomedimni who made from their own land 500 measures—solid or liquid. Knights were those who made 300 measures;[4] Zeugitae those who made 200 measures; and Thetes the remainder who were not eligible for any office.[5]

[8] Solon provided (B) that election to the various magistracies should be by lot, from candidates chosen by each of the

[1] This is the origin of an oath still taken by the archons [see page 296].—(A.)
[2] The first of these names is explained by the qualification (500 measures) mentioned below. Both explanations [footnote 4 *infra*] of the term 'knights' are correct, inasmuch as 300 measures would enable them to keep a horse. The 200 measures of a Zeugites enabled him to keep a *yoke* of oxen. The Thetes were originally serfs attached to the land.
[3] They were superintendents of the state prison (see page 292).
[4] Some hold, on etymological grounds, that knights were those who could afford to maintain a horse; and they back their argument with the evidence of some ancient votive offerings, e.g. that of Anthemion on the Acropolis, which bears the following inscription: 'Anthemion, son of Diphilus, being raised from the Thetes to the rank of Knight, offered this horse to the gods as a thank-offering for his promotion.' The man is shown with a horse, implying, it is held, that possession of a horse was the qualification for knighthood. All the same, it is reasonable to suppose that knights, like Pentacosiomedimni, attained their rank by possessing an income of so many measures.
[5] Except in so far as membership of the popular assembly and of the law-courts could be reckoned as holding office.

tribes. For the nine archonships each tribe nominated ten candidates, among whom the lot was cast. This method is still in use to-day, the tribal nominations also being made by lot. That Solon regulated elections to office according to the property classes is proved by the surviving law which confines the office of treasurer to the Pentacosiomedimni.[1] So much for his legislation respecting the nine archons; in very early times [2] the Council of Areopagus used to summon those whom it considered suitable and appoint them to the different offices for the ensuing year.

(C) There were, as of old, four tribes and as many tribe-kings. Each tribe, again, continued to be divided into three trittyes containing twelve naucraries apiece.[3] These last sub-divisions had their own officials called Naucrari, whose duty it was to superintend current receipt and expenditure.[4]

(D) Solon likewise instituted a council (*boule*) of four hundred members, one hundred from each tribe; but he confirmed the Areopagus in its ancient right of superintending the laws and acting as general guardian of the constitution. It kept watch and ward over public affairs in most matters of out-standing importance, enjoying at the same time full powers to correct offenders by the imposition of fines or the infliction of personal chastisement. Moneys derived from fines were deposited in the Acropolis without record of the offences for which they had been exacted. The Areopagus also tried cases of conspiracy against the constitution, for which purpose Solon had instituted a special process of impeachment. Experience had also taught him that in times of civil commotion many citizens were led by a spirit of indifference to accept whatever situation might result. He therefore enacted a law whereby anyone who, in the event of internal disputes, failed to take arms on one side or the other lost his civic rights and no longer formed part of the body politic.

[9] Passing from Solon's legislation on the subject of magistracies, I notice three points in his constitution which are peculiarly democratic. Most important of these was (A) the prohibition of loans on security of the debtor's person. Then

[1] In the 4th century B.C. this rule was purely nominal (see page 288).
[2] i.e. before Draco.
[3] Cf. Herodotus, v. 71. The naucraries were local divisions which were replaced by the demes of Cleisthenes.
[4] Among the obsolete laws of Solon it is more than once stated that the Naucrari shall receive and disburse the Naucraric fund.—(A.)

(B), all who cared to do so were entitled to claim redress on behalf of any person who was the victim of injustice. Finally (C) there was the institution of appeal to the courts. This, they say, was the key to the future strength of the masses; for when the people control the ballot-box, they are likewise masters of the constitution. Moreover, since the laws were framed in somewhat obscure and ambiguous terms—like the one concerning inheritances and wards [1]—disputes inevitably followed, and the courts found themselves having to decide every kind of suit, public and private. It has even been argued that Solon purposely made his laws indefinite, so as to leave the people with their final interpretation. This is not likely; he no doubt had in mind [2] the impossibility of rising to absolute perfection in the framing of a general law.

[10] These appear to be the democratic features of Solon's constitution, which was preceded by the cancellation of debts, and followed by an increase in the currency measures. Under Solon's regime a standard of currency larger than that of Pheidon was introduced; and the mina, which formerly rated seventy, was advanced to one hundred drachmas.[3] The standard coin in earlier times was the didrachma. He also established weights corresponding with the coinage, raising the value of the talent to sixty-three minae and distributing the additional three minae among the stater and lower values.[4]

[11] Having reorganized the constitution, etc., as above, Solon was pestered with complaints and questions about his laws. Reluctant to go back on what he had done, but equally reluctant to incur the hostility of both parties by remaining at Athens, he left for Egypt after giving notice that he would be absent for ten years. He hoped to reap the twofold benefit of trade and travel. There was, it seemed, no call for him to stay and interpret laws which should command universal obedience as they stood. Besides, he was in a most unenviable position: many of the notables had deserted him because of the Seisachtheia; and both sides had withdrawn their support through discontent with the newly established order. The masses had looked for a

[1] See pages 285, footnote 1; 286.
[2] His intention must be gathered from the tone of his legislation as a whole, not from its present-day results.—(A.)
[3] This means that Solon replaced the Aeginetan with the Euboic system. In both the mina consisted of one hundred drachmas; but the Aeginetan mina had the value of only seventy Euboic drachmas.
[4] In both systems the talent had sixty minae; but the Euboic talent was equal to sixty-three Arginetan minae.

complete redistribution of property, while the notables had expected him to make little or no change.   Solon, however, had disappointed both classes.   It was in his power to become tyrant of Athens by siding with one or the other; but he chose instead to earn the hostility of both, in order to stand forth as the ideal legislator who would save his country.

[12] All now recognize that this was Solon's aim, an aim which his own poems make clear.   For example:

> I gave the people rights that are their due,
> Not niggard nor yet lavish of my gift.
> Still were the rich and mighty my fond care,
> That they should suffer no unseemly shame.
> I stood with strong shield sheltering each host.
> And neither won an unjust victory.

The following lines show us his view of how the masses ought to be treated:

> The people will follow its leaders best
> When firmly restrained but not harshly opprest.
> Let prosperity shine on restlessness,
> And arrogance comes from the womb of excess.

In another place he refers to those who sought a redistribution of land:

> The pillagers came filled high with hope: each would win a great fortune;
> And I, they thought, though I smoothly coaxed, would soon reveal a harsh purpose.
> Vain were their imaginings then.   And now, in their anger against me,
> They eye me askance as an enemy man; unjustly too, for th' immortals
> Have helped me achieve what I swore to do, and much beside that I shouldered.
> Tyranny, sure, is no way to success, paved as it is with violence;
> Nor think I that the wicked should share in the good rich soil of my country.

And here are some verses on the cancellation of debts and on those whom the Seisachtheia delivered from servitude:

> You ask me why, as shepherd of the flock,
> I ceased to strive before I'd reached the end.
> There *was* no ceasing.   In the court of Time
> Bear witness, mighty Mother of the Gods,
> Black Earth!   For from thy bosom once I tore
> The mortgage-pillars planted everywhere;
> And thou, erst held in bondage, now art free.

How many men to Athens I restored
(Their native city, founded from on high),
Men who in justice, or despite thereof,
Were sold abroad, or, into exile driven
By stern necessity, wandering far and wide,
No longer spake the tongue of Attica.
Those here at home reduced to slavery,
Who trembled at their master's nod, I freed.
These things—all these—by main strength have I wrought,
Fashioning force and justice into law.
Yea, I went through as I had promised you;
Enacted rules for good and bad alike,
A line of jurisdiction straight and true
Fitting to every man.
Yet, had another, villain covetous,
Grasped, as did I, the goad—what think you then:
Would he like me have held the people back?
Had I at that time yielded to my foes,
Or later to the counsel of my friends,
Athens had been bereaved of many sons.
Wherefore I stood at bay, a wolf 'mid hounds,
Fending them off on this side and on that.

Now he rebukes both parties for their subsequent discontent:

> This folk—if I must openly rebuke—
> Had ne'er beheld the boons which now they hold,
> Not in their dreams; while those of higher rank
> And greater power would all commend my deeds
> And seek my friendship.

For, says he, if any other man had been exalted as he himself had
been:

> He'd not have checked the people, nor have stopped
> Before he'd stirred the milk and drawn its fat.
> But I stood as a stone in No-man's Land,
> A boundary-stone betwixt the parties twain.

[13] After Solon had withdrawn from Athens, for the reasons
stated above, opinion remained divided; and although the constitutional machinery continued to function for the first four
years after his archonship, the fifth and ninth years witnessed
such violent conflict that no archon was elected. Eventually
Damasias was chosen; but after holding office for a year and two
months he was expelled. It was then agreed to compromise by
electing ten archons, five from the nobility, three from the agriculturists, and two from the manual labourers. They held office
for a year after the expulsion of Damasias.

These events go to show that the archonship was at that time the most important magistracy: we find that trouble invariably arose in connection therewith. But the state was in the grip of almost incessant turmoil. Some malcontents attempted to justify their attitude by the penury to which they had been reduced through Solon's cancellation of debts. Others lamented revolutionary changes in the constitution. Others again were simply giving rein to spite. There were at this time three distinct parties, called after the districts where their lands were situated. The party of the Coast, led by Megacles the Alcmaeonid, appeared to be striving after a moderate form of government; that of the Plain, under Lycurgus, wanted an oligarchy. But the party of the Highlands were led by Peisistratus, who had the reputation of an extreme democrat; and their ranks were swelled by creditors who claimed to have been impoverished by the cancellation of debts, as well as by those who had reason to fear the consequences of their impure descent.[1] Nor were the apprehensions of this last group unfounded; for after the expulsion of the Peisistratids the citizen roll underwent revision on the ground that many were exercising civic rights who were not entitled thereto.

III. THE PEISISTRATID TYRANNY

(CHAPTERS 14–19)

[14] Not only was Peisistratus looked upon as an extreme democrat, but he had served with distinction in the Megarian war. Using this fact as a handle, he wounded himself and gave out that his injuries had been inflicted by his political rivals. The people took his word for it, and passed a measure introduced by Aristion to assign him a bodyguard. With these so-called club-bearers he turned on the people, and got possession of the Acropolis during the archonship of Comeas, thirty-one years after Solon's legislation.[2] The story goes that Solon resisted the demand of Peisistratus for a bodyguard. 'In doing this,' he claimed, 'I am wiser than one-half of you and braver than the rest: wiser than those who are blinded to the fact that Peisistratus intended to make himself tyrant, and braver than those who see it but remain silent.' His words fell on deaf ears, and

[1] They foresaw that their right to the franchise might be challenged.
[2] 560 B.C.

Solon (who was now a very old man) brought out his armour, hung it up outside his house, declared he had done everything possible for his country, and invited all his fellow citizens to follow his example. Again he was ignored, and Peisistratus stood forth supreme.

The government of Peisistratus was more like that of a constitutional monarch than of a tyrant; but five years later, before he was firmly in the saddle, Megacles and Lycurgus with their followers combined to expel him. This event took place in the archonship of Hegesias.[1] At the end of another four years Megacles found himself embroiled with Lycurgus, and therefore approached Peisistratus with an offer of his daughter's hand in marriage. Peisistratus agreed, and was accordingly brought back to Athens by means of an almost childish ruse. Megacles announced that Athena herself was bringing back Peisistratus. He then found a woman of great stature and beauty,[2] dressed her up to resemble the goddess, and introduced her to the city riding in a chariot with Peisistratus. The inhabitants were duly impressed and welcomed him with acclamation!

[15] That was the manner of his first return. But his authority was again short-lived, and six years later he went into exile for a second time. Refusing to treat Megacles' daughter as his wife, he feared a coalition of the other parties and fled the country—first to Rhaicelus near the Thermaic gulf (where he founded a colony), and thence to the neighbourhood of Mt Pangaeus in Thrace. In this latter place he made a fortune,[3] and was thus enabled to raise a band of mercenaries; but it was not until ten years had passed that he arrived at Eretria in Euboea and attempted to reinstate himself by force of arms. Chief among his numerous allies on this occasion were the Thebans and Lygdamis of Naxos, together with the knights who enjoyed sovereign power under the Eretrian constitution. Victorious at the battle of Pallene, Peisistratus took Athens and disarmed the people.[4] When his rule was firmly re-established he captured Naxos and set up Lygdamis as tyrant there.

[1] 555 B.C.
[2] Her name was Phyē. Herodotus [i. 60] says she belonged to the deme of Paeania. Others affirm that she was a Thracian flower-seller of the deme of Collytus.—(A.)
[3] Pangaeus was celebrated for its gold-mines.
[4] This was done as follows. Peisistratus ordered a parade in full armour at the Theseum, where he began to address the people. He had not been speaking for long when his audience began to shout that they could not hear him; so he told them to ground their arms and come up to the entrance of the

[16] I pass now from the origin and varying fortunes of the tyranny to the *administration* of Peisistratus. It was, as I said above, more like that of a constitutional ruler. Always kindly, restrained, and prepared to forgive an enemy, he also lent money to the poorer classes to help them make a living as farmers; and in this his object was twofold. First, it would scatter them over the countryside and prevent a crowd of indigent folk from idling away their time in the capital; and secondly, by making sure that they were reasonably well off and busy about their private occupations, it would deprive them of the time and even of the wish to meddle in affairs of state. Simultaneously, the tyrant's own revenues were thereby increased, for he levied a tax of one-tenth on all agricultural produce. The same considerations moved Peisistratus to establish local justices,[1] and also to make frequent progresses through the countryside in order both to keep an eye on its condition and to settle disputes which might otherwise have obliged the litigants to neglect their farms while absent in the capital. It was in course of one such journey that the episode of Tax-Free Farm is supposed to have occurred. Peisistratus saw a farmer of Hymettus trying to cultivate a stony plot; and being curious, he sent one of his attendants to ask the man what he got out of this piece of ground. 'Aches and pains,' was the reply, 'and I hope Peisistratus gets the same out of his tenth!' The farmer, of course, had no idea from whom the question came; and Peisistratus was so impressed by the man's outspokenness and hard work that he forthwith exempted him from all taxes. Hence the name of the farm.

Generally, in fact, Peisistratus governed in such a way as to cause a minimum of inconvenience to his people. He always fostered peace and contentment; and for this reason his tyranny was often referred to as a proverbially 'golden age,' especially under the much harsher rules of his two sons who succeeded him.

Above all, Peisistratus had an agreeable and friendly disposition.

Acropolis, where he would be more audible. They did so; but while he continued his long speech certain men whom he had chosen for the purpose went round and collected the arms, which they locked up in the nearby chambers of the Theseum. When they had completed their task they came and made a sign to Peisistratus, who finished what he had to say and then informed the people what had happened to their arms. He told them not to be frightened, but to return home and in future to mind their own business while he attended to affairs of state.—(A.)

[1] See pages 268; 293, footnote 1.

He was scrupulous in his observance of the laws, and claimed no special privilege. On one occasion, for example, he was summoned before the Areopagus on a charge of homicide, and went in person to defend himself. The prosecutor dared not put in an appearance, and the case was dropped.

All these factors account for his long tenure of power, and for the ease with which he recovered his authority after being twice expelled. He was supported by most of the notables and by a large majority of the common people: by the former because he mixed with them on equal terms, and by the latter because of the financial help they received from him. His personality appealed to all alike. Furthermore, the attitude of the law at this time to would-be tyrants was moderate in the extreme; notably in the provision against attempts to create a new tyranny, which ran as follows: 'These are the ancient statutes of the Athenians; if any-one tries to establish a tyranny, or has a hand in any such attempt, he and all his family shall forfeit civic rights.'

[17] And so Peisistratus continued to hold the reins of government until his death from natural causes at a ripe old age, in the archonship of Philoneos.[1] It was thirty-three years since he first came to power; he had ruled for nineteen of them, and spent the remainder in exile. We may therefore disregard the story that as a young man he was Solon's favourite and was general in the Megarian war for the subjugation of Salamis. It is a chronological impossibility, considering their respective ages and dates of death.[2]

Peisistratus was succeeded in the tyranny by his two sons, Hippias and Hipparchus, who were born of his first and legitimate wife.[3] [18] They took over the government jointly, on grounds both of dignity and age; but Hippias was de facto ruler, owing to his natural statesmanship and shrewd disposition. Hipparchus had a more youthful outlook; he was amorous and

---

[1] 527 B.C.
[2] Solon died c. 559 B.C. at the age of about 80 years.
[3] He had two sons by his second wife, Iophon and Hegesistratus, who was surnamed 'Thessalus.' She was an Argive [and therefore in Athenian law not his legitimate wife] named Timonassa. Daughter of one Gorgilus, she had previously been married to Archinus of Ambracia, a descendant of Cypselus. Hence the friendship between Peisistratus and the Argives, one thousand of whom, under Hegesistratus, fought on his side at the battle of Pallene. Some authorities believe that this second marriage was contracted during his first period of exile; others favour a date while he was in power. —(A.)

passionately fond of literature.[1] Thessalus, many years their junior [2] and a firebrand, was afterwards responsible for the disaster that overtook his family.[3] Falling in love with Harmodius, in whom he could arouse no reciprocal affection, Thessalus abandoned himself to an outburst of ungovernable rage: he went so far as to prevent Harmodius's sister from taking part as a basket-bearer in the Panathenaic procession, on the grounds that her brother was a profligate. This aroused the fury of Harmodius and his friend Aristogeiton, who, together with a number of confederates, undertook their celebrated deed. But as the two lay in wait for Hippias on the Acropolis during the Panathenaea,[4] they noticed one of their fellow conspirators chatting with him. Supposing that this man was in the act of revealing their plot, and anxious to forestall their arrest, they ran down and attacked at once without waiting for the others. They slew Hipparchus near the Leocoreum as he was marshalling the procession; but the design as a whole had failed. Harmodius was immediately cut down by the guards. Aristogeiton was arrested; he died after a long ordeal under torture, though not before he had accused many persons of the highest birth who were close friends of the tyrants. Meanwhile it was impossible to identify the other conspirators. One may dismiss the commonly accepted [5] story that Hippias ordered all taking part in the procession to lay down their arms and then had them searched for hidden daggers; arms were not carried in the Panathenaic procession until later, after the establishment of democracy.

The popular party maintain that Aristogeiton accused the tyrants' friends for the express purpose of weakening Hippias and Thessalus by implicating them in the crime of putting to death their innocent associates; others say he told nothing but the truth, betraying only his actual accomplices. At length, when he understood that only by informing against others hitherto unnamed could he win release from his sufferings by death, he asked Hippias to give him his hand as token of his good

---

[1] It was at the invitation of Hipparchus that Anacreon, Simonides, and other poets settled in Athens.—(A.)

[2] Since Iophon is not mentioned we may perhaps assume that he had predeceased his father.

[3] Compare the different version of this story given by Thucydides (vi. 54–8).

[4] He was awaiting the arrival of the procession while Hipparchus saw to its departure.—(A.)

[5] Cf. Thucydides, vi. 58.

faith. No sooner had he grasped it than he began to revile the tyrant for shaking hands with his own brother's murderer. Whereupon Hippias saw red: he plucked out his dagger and slew Aristogeiton.

[19] The tyranny now became much more severe. The vengeance exacted by Hippias for his brother's death, in the shape of numerous executions and banishments, brought him into hatred and contempt, which in turn embittered him. Three years or so after the death of Hipparchus, fearing for his safety in the capital, he began the fortification of Munychia,[1] where he intended in future to reside. But this work was still incomplete when he was driven out by King Cleomenes of Sparta, whose subjects had been repeatedly urged by the Delphic oracle to overthrow the tyranny.

Here is the story of those oracles. The Athenian exiles, led by members of the Alcmæonid family, made several unaided and therefore abortive attempts to effect their return.[2] Accordingly they contracted [3] to rebuild the temple at Delphi, and thereby obtained sufficient funds to purchase the help of Sparta. Meanwhile the oracle again and again told its Spartan clients that they must free Athens. Eventually Sparta determined to obey, notwithstanding the ties of hospitality which bound her to the family of Peisistratus.[4] She began, therefore, by dispatching a sea-borne expeditionary force under Anchimolus; but it was defeated, and its commander killed, through the arrival of Cineas from Thessaly with 1,000 horsemen in support of the Peisistratids. Indignation at this set-back moved the Spartans to send one of their kings, Cleomenes, in command of a more powerful force by land. He routed the Thessalian cavalry which

---

[1] The smallest and most easterly of the three harbours of Athens.
[2] One of these attempts was marked by the fortification of Lipsydrium, on Mt Parnes in Attica. Here they were joined by some guerrillas from Athens itself, but were besieged by the tyrants and forced to surrender. Whence a contemporary drinking song:

'Woe to thee, Lipsydrium,
What men thou hast slain,
Noble of birth, mighty in war!
In that hour they proved
Whose sons they were.'—(A.)

[3] With the Amphictyons. The temple of Delphi had been accidentally burned down in 548 B.C. (See Herodotus, ii. 180.)
[4] This resolution, however, must be attributed equally to the friendship between the Peisistratids and Argos [see page 259, footnote 3].—(A.)

attempted to bar his way into Attica; shut up Hippias within the so-called Pelargic wall; [1] and blockaded him with Athenian help. During the siege the grandsons of Peisistratus were captured while trying to make their way through the Spartan lines; the tyrants capitulated in return for the safety of their children, and surrendered the Acropolis to the Athenians after five days' grace had been allowed in which to remove their personal belongings.

This occurred in the archonship of Harpactides,[2] the sons of Peisistratus having ruled for about fifteen years after their father's death. The whole tyranny (including the latter's reign) had lasted forty-nine years.

IV. The Constitution of Cleisthenes

(CHAPTERS 20, 21)

[20] The overthrow of the Peisistratid tyranny left the city split into two factions under Isagoras and Cleisthenes respectively. The former, a son of Tisander, had supported the tyrants; the latter was an Alcmæonid. Cleisthenes, defeated in the political clubs, won over the people by offering citizen rights to the masses. Thereupon Isagoras, who had fallen behind in the race for power, once more invoked the help of his friend Cleomenes and persuaded him to exorcise the pollution, i.e. to expel the Alcmæonidae, who were believed still to be accursed. Cleisthenes accordingly withdrew from Attica with a small band of adherents, while Cleomenes proceeded to drive out seven hundred Athenian families. The Spartan next attempted to dissolve the Council and to set up Isagoras with three hundred of his supporters as the sovereign authority. The Council, however, resisted; the populace flew to arms; and Cleomenes with Isagoras and all their forces took refuge in the Acropolis, to which the people laid siege and blockaded them for two days. On the third day it was agreed that Cleomenes and his followers should withdraw. Cleisthenes and his fellow exiles were recalled.

The people were now in control, and Cleisthenes, their leader, was recognized as head of the popular party. This was not surprising; for the Alcmæonidae were largely responsible for the

---

[1] The ancient wall of the Acropolis.   [2] 510 B.C.

overthrow of the tyrants, with whom they had been in conflict during most of their rule.[1]

[21] The people, therefore, had every grounds for confidence in Cleisthenes. Accordingly, three years after the destruction of the tyranny, in the archonship of Isagoras,[2] he used his influence as leader of the popular party to carry out a number of reforms. (A) He divided the population into ten tribes instead of the old four. His purpose here was to intermix the members of the tribes so that more persons might have civic rights;[3] and hence the advice 'not to notice the tribes' which was tendered to those who would examine the lists of the clans. (B) He increased the membership of the Council from 400 to 500, each tribe now contributing fifty instead of one hundred as before. His reason for not organizing the people into *twelve* tribes was to avoid the necessity of using the existing division into trittyes,[4] which would have meant failing to regroup the population on a satisfactory basis. (C) He divided the country into thirty portions—ten urban and suburban, ten coastal, and ten inland—each containing a certain number of demes. These portions he called trittyes, and assigned three of them by lot to each tribe in such a way that each should have one portion in each of the three localities just mentioned. Furthermore, those who lived in any given deme were to be reckoned fellow demesmen. This arrangement was intended to protect new citizens from being shown up as such by the habitual use of family names. Men were to be officially described by the names of their demes; and it is thus that Athenians still speak of one another. Demes had now supplanted the old naucraries, and Cleisthenes therefore appointed Demarchs whose duties were identical with those of the former Naucrari. He named some of the demes from their localities, and others from their supposed founders; for certain areas no longer corresponded to named localities. On the other

[1] Incidentally, before that time one Cedon had rebelled against the tyranny; whence another drinking song, this time in *his* honour:
> 'Come now, boy, fill up
> The cup for Cedon's health;
> A toast is ever due
> To all good men.'—(A.)

[2] 508 B.C.

[3] Cleisthenes was resolved to do away with the family and tribal prejudices which had caused most of the earlier unrest. To this end he created many new citizens from emancipated slaves and resident aliens, who could not have been introduced into a system of tribes corresponding to a subdivision of the old ones.

[4] There were three trittyes in each of the four tribes.—(A.)

hand, he allowed everyone to retain his family and clan and
religious rites according to ancestral custom.   He also gave the
ten tribes names which the Delphic oracle had chosen out of one
hundred selected national heroes.

V. Ostracism

(CHAPTER 22)

[22] The foregoing measures rendered the constitution far
more democratic than that of Solon.   The laws of Solon had
been abrogated through disuse during the tyranny, and were
replaced by those [1] of Cleisthenes, who sought thereby to curry
favour with the masses.

Seven years after the reforms of Cleisthenes, in the archonship of Hermocreon,[2] the Athenians first imposed on the
Council of Five Hundred an oath which is still in force.   Next,
they began in the same year to elect the generals by tribes, one
from each, though the Polemarch continued to command the
army as a whole.   Eleven years later, in the archonship of
Phaenippus,[3] they won the battle of Marathon; and two years
after that victory, on the flood-tide of self-confidence, they for
the first time made use of the law of ostracism.[4]   In the very
next year, when Telesinus was Archon,[5] and for the first time
since the abolition of tyranny, they elected the nine archons by
tribes.   The choice was made by lot [6] out of one hundred candidates put forward by the demes.   Megacles,[7] son of Hippocrates of the deme Alopece, was ostracized in this same year.
Thus for three years [8] they continued ostracizing ex-partisans of

[1] Including the law concerning ostracism.—(A.)
[2] 501 B.C.
[3] 490 B.C.
[4] This law was originally intended as a shield against the ambition of men
in high places.   Peisistratus, for example, had used his influence as general
and leader of the popular party to make himself tyrant.   The first person to
be ostracized was one of his relatives—Hipparchus, the son of Charmus, of
the deme Collytus—with an eye to whose removal in particular Cleisthenes
had introduced the law.   Hipparchus had escaped until now, because the
Athenians, with true democratic forbearance, had refrained from actually
banishing those of the tyrants' supporters who had not shared their guilt
during the troubles and whose chosen leader he was.—(A.)
[5] 487 B.C.
[6] All previous elections under the constitution of Cleisthenes had been by
vote.—(A.)
[7] He was nephew of Cleisthenes, and uncle of Pericles.
[8] 488–486 B.C.

the tyrants, against whom the law was originally directed; but
in the fourth year [1] they began removing others also who
appeared too influential.   The first of these victims unconnected
with the tyrants was Xanthippus, son of Ariphron.   Two years
later, in the archonship of Nicodemus,[2] the mines of Maroneia [3]
were discovered, and from their working the state made a profit
of one hundred talents.   It was urged that the whole amount
should be distributed among the people; but Themistocles
intervened.   He refused to say exactly how he proposed to spend
the sum; but he urged that it be lent to the hundred wealthiest
men in Athens, one talent each.   If their use of it satisfied the
people, the cost should be reckoned as chargeable to public
funds; otherwise the borrowers should repay the state.   Well,
the money was granted on these conditions; Themistocles had
one hundred triremes built, each of the hundred rich men
providing one; and with these ships the battle of Salamis was
fought against the barbarians.[4]

About this time also [5] Aristides, son of Lysimachus, was
ostracized.   But three years afterwards, in the archonship of
Hypsichides,[6] Xerxes began his expedition, and all those who
had been ostracized were recalled.   It was, however, resolved
that in future all persons under sentence of ostracism must reside
beyond a line drawn from Geraestus to Scyllaeum,[7] or suffer
irrevocable loss of civic rights.

VI. SUPREMACY OF THE AREOPAGUS.   ARISTIDES
AND THEMISTOCLES

(CHAPTERS 23, 24)

[23] The Athenian state had hitherto advanced parallel with
the gradual progress of democracy.   After the Persian war, however, the Council of Areopagus was once again in the ascendant
and dominated the political scene; not by virtue of any formal
decree, but because it had made possible the battle of Salamis.

---

[1] 485 B.C.
[2] 483 B.C.
[3] Five miles north of Sunium.
[4] 480 B.C.
[5] 484 B.C.
[6] 481 B.C.
[7] Geraestus, a cape at the south-western extremity of Euboea; Scyllaeum,
a cape at the eastern extremity of Argolis.

When the generals were at a loss how to meet the challenge, and issued a proclamation that everyone should look to his own safety, the Areopagus provided a sum of money, distributing eight drachmas to each member of the fleet, and so persuaded them to go aboard. The Areopagus, therefore, won the people's respect, and Athens enjoyed a period of sound govern-' ment. At this time she bent all her efforts to the prosecution of the war; she had a splendid reputation throughout the Greek-speaking world, and was therefore given maritime command, notwithstanding the opposition of Sparta.

The popular leaders at the date in question were Aristides, son of Lysimachus, and Themistocles, son of Neocles. The latter was recognized as a soldier of genius; the former was known as a brilliant statesman and the most upright man of his age. The one was therefore employed in military affairs, the other as a political adviser. Although they did not always see eye to eye, they combined in pushing forward the rebuilding of the walls. But it was Aristides who, taking advantage of the discredit into which Sparta had fallen through the conduct of Pausanias, shaped the policy of Athens towards the defection of the Ionian states from the Spartan bloc. He it was, therefore, who drew up the first assessment of tribute to be paid by the allied states, two years after the battle of Salamis, in the archon-ship of Timosthenes.[1] He also it was who swore the oath of offensive and defensive alliance with the Ionians, at which ceremony lumps of iron were thrown into the sea.[2]

[24] After this, when the state began to grow in self-confidence and wealth, he advised the people to assume control of the league and abandon the countryside for the city. All, he promised, would find a means of livelihood, either by military service at home or in the garrison towns, or else by sharing in political life. Only thus would they achieve hegemony. The people accepted his advice, and having assumed supreme control they began to treat their allies more high-handedly. Chios, Lesbos, and Samos alone, as bastions of the Athenian empire, were allowed to retain their constitutions and their overseas territory.

The masses received ample provision in the way suggested by Aristides: tribute, taxes, and contributions of the allies were

---

[1] 478 B.C.

[2] To symbolize an irrevocable oath. (Cf. Herodotus, i. 165; Horace, *Epode*, xvi. 25, 26.)

sufficient to maintain more than 20,000 persons. These included 6,000 jurymen, 1,600 archers, 1,200 cavalry, 500 members of the Council, 500 dockyard guards, 50 guards of the Acropolis, 700 magistrates at home and an equal number abroad. Afterwards, when the state was on a war-footing, there were, in addition, 2,500 heavy infantry, as well as the crews of 20 guard-ships and vessels for transporting garrison troops, to the number of 2,000 men chosen by lot. Besides these there were the individuals maintained in the Prytaneum, the children of those killed in action, and the prison authorities. All these were chargeable to public funds.

VII. Ephialtes

(CHAPTER 25)

[25] The Areopagus, though in gradual decline, continued supreme for about seventeen years after the Persian war. But as the masses grew in strength Ephialtes [1] took over leadership of the popular party and set about undermining that Council. His first step was to ruin many of its members by charging them with maladministration. Then, in the archonship of Conon,[2] he deprived the Areopagus of all its more recently acquired privileges which made it guardian of the constitution. Some of these he conferred upon the Council of Five Hundred, others upon the Assembly and the courts. Themistocles [3] had a hand in these proceedings. Himself an Areopagite, he was awaiting trial on a charge of treasonable negotiations with Persia, and was therefore anxious for the Council's overthrow. He set to work as follows.

Themistocles told Ephialtes that the Areopagus was going to arrest him, and likewise informed the Areopagus that he would discover to them certain persons who were conspiring against the state. He then escorted the Council's representatives to the house of Ephialtes, promising to point out the assembled

[1] Son of Sophonides, he was known to be incorruptible and a man of pre-eminent civic virtues.—(A.)

[2] 462 B.C.

[3] The part alleged in this chapter to have been taken by Themistocles in the overthrow of the Areopagus cannot be admitted as historical: it implies a chronology at variance with the accepted narrative of Thucydides, and is not mentioned in *Politics* 1274ᵃ7. There is no compelling evidence upon which to reject the passage as an interpolation.

conspirators, and began conversing with them in great earnest. When Ephialtes noticed this he panicked and took refuge in suppliant guise [1] at the family altar.   There was general excitement.   Presently the Council of Five Hundred met; Ephialtes and Themistocles fulminated against the Areopagus, and then went on to do the same before the popular Assembly, until they succeeded in depriving it of all effective power.   Not long afterwards Ephialtes was assassinated by Aristodicus of Tanagra.

VIII. CIMON

(CHAPTER 26)

[26] Once the Areopagus had been deprived of constitutional authority the administration became increasingly lax, owing to the violent animosity of rival demagogues.   It so happened at this period that the better classes had no real head.   Their nominal leader was Cimon, son of Miltiades; but his character was unstable, and he had been rather late in entering public life. Moreover the common people suffered heavy casualties in war. The army at that time was recruited from the list of citizen hoplites; and since they were commanded by inexperienced generals who owed their position exclusively to their social standing, it continually happened that upwards of 2,000 or 3,000 troops lost their lives in the course of an expedition.   The flower of both the upper and lower classes was therefore exhausted, and in most departments of administration there was less adherence to the laws than formerly.   The method of electing the nine archons, however, was not altered; save that five years after the death of Ephialtes [2] candidature for submission to the lot was extended to the Zeugitae,[3] and the first Archon from that class was Mnesitheides.[4]

Four years later, in the archonship of Lysicrates,[5] the thirty so-called local justices [6] were re-established; and two years after

[1] i.e. wearing the *chiton* only, without the *himation*.
[2] i.e. in 457 B.C.
[3] Hitherto the archons had always been chosen from the Pentacosiomedimni and the knights.   The Zeugitae had been restricted to inferior offices, except when some evasion of the law was overlooked.—(A.)
[4] In the same year, 457.
[5] 453 B.C.
[6] See pages 258; 293, footnote 1.

that, in the archonship of Antidotus,[1] the population had increased to such an extent that it was resolved on the motion of
Pericles to exclude from civic rights all who were not born of
two citizen parents.[2]

IX. PERICLES

(CHAPTER 27)

[27] Pericles now came forward as leader of the popular
party. He had first made his name by prosecuting Cimon on
the audit of his official accounts as General. Under him the
constitution became still more democratic: he took away some
of the privileges remaining to the Areopagus; but above all he
turned the state's attention to the acquisition of sea-power, and
thereby gave the masses that confidence in themselves which
caused them to assume a steadily increasing measure of control
in public affairs. Moreover, forty-nine years after the battle of
Salamis, in the archonship of Pythodorus,[3] the Peloponnesian
war broke out, during which the people were shut in the city and
became used to earning their livelihood by military service; and
so, willingly or unwillingly, they resolved to take the administration into their own hands.

Pericles was also the first to introduce pay for service in the
courts. He did this as a bid for popular favour against the
influence of Cimon's wealth.[4] Some [5] have accused him of
thereby debasing the character of juries, since it was invariably
the common people rather than members of the upper class who
offered their services in this capacity. Then, too, it was after the

[1] 541 B.C.
[2] Several scholars have maintained that this statement is inaccurate, and
that this 'law' of Pericles was no more than a revision of the list of citizens,
dating not from 451 but from 445 B.C.
[3] 431 B.C.
[4] Cimon, who had princely possessions, fulfilled the regular state services
on a magnificent scale, and also supported many of his fellow demesmen.
Any member of the deme Laciadae might visit Cimon's residence every day
and there receive moderate provision. The fences were also removed in
order that anyone who chose to do so might help himself to its fruits Now
all this lavishness was beyond the private means of Pericles. He therefore
took the advice of Damonides of Oea, who was afterwards ostracized on
suspicion of having inspired most of Pericles' legislation. On the present
occasion he told Pericles: 'You are left at the post so far as personal wealth is
concerned; very well, then make the people a present of their own property!'
That was how pay for jury service came to be introduced.—(A.)
[5] Cf. Plato, *Gorgias*, 515 E.

introduction of this measure that bribery reared its head. The first offender was Anytus after his command at Pylos: [1] prosecuted for the loss of that place, he secured an acquittal by bribing the jury.

X. THE SUCCESSORS OF PERICLES

(CHAPTER 28)

[28] So long as Pericles was at the helm, Athens did not do so badly; but with his death a grave deterioration set in. Up to that time leaders of the democracy had always been respected in higher circles; now for the first time the people chose one who had no such reputation.

First of these popular leaders was Solon, and second Peisistratus, both of whom were men of good birth and position. After the abolition of tyranny there was Cleisthenes, a member of the Alcmæonid family, who had no rival after the expulsion of Isagoras and his adherents. Then came Xanthippus, the highborn Miltiades, Themistocles and Aristides, Ephialtes, and Cimon, the wealthy son of Miltiades. They were followed by Pericles, whose opposite number was Thucydides [2] as head of the notables.

After the death of Pericles,[3] Cleon, son of Cleaenetus, took over leadership of the people, and Nicias, who afterwards perished in Sicily, that of the nobility. Now Cleon appears more than anyone else to have been responsible for lowering the standards of democracy by his excesses.[4] He was the first to indulge in shouting and scurrilous abuse from the Bema,[5] and to address the people with his clothes tucked up like a common labourer, whereas all his predecessors had spoken with dignity and properly dressed.

Nicias and Cleon were followed respectively by Theramenes, son of Hagnon, and the lyre-maker Cleophon. It was the latter who first granted the two-obol allowance for theatre seats,[6] and

[1] 411 B.C.   Anytus was afterwards one of the prosecutors of Socrates.
[2] Son of Melisias, ostracized in 444 B.C.
[3] 429 B.C.
[4] Besides those next mentioned, Cleon raised the pay for jury service to three obols (428 B.C.).
[5] The platform from which orators addressed the people.
[6] Paid out of the so-called Theoric Fund.

this continued for some time as the standard rate, until Calli-crates, the Paeanian, stepped in with a promise to make it *three* obols. Both these characters were afterwards condemned to death;[1] the people may be deceived for a while, but they ultimately come to hate those who have inveigled them into evil paths.

After Cleophon, the popular leadership was held successively by men who were prepared to boast the loudest and court the favour of the masses with a view to immediate advantage. Nicias, Thucydides, and Theramenes are commonly recognized as the best Athenian statesmen of modern times. It is almost universally agreed that Nicias and Thucydides, besides being perfect gentlemen, governed Athens with paternal solicitude. About Theramenes there is some difference of opinion, owing to the unsettled conditions then prevailing. But a careful study of events will show him to have been no destroyer of all constitu-tions, as his enemies maintain, but a man who would support any form of government so long as it respected the laws. He showed in this way that he was able, as every good citizen should be, to live under any constitution, while setting his face against illegality, of which he was an inveterate enemy.

XI. REVOLUTION OF THE FOUR HUNDRED

(CHAPTERS 29–33)

[29] So long as Athens prospered in the war her democracy survived. But after the Sicilian debacle[2] Sparta gained the upper hand, thanks to an alliance with the King of Persia. The Athenians were compelled to abolish the democracy and set up the constitution of the Four Hundred.[3] Melobius[4] also was in favour of this measure, which was proposed by Pythodorus of Anaphlystus; but the rank and file were driven to agree mainly by a belief that the Persian monarch would be more dis-posed to ally himself with Athens if her constitution were modelled on an oligarchical pattern.

The motion of Pythodorus contained the following provisions.

[1] Cleophon was put to death in 404 B.C. for neglect of military duty. Nothing else is known of Callicrates's execution.
[2] 413 B.C.
[3] See Thucydides, viii. 1.
[4] Afterwards one of the Thirty.

(A) The Assembly would elect twenty men, over forty years of age, who, jointly with the existing Board of Ten,[1] would take an oath to frame such measures as seemed best for the state, and then take appropriate steps for the public safety.   (B) Anyone else might offer his own suggestions, so that the people should have an opportunity of selecting the best scheme of all those submitted.

Cleitophon seconded this proposal; but he also moved an amendment as follows: 'The joint committee should at the same time study the laws enacted by Cleisthenes when he inaugurated the democracy—laws which would be an additional help in reaching a satisfactory decision.'   His amendment was based on the view that the constitution of Cleisthenes, so far from being really democratic, was closely akin to that of Solon.

The newly elected committee took the following preliminary steps.   (A) They laid down that the Prytanes [2] should be compelled to put to the vote any and every measure submitted in the interests of public safety.   (B) They suspended (1) all indictments for illegal proposals, (2) denunciation for certain offences, and (3) all summonses, in order that any Athenian who wished might tender his advice on the situation.   (C) They decreed that anyone reported as having tried to get another fined for making any proposal he thought proper, or as having attempted to denounce him or summon him before a court, should be summarily arrested, haled before the generals, and turned over by them to the Eleven for execution.

The committee then proceeded to enact the following constitutional measures.   (A) The state revenues were to be spent exclusively on the war.   (B) Magistrates would serve without pay during the period of hostilities, excepting the nine archons and the Prytanes, who would each receive three obols a day. (C) While the war lasted all other administrative departments would be entrusted to those Athenians who could best serve the state in purse or person, to the number of not less than 5,000; and this body would have sovereign power, being entitled even to make treaties with whom they saw fit.   (D) The list of these 5,000 would be drawn up by ten persons chosen from each tribe; they would be over forty years of age, and would not set to work until they had taken an oath over full-grown sacrificial victims without blemish.

[1] Cf. Thucydides, viii. 67.   This board was merged in the Four Hundred.
[2] See pages 285, 286.

[30] After these recommendations of the committee had been ratified, the Five Thousand [1] chose from among themselves one hundred representatives to draw up the constitution, and these in turn submitted the following draft resolutions.

(A) There should be a Council of Four Hundred, holding office for one year, unpaid, and consisting of men over thirty years of age. It would include the ten generals; the nine archons; the Amphictyonic secretary; [2] the ten taxiarchs, the hipparchs, and the ten phylarchs; [3] the nine garrison commanders; the board of ten stewards responsible for the temple treasuries of Athena and other deities; the twenty treasurers of other (non-sacred) moneys; the ten commissioners of sacrifices; and the ten superintendents of public ritual.

(B) The Council itself would appoint all these officials out of a number of selected candidates, choosing a larger number than those actually required out of the members of the Council for the time being.[4] All other magistracies would be filled by lot, and not from members of the Council. To this latter the Hellenic Treasurers,[5] who handled the safe-keeping and necessary disbursement of funds, would not belong.

(C) In future there would be four Councils, the members, as before, being over thirty years of age. One of these would be chosen by lot to take office forthwith; the others would do so in turn, the order being decided by lot. For this purpose the hundred commissioners would distribute themselves, and the rest of the Five Thousand over thirty years of age, as nearly as possible into four equal parts and cast lots for precedence. The selected body would hold office for one year. They would have

---

[1] We learn from a subsequent passage in the text (page 275, confirmed by Thucydides viii. 92) that the Five Thousand were only nominally chosen. Sir Frederick Kenyon explains this present reference to the Five Thousand as follows: 'Either all persons possessing the necessary qualification of being able to furnish arms were temporarily called "the Five Thousand" (thus the so-called Five Thousand which took over after the fall of the Four Hundred actually included all persons able to furnish arms); or the Five Thousand nominated by the hundred persons mentioned at the end of the last chapter was only a provisional body, and a fresh nomination was to be made when the constitution had been finally drawn up.'

[2] He was one of the two members sent by each Amphictyonic state to the general councils. The other, known as the Pylagoras, was his superior and actually represented his state.

[3] See page 301.

[4] This means that 'the Council was (1) to nominate candidates out of its own body to succeed these officials, and (2) to choose such successors out of the number so nominated' (Sir J. E. Sandys, ed. 1893).

[5] These *Hellenotamiae* were a special board for managing the tributes.

full discretion in the exercise of that office, both as regards the safe custody and necessary expenditure of funds, and generally would act to the best of their ability. If they wished to consult a larger body, each member might invite one co-opted member of his own choice, provided the latter was more than thirty years old.

(D) The Council would sit once every five days, unless more frequent sessions became necessary.

(E) The nine archons would superintend the sortition of the Council, whose divisions (taken by show of hands) would be decided by five tellers chosen by lot from the Council itself. One of these tellers would be chosen by lot every day of session, to act as president. All five of them would draw lots to decide precedence among those who wished to appear before the Council; but they would give first place to sacred matters, second to heralds, third to embassies, and fourth to other persons. On the other hand, matters concerning the war might be dealt with, on a motion of the generals, whenever necessary and without balloting.

(F) Any member of the Council who absented himself from the chamber at the appointed time would be fined one drachma for each day of such non-attendance, unless he had been granted leave of absence.

[31] The foregoing provisions represented a future constitution; but for the time being the following scheme was drawn up.

(A) There would be a Council of Four Hundred, as under the constitution of Solon; its members would include forty from each tribe, chosen from candidates over thirty years of age who had been selected by the members of the tribes.

(B) This Council would appoint the executive magistrates and determine what oath they should take. It would also have full discretion in all matters concerned with the laws and the examination of official accounts. But it would have to observe any constitutional laws that might be enacted; these it could neither alter not supersede with others.

(C) The generals were for the present to be elected from the whole body of Five Thousand; but when the Council had been established it would carry out an inspection of military equipment and then proceed to choose ten persons

and a secretary.   These would hold office for the ensuing
year with full powers, together with the right, if so desired,
of attending Council meetings.

(D) The Five Thousand would also elect one hipparch [1]
and ten phylarchs; but in future these would be elected by
the Council, as recorded in (C) above.

(E) No magistracy, except membership of the Council
and the office of General, might be held more than once,
either by its first holder or by his successors.

(F) As regards the future distribution of the Four
Hundred into the four divisions,[2] the hundred commissioners would have to make that distribution as soon as
it became possible for them to sit in council with the Five
Thousand.

[32] The hundred commissioners elected by the Five
Thousand drew up the constitution as above; and when it had
been ratified by the people, under the presidency of Aristo-
machus, the existing Council (that of Callias's year [3]) was dis-
solved before the completion of its term of office.   The dissolution took place on 14 Thargelion; [4] and the Four Hundred
entered into office on 21st of that month, although the regular
Council chosen by lot should have begun their duties on 14th
Scirophorion.[5]

Thus was established the oligarchy, in the archonship of
Callias, very nearly one hundred years after the expulsion of the
tyrants.   The principal authors of the revolution were
Peisander, Antiphon, and Theramenes—all men of good birth,
outstanding intelligence, and pre-eminent ability.

But once this constitution had been established, the Five
Thousand were only *nominally* selected.   The Four Hundred,
together with the ten generals who had been granted full
powers,[6] took over the council house and carried on the business
of government.   Dispatching representatives to Sparta, they
proposed an end of hostilities without concessions on either side.
Negotiations, however, were broken off, because the Spartans
insisted that Athens must first surrender her command of the
sea.

[33] The constitution of the Four Hundred lasted for about
four months, with Mnesilochus as Archon by their appointment

[1] There were normally two.   [2] See page 273.
[3] 412–411 B.C.   [4] i.e. late in May 411.
[5] i.e. towards the end of June.   [6] See pages 274, line 38; 275, line 3.

for two months of the year of Theopompus, who held that office for the remaining ten.   But the naval defeat off Eretria and the revolt of Euboea (Oreum excepted) aroused more indignation than any previous set-back; for the Athenians at that time relied more upon Euboea than on Attica itself.   The Four Hundred were accordingly deposed.   The administration was entrusted to the Five Thousand, who consisted of men possessing military equipment; and it was voted that no office should carry a salary. The chief architects of *this* revolution were Aristocrates and Theramenes, both of whom had frowned on the proceedings of the Four Hundred in monopolizing the direction of affairs without reference to the Five Thousand.   Under this new regime Athens would seem to have been well governed; it was a time of war, and the constitution was on a military footing.[1]

XII. Arginusae and Aegospotami

(CHAPTER 34)

[34] It was not long before the Five Thousand also were ousted by the people.[2]   Then, five years after the overthrow of the Four Hundred, in the archonship of Callias of Angele,[3] the battle of Arginusae was fought, with two results.   (A) The ten generals who won the victory were all [4] condemned by a single vote taken by show of hands.   Some of them had taken no part in the action, while some had themselves been rescued by other ships; but agitators had been at work to rouse the people's indignation.   (B) The Spartans offered to evacuate Decelea and conclude a peace without concessions on either side; and some Athenians were ready to back this proposal.   The majority, however, would not listen to them; they were led astray by Cleophon.   He entered the assembly drunk and wearing his breastplate, declared he would never agree to the proposal unless Sparta gave up all claims upon her allied states, and thereby prevented the conclusion of peace.

[1] See Thucydides, viii. 97.
[2] 410 B.C.
[3] 406 B.C.
[4] This is obviously wrong.   Only eight of the generals were present at Arginusae.   Only six stood their trials; the remaining two would not return to Athens, and were probably condemned in their absence.   See the account of these proceedings in Xenophon's *Hellenica*.

Well, Athens had missed an opportunity, and she quickly realized her mistake. Next year, in the archonship of Alexias,[1] she suffered the naval disaster of Aegospotami, with the result that Lysander became master of the city and appointed the Thirty to govern her. This is what happened. The peace treaty included a stipulation that Athens 'should be governed *according to the ancient constitution.*' The modern democrats therefore endeavoured to preserve the democracy. Those of the notables who belonged to political clubs, together with the exiles who had returned after the peace, desired an oligarchy; while those of them who were not members of any club (though in other respects they looked upon themselves as no whit inferior to other citizens) wanted the old Solonian constitution. Among these latter were Archinus, Anytus, Cleitophon, Phormisius, and many others; but their principal leader was Theramenes. Lysander, however, favoured the oligarchical party; and the people were browbeaten into voting for an oligarchy on a motion proposed by Dracontides of Aphidna.

XIII. THE THIRTY

(CHAPTERS 35–7)

[35] So the Thirty came to power in the archonship of Pythodorus;[2] but as soon as they were firmly established in authority they ignored all the constitutional enactments that had been passed. They began by appointing a Council of Five Hundred, and other officials, from a number of selected candidates. Next, they enlisted the services of the ten magistrates at Peiraeus and the Eleven, with whose support, and that of three hundred attendant 'whip-bearers,' they obtained control of the city. At first, indeed, they behaved with moderation towards the inhabitants, and made a show of governing in obedience to the ancient constitution. Accordingly, they took down from the Hill of Ares the laws of Ephialtes, which had curtailed the powers of the Areopagus. They also repealed the more obscure ordinances of Solon, and did away with the supremacy of the law-courts. These measures were a pretence of 'restoring' the constitution and freeing it from ambiguities. Testators, for example, were given the absolute right to bequeath their

---

[1] 405 B.C. [2] 404 B.C.

property as they pleased; and (in order to frustrate the designs of professional accusers) there were also abolished the inconvenient limitations attaching to that right in cases of insanity, senility, and undue female influence.

These are only a few examples of the policy adopted by the Thirty; [1] and the whole city was delighted, believing it to have been inspired by the very best motives. But as soon as the Thirty had tightened their hold upon the state, they showed no mercy to any class of citizens, putting to death any whose wealth, birth, or character was above the average. Their purpose in doing so was to get rid of all whom they had cause to fear, and to lay hands on their estates. Within quite a short time no fewer than 1,500 persons had been executed.

[36] Theramenes, however, watching Athens overtaken by this fate, was horrified at their proceedings. He advised them to cease their abominations and allow the better classes some share in the government. At first they resisted; but his proposals became known to the general public, and the masses began to side with him. The Thirty were now gravely alarmed: Theramenes was on the way to making himself leader of the people and overthrowing their despotic rule. Accordingly, they drew up a list of 3,000 citizens who, they said, would be granted constitutional rights. But Theramenes was far from satisfied with the scheme. True, it was proposed to enfranchise the best people; but 'the best people' in this case included a mere 3,000 souls, as if no merit existed outside that number. Besides, the measure involved an inconsistency: theoretically the government was founded upon force, but the new scheme would leave the rulers weaker than their subjects.

The Thirty, however, turned a deaf ear to his criticisms, and repeatedly delayed publication of their list, concealing the names of those whom it would ultimately include. Whenever they did decide to publish, they would strike out some of those originally included and substitute others hitherto omitted.

[37] Now in the first days of winter Thrasybulus and the exiles occupied Phyle. The Thirty went out to attack them at the head of an abortive expedition, and thereupon resolved to disarm the population and get rid of Theramenes. This is how they set to work. The Council was ordered to pass the following

[1] They removed the blight not only of professional accusers, but also that of certain mischievous and evil-minded persons who had ruined the democracy by their fawning attachment.—(A.)

laws submitted for its consideration: (A) The Thirty should have absolute power to put to death any citizen not included in the list of 3,000; and (B) those persons who had taken part in demolishing the fortifications of Eetioneia,[1] or who had in any way opposed the previous oligarchy of Four Hundred, should be denied constitutional rights.   Theramenes had done both; so that the passage of these laws not only placed him outside the constitution, but empowered the Thirty to order his removal.[2] Theramenes was accordingly put to death.   The populace, excepting the 3,000, were then disarmed, and the Thirty began to wade still deeper into every sort of cruelty and crime.   Next, ambassadors were sent to Sparta, to calumniate Theramenes and ask for help.   The Spartans answered their appeal by dispatching Callibius as military governor with about 700 troops.   He entered Athens and occupied the Acropolis.

XIV. THE TEN AND THE RESTORATION.
OF DEMOCRACY

(CHAPTERS 38–41)

[38] Munychia was now occupied by the exiles from Phyle, who defeated the Thirty and their supporters.   Following this reverse the city force retreated; next day they held a meeting in the market-place, where they deposed the Thirty and elected ten citizens with authority to end the war.   These Ten took over the government, but did nothing to carry out their task; they merely sent representatives to Sparta, asking for help and a loan of money.   Finding, moreover, that those of the citizens who possessed the franchise were dissatisfied with their conduct, the Ten began to fear their dismissal.   In order, then, to intimidate their opponents, they arrested Demaretus, one of the most eminent citizens, and put him to death, thus achieving their purpose and obtaining a firm hold on the government.   They were supported not only by Callibius and his troops, but also by several of the knights; for certain members of that class were more anxious than anyone else at Athens to prevent the exiles returning from Phyle.   The entire populace, however, gradually went over to the party in Munychia and Peiraeus, whose

---

[1] These consisted of a projecting mole which constricted and commanded, on the northern side, the narrow entrance of Peiraeus.

[2] But see Xenophon, *Hellenica*, ii. 3, 23–56.

military strength was thereby greatly increased.   Consequently, the upper city deposed the original Ten and elected an equal number in their place.   The latter were all citizens of the highest repute.   Under their administration, and thanks to their untiring zeal, hostilities were ended and the populace flocked back to the city.   The most outstanding members of the new Ten were Rhinon of Paeania and Phayllus of Acherdus. Even before the arrival of Pausanias, King of Sparta, they began negotiations with the party in Peiraeus, and after his arrival they did all they could to help him repatriate the exiles.   Pausanias, however, acting in conjunction with a board of fifteen arbitrators whom he had instructed to follow him from Sparta, was the man who brought negotiations to the point of settlement and reconcilation.

Rhinon and his colleagues were accorded a vote of thanks for their generous services to the people.   They had taken office under an oligarchy, and rendered their accounts to a democracy; but no voice was raised against them, either among those who had remained in the upper city or among the exiles who had returned from Peiraeus.   Rhinon, in fact, was then and there elected General as a reward for his conduct.

[39] The reconciliation was effected in the archonship of Eucleides,[1] on the following terms:

(A) Those Athenians who had stayed on in the upper city, but now wished to leave, should be free to take up residence at Eleusis.   There they would continue to enjoy civic rights, together with unrestricted powers of self-government and the fruits of their own property.

(B) The temple of Demeter at Eleusis would be common ground for both parties, under the supervision of the Ceryces and Eumolpidae [2] in accordance with ancient custom.

(C) Those who seceded to Eleusis should not be allowed to enter Athens, nor those resident in Athens to visit Eleusis; except when the mysteries were being celebrated, and then the prohibition should be suspended in favour of both parties.

(D) The secessionists, like the rest of the Athenians, should contribute from their revenues to the fund for common defence.

[1] Late summer, 404 B.C.
[2] Hereditary guardians and priests of the temple.

(E) If any secessionist desired to take a house at Eleusis, the people would help him to obtain the owner's consent; and if they could not reach agreement, each side should appoint three valuers, whose decision as regards a price should be binding on the owner.

(F) Of the original inhabitants of Eleusis, those whom the secessionists desired to continue as part of their community should be allowed to do so.

(G) The list of those wishing to secede should be compiled within ten days of their taking the oaths of pacification, in the case of persons then resident in the country, and they should leave Athens within twenty days. Persons not so resident should be granted the same conditions as from the date of their return.

(H) No one who settled at Eleusis should be eligible for any magistracy at Athens until he had registered himself as again resident there.

(I) Trials for homicide and unlawful wounding should follow the traditional procedure.

(J) No one should be victimized for his share in past events—excepting the Thirty, the first Ten, the Eleven, and the magistrates of Peiraeus; and even they should be included in the amnesty provided they submitted their accounts as follows: (1) the magistrates of Peiraeus to the courts held there; and (2) the magistrates of the upper city [1] to a court consisting of those who could show they possessed rateable property there.

Such were the terms upon which those who wished to do so might secede. Each party was to make separate repayment of the moneys it had borrowed for the war.

[40] As soon as this reconciliation had been effected, those who had fought for the Thirty were filled with apprehension, and many of them determined to secede. On the other hand, they postponed entering their names until the very last moment, as men invariably do. Archinus, therefore, who observed that they were very numerous, and disliked the idea of losing so many citizens, seized this opportunity of cancelling the remaining days of grace; so that many persons were obliged to remain—though most unwillingly until their fears began to evaporate.

[1] i.e. members of the Thirty, the first Ten, and the Eleven.

Archinus seems to have acted in this matter like a true states-man. His conduct was equally commendable in his subsequent prosecution of Thrasybulus on a charge of having illegally pro-posed to confer the franchise on *all* who had taken part in the return from Peiraeus, some of whom were well known to be slaves. A third example of his statesmanship appears in the episode of a certain returned exile who began to violate the amnesty. Archinus haled this man before the Council and persuaded them to have him executed without trial. 'You must now,' he said, 'show whether you mean to preserve the demo-cracy and abide by your oaths. If you acquit the accused you will be inviting others to follow his example; but put him to death, and you will give a concrete warning to others.' The admonition was fully justified; for after the fellow had been executed there was no further attempt on the part of anyone to violate the amnesty. The Athenians appear, in fact, both publicly and privately, to have behaved with unsurpassed moderation and fairness towards those who shared the guilt of earlier misfortunes. They not only abstained from any form of victimization, but actually drew on state funds to repay Sparta a war loan raised by the Thirty, notwithstanding the treaty which made each party (i.e. of the upper city and of the Peiraeus) separately responsible for its own debts. This gesture on the part of Athens arose from her conviction that without some such initial step true harmony could never be restored. Examine the history of other states, and you will find that when a democracy comes to power, so far from delving into its own pocket, it nearly always makes a general redistribution of the land.

A final reconciliation with the secessionists was brought about two years after their departure from Athens, in the archonship of Xenaenetus.[1] [41] But this is to anticipate. As soon as the democracy had been re-established, the present constitution was enacted in the archonship of Pythodorus.[2] The people's re-sumption of authority seems justified by the fact of their having done so by their own unaided exertions. This was the eleventh change in the Athenian constitution, omitting the work of Ion and his companions [3] who initiated communal life, divided the people into four tribes, and created the tribal kings.

[1] 401 B.C.
[2] 403 B.C.
[3] The so-called constitution of Ion, and also that of Theseus mentioned below, was described in the pages now lost from the beginning of the manuscript.

XV. Summary

(CHAPTER 41, LINE 10 TO END,

The first constitutional milestone worthy of the name is the slight deviation from absolute monarchy in the reign of Theseus. The second is the codification of the laws by Draco. The third is Solon's establishment, which followed a period of civil war and is the origin of Athenian democracy. The fourth is represented by the Peisistratid tyranny; and the fifth by the reforms of Cleisthenes, which followed its overthrow and were of a more democratic character than the provisions of Solon. Sixth comes the supremacy of the Areopagus after the Persian wars. Aristides designed the seventh. It was perfected by Ephialtes, who curtailed the powers of the Areopagus; but under it Athens, misled by demagogues, committed the gravest errors . . .[1] on account of her maritime empire. The eighth and ninth constitutional milestones are represented respectively by the government of the Four Hundred and the temporary revival of democracy; the tenth by the reign of terror under the Thirty and the Ten. Finally, there is the eleventh, which followed the return of the exiles from Phyle.

The constitution then established has continued until to-day, accompanied by a steady growth in the power of the masses. The democracy controls public life in every sphere by means of its votes in the Assembly, as well as by its hold upon the courts. Even the judicial functions of the Council have been taken over by the people—a wise step, I think, because small bodies are more easily corrupted by money or influence than large ones.

When the democracy was first restored, no payment was allowed for attendance at the Assembly, with the result that absenteeism was common. The Prytanes tried all sorts of tricks to get the citizens to come and ratify the votes, but in vain. Agyrrhius, therefore, introduced a system of payment at the rate of one obol a day. Heracleides of Clazomenae, who was nicknamed 'the King,' raised it to two obols, and Agyrrhius again to three.

[1] Lacuna in the text.

PART II

THE CONSTITUTION OF ATHENS,
CIRCA 325 B.C.

I come now to the present state of the Athenian constitution, which extends its franchise to males born of two citizen parents.

I. Enrolment and Training of Ephebi
(CHAPTER 42, LINE 3 TO END)

[42] Enrolment among the demesmen takes place at the age of eighteen, and the process is as follows.   (A) The demesmen vote on oath (1) as to whether the candidates appear to be of legal age (if not, they resume the rank of boys), and (2) as to whether the candidate is free-born, i.e. of such parentage as required by law. With regard to (2), if it is decided that he is not a freeman, he appeals to the law-courts.   The demesmen now appoint five of their own number to act as accusers; if the court finds that he is not entitled to enrolment, the state sells him into slavery, but if he wins his case he must be forthwith enrolled among the demesmen.   (B) The new ephebi are next examined by the Council: if it forms an opinion that any of them is under eighteen years of age, it fines the demesmen who enrolled him.

(C) When the young men have been thus examined, their fathers meet by tribes and appoint on oath three of their fellow tribesmen, over forty years of age, whom they consider the best and most competent persons to take charge of the ephebi.   From the number so appointed the Assembly elects by open vote [1] one from each tribe as *guardian*, and also a *director*, from the general body of Athenian citizens, to manage all the ephebi in their respective tribes.

Conducted by these persons, the young men begin by making a round of the temples; then they set out for the Peiraeus, where some of them garrison Munychia, and others the peninsula of Acte.[2]   The Assembly meanwhile has also elected two [3]

---

[1] *Cheirotonei*, 'votes by show of hands,' which is the regular term used in this treatise to describe election by open vote as opposed to appointment by lot.
[2] The southern peninsula of the Peiraeus.
[3] Reduced to one in 305 B.C.

trainers with their subordinate instructors to teach the youths how to fight in heavy armour, how to wield the bow and javelin, and how to fire a catapult.

The state provides each guardian with one drachma apiece for their keep, while the ephebi themselves are paid four obols apiece. Each guardian receives the allowance for all the ephebi belonging to his own tribe, and buys the provisions necessary for the common table at which they eat.

(D) So the first year passes. Next year, when the Assembly meets in the theatre, the ephebi give a public demonstration of their drill, and each one is afterwards presented by the state with a shield and spear. They spend the next two years patrolling the country or on garrison duty, during which time they wear the short military cloak. Throughout this period also they are exempt from taxation; nor may they sue or be sued in the courts.[1] At the end of it they take their place in the citizen body. So much for the enrolment and training of ephebi.

II. MAGISTRATES CHOSEN BY LOT: THE LEGISLATURE AND EXECUTIVE

(CHAPTERS 43–60)

[43] All the magistrates concerned with day-to-day administration are chosen *by lot*.[2] They are as follows:

(A) THE COUNCIL OF FIVE HUNDRED MEMBERS, fifty from each tribe. Each of these groups of fifty serves as Prytanes [3] in an order determined similarly by lot. Since the reckoning is by lunar years,[4] the first four prytanies last for thirty-six days each, and the other six for thirty-five. The Prytanes for the time being share a common table in the Tholus, for which purpose they receive a sum of money from the state. They also summon

---

[1] This is in order that they may have no occasion to ask for leave. Exception, however, is made in cases of actions concerning inheritances and wards of state, and also in the event of sacrificial rites connected with the youth's own family.—(A.)

[2] Excepting the Military Treasurer, the Treasurers of the Theoric Fund, and the Superintendent of Springs. They are elected by open vote, and hold office from one Panathenaic festival to the next [i.e. for four years]. All military offices are filled likewise by open vote [see pages 301–2].—(A.)

[3] i.e. sits as a presiding or superintending subcommittee of the whole Council.

[4] The normal Attic year consisted of 12 months of 29 and 30 days alternately, making a total of 354 days. The tenth part of 354 is 35 days, and 4 over. These latter were assigned to the first four prytanies.

meetings of the full Council every day except holidays, prepare its agenda, and decide where the meetings are to be held.

(1) *The Council and the Assembly*. The Prytanes convoke the Assembly four times in each prytany, and draw up its agenda. One of the four meetings is called the 'sovereign,' at which the people must confirm in office those magistrates whom they consider to be performing their duties satisfactorily. On this day also impeachments are introduced by any who wish to do so; inventories are read of property confiscated by the state; and claims to inheritances and wards of state are heard, so that all may have cognizance of any vacancy in an estate. At the 'sovereign' meeting in the sixth prytany, besides the foregoing items of business, a vote is taken as to whether or not the power of ostracism shall be exercised.[1] Complaints against professional accusers (whether Athenian citizens or resident aliens) are also heard on this occasion, to the maximum of three in either class, together with cases involving non-performance of promises made by individuals to the state.

The second meeting of the Assembly in each prytany is devoted to the hearing of formal petitions. Then anyone is free, on depositing the suppliant's staff,[2] to address the people on any matter, public or private.

The last two meetings are assigned for other purposes, but are bound by law to discuss three religious matters, three secular, and three arising from the introduction of foreign representatives.[3]

[44] There is a single president of the Prytanes, chosen by lot, who presides for a night and a day; he may not exercise that function for a longer period, nor may the same man hold the office more than once. He keeps the keys of the temples in which the public treasure and state records are preserved, and also the public seal; and he must remain in the Tholus, together with a third of the Prytanes, whom he himself appoints.

Whenever the Prytanes convoke a meeting of the Council or of the Assembly, their president chooses by lot nine Proedri, one from each tribe excepting that of the Prytanes for the time being, and out of their number he likewise chooses one as president.

---

[1] If the decision was in favour, the actual votes for and against ostracism of particular individuals were taken in the eighth prytany.

[2] An olive-branch bound with wool, which was laid on the altar in the place of assembly.

[3] Heralds and envoys call first on the Prytanes, who also receive dispatches brought in by messengers.—(A.)

He then delivers the agenda for the meeting to the Proedri, who thereafter maintain order in the assembly, bring forward the various items of business, decide the results of the voting, supervise the proceedings generally, and are even empowered to dissolve the meeting.   No one may serve as president of the Proedri more than once in the year, but anyone may act as a simple Proedrus once in each prytany.

(2) *Other Functions of the Council.*   [45] The Council once had power to inflict fines, imprisonment, and even death . . .[1] But on one occasion it was in the act of delivering Lysimachus for execution the same day, when Eumelides of Alopece saved his life by proclaiming that no Athenian citizen ought to suffer the death penalty except by sentence of a court of law.   In due course Lysimachus was brought to trial; he was acquitted, and known thereafter as 'the man who escaped the bastinado.'   The people then deprived the Council of its right to punish by death, imprisonment, or fine; they passed a law that if the Council condemned anyone for an offence, or imposed a fine, the Thesmothetae should submit the sentence to a court of law, whose decision should be final.

But the Council still (*a*) passes judgment on most of the magistrates, especially those who handle public funds.   Its judgment, however, is not final; there is a right of appeal to the courts.   Even private individuals may lay before it an information against any magistrate for non-observance of the laws; but here again there is an appeal to the courts if the Council finds the magistrate in question guilty.

The Council (*b*) examines those who are to succeed it in the following year, as well as the nine archons.[2]   Once upon a time it had power to reject candidates out of hand, but now they may appeal to the law-courts.

Although the Council can pass no final judgment in the above cases, it (*c*) takes preliminary cognizance of all matters coming before the Assembly.   Nor may the latter vote on any question that has not first been considered by the Council and placed on the agenda by the Prytanes.   If this procedure is omitted, anyone who carries a motion in the Assembly is liable to an action for illegal proposal.

[46] The Council (*d*) is responsible for triremes already in commission, as well as for their tackle and sheds.   It likewise sees to the building of new triremes or quadriremes, according

---

[1] Lacuna in the text.   [2] See page 295.

as the Assembly directs, and to the provision of their tackle and sheds.   The appointment of master-shipbuilders is carried out by vote in the Assembly; and unless the Council hands over the completed vessels to its successor it cannot receive the donation which is normally given after the new Council has taken office.   The actual building of the triremes is supervised by ten commissioners appointed by the Council from the whole people.[1]

The Council (e) inspects all public buildings under construction.   If it is of opinion that the state is being defrauded it formally denounces the offender to the Assembly and, if he is found guilty, turns him over to the law-courts.

[47] The Council (f) co-operates in most of the duties carried out by the following magistrates, *all of whom are chosen by lot*.

(i) The ten *Treasurers of Athena*, one from each tribe.   Under a law of Solon which is still in force they must be Pentacosiomedimni; in practice, however, anyone upon whom the lot falls assumes the office, however poor he may be.   These officials take charge of the statue of Athena, the figures of Victory, and other treasures of the Parthenon (including money) in presence of the Council.

(ii) Ten *Commissioners for Public Contracts*, one from each tribe, who farm out the public contracts.   (a) In conjunction with the Military Treasurer and the Treasurers of the Theoric Fund, and in presence of the Council (which indicates the lessee by open vote), they ratify the lease of taxes, and also of mines let out by the state—including those which are still workable (on three-year leases) and those which are the subject of special concessions (on ten-year leases).[2]   (β) Again in presence of the Council, they sell the property of those who have withdrawn from Attica while on trial before the court of Areopagus,[3] and

---

[1] It appears from Aeschines, *Contra Ctesiphonta*, 30, that these commissioners were chosen by the tribes from candidates nominated by the demes; so that this 'appointment' by the Council probably amounted to no more than a ratification of the tribes' choice.
[2] This may refer to exhausted mines with heaps of scoriae near by, which, having reverted to the state, were leased on more favourable terms than those that were still workable.
[3] A person accused of wilful murder before the Areopagus might (except where the charge was parricide) leave the country, according to Demosthenes, 'after making his first speech.'   But his property was confiscated and he was never allowed to return.   In the event of a decree for the repatriation of exiles, such people were always and expressly excluded.

of persons indebted to the Treasury,[1] subject to ratification of these contracts by the nine archons. (γ) They deliver to the Council lists of the taxes farmed out for the year, entering on whitened tablets the name of the lessee and the amount to be paid. These lists are made up as follows: *first*, those who have to pay their instalments in each prytany, on ten separate tablets; *second*, those who are to pay three times in the year, with a separate tablet for each instalment; and *third*, those who pay in the ninth prytany. (δ) They draw up a schedule of farms and dwelling-houses which have been confiscated by order of the court and afterwards let out by them in the course of their official duties. The full value of dwelling-houses must be paid up within five years, and of farms within ten, the instalments becoming due in the ninth prytany.

Leases of the sacred enclosures, written on whitened tablets, are submitted to the Council by the King-Archon.[2] These leases also are for ten years, with instalments payable in the ninth prytany; so that more money is collected at that time than at any corresponding period.

The tablets containing the lists of instalments are carried in to the Council, where the public clerk takes charge of them. Whenever a payment falls due he takes down from the pigeon-holes only the particular list of instalments to be paid and written off on that day, and hands it over to the Receivers-General. The others are kept apart, in order that no debt may be marked as settled before it has actually been paid.

[48] (iii) Ten *Receivers-General*, one from each tribe. In the Council Chamber, and in presence of the Council, they receive the tablets as above, strike off the instalments as they are paid in, and hand back the tablets to the public clerk. If anyone fails to pay an instalment, the fact is noted on the tablet. The debtor must then pay twice the amount of his arrears; and the Council is empowered by law to pass this sentence as well as to exact the double sum. On one day, therefore, the Receivers accept the instalments and apportion the money among the various magistracies. Next day they bring into the Council Chamber a schedule of their apportionment, written on a wooden notice-board. After reading it out, they put this

---

[1] A debt to the Treasury which had not been paid by the ninth prytany was doubled and the debtor's property sold.

[2] For his principal functions, most of which were religious, see pages 297–298.

formal question: 'Does anyone know of any malpractice with regard to the apportionment, on the part either of a magistrate or of a private person?' If anyone is charged with such conduct they proceed to take a vote on the accusation.

(iv) *Ten Auditors*, chosen by the Council from its own members, who audit the accounts of magistrates in every prytany.

(v) From each tribe the Council likewise chooses an *Examiner of Accounts*, together with two assessors for each Examiner. Their duty is to sit at the regular tribal meetings, each one opposite the statue of his tribe's eponymous hero. Suppose now that someone wishes to bring a charge, either on public or on private grounds, against any magistrate who during the last three days has passed his audit before a court of law. He writes on a whitened tablet his own name and that of the magistrate against whom he prefers the charge, together with a note of the alleged offence, and adds a statement of whatever penalty he thinks should be imposed. He then hands the completed form to the Examiner, who, having satisfied himself that the charge is justified, proceeds as follows. (α) If the case is a private one he hands over the record to the local justices who introduce cases for the tribe concerned. But (β) if the case is a public one he registers it with the Thesmothetae; and if the latter accept it they once again lay the accused magistrate's accounts before the court, whose decision is final.

[49] The Council (*g*) carries out an inspection of cavalry. Anyone who possesses a good horse, but is found to be neglecting it, has his allowance of corn reduced. Those horses which cannot keep up, or will not stand steady, are branded with a wheel on the jaw and thereby marked as unserviceable. The inspection also includes those whom the Council believes fit for duty as mounted skirmishers; but anyone whom it rejects is deprived of his horse. Infantrymen who fight in the cavalry ranks are likewise inspected, and anyone turned down is struck off the pay-roll.

The cavalry register is drawn up by ten *Commissioners of Enrolment* who are elected *by open vote* in the Assembly. They hand it over for submission to the Council by the Hipparchs and Phylarchs. These officers begin by opening the sealed tablet, which contains the names of all cavalrymen except those newly enrolled; and if anyone declares on oath that he is no longer physically fit for service with the cavalry, his name is struck out.

Then they summon the newly enrolled. Any who declare themselves on oath to be physically or financially incapable of cavalry service are dismissed. As to the remainder, the Council then votes on each one separately, to determine whether or not he is suitable. An affirmative vote means that his name is forthwith entered on the tablet; otherwise he too is dismissed.

At one time the Council used also to decide on plans for public buildings and on the contract for weaving the *peplos*; but these duties are now performed by a jury (chosen by lot) in the law-courts, because the Council was suspected of favouritism in its decisions.

The Council (*h*) examines destitute cripples. There is a law providing that those whose property is worth less than ten minae, and who are so infirm as to be incapable of doing any work, shall be examined by the Council and thereafter receive from public funds two obols a day for their support. They have a treasurer appointed by lot.

Broadly speaking, then, we may say that the Council has a very large share in the duties of all other magistrates; and this ends our account of its functions.

(B) MINOR OFFICIALS. [50] The following magistrates also are chosen *by lot*:

(1) Ten *Commissioners for Temple Repairs*, who receive thirty minae from the Receivers-General and use it to carry out the most necessary repairs to sacred buildings.

(2) Ten *City Commissioners*, five for the Peiraeus and five for the upper city. Their duties are as follows: (*a*) To see that female flautists, harpists, and lute-players are not hired at more than two drachmas a time; and, if more than one person seeks to hire a particular girl, to determine by lot who shall have first call upon her services. (*b*) To see that no collector of sewage dumps any of his filth within ten stadia of the walls. (*c*) To prevent people encroaching on the streets with buildings, and from endangering them by means of projecting balconies, overhead drain-pipes that discharge into the street, or windows that open outwards. (*d*) To remove and bury the corpses of those who drop dead in the streets, for which purpose they employ a band of public slaves.

(3) [51] *Market Commissioners*, five for the Peiraeus and five for the upper city. The laws direct them to see that all commodities on sale in the market are clean and unadulterated.

(4) *Commissioners of Weights and Measures*, five for the Peiraeus and five for the upper city, who must see that tradesmen use correct weights and measures.

(5) *Corn Commissioners*.   There were originally ten of them, five for the Peiraeus and five for the upper city; but now the latter has twenty, and the former fifteen.   Their functions are: (*a*) to see that the unprepared corn in the market is offered for sale at fair prices; (*b*) to see that the millers sell barley meal at a price related to that of barley, and that the bakers sell their loaves not only at a price proportionate to that of wheat, but also of such weight as is laid down by the Commissioners in course of their statutory duties.

(6) Ten *Superintendents of Wholesale Warehouses*,[1] whose title is self-explanatory.   They must, among other things, take care that importers supply the upper city with two-thirds of all grain reaching the Peiraeus from overseas.

(7) [52] *The Eleven* (*a*) have charge of prisoners in the state jail.   (*b*) Thieves, kidnappers, and pickpockets are brought before them, and on pleading guilty are put to death.   But if they deny the charge, the Eleven bring the case before the courts; acquitted, the prisoners are discharged, otherwise they are handed back for execution.   (*c*) The Eleven bring up before the law-courts a list of farms and houses marked down for confiscation by the state; and they deliver to the Commissioners of Public Contracts those of the aforesaid properties in respect of which the court upholds their claim.   (*d*) They also bring up certain informations laid against magistrates; but although this forms part of their duties, some such matters are brought up by the Thesmothetae.

(8) Five *Introducers*, each one acting for two tribes, who bring up before the courts the following cases which have to be decided within a month: (*a*) actions for restitution of dowry; (*b*) actions for the recovery of debts where the rate of interest is not more than 12 per cent; (*c*) actions to recover capital lent for the purpose of helping someone to set up a business in the market place; (*d*) actions for slander; (*e*) actions for the recovery of friendly loans, or for the decision of disputes between members of a partnership; (*f*) suits against corporations; (*g*) actions arising out of damage done by slaves and beasts of draught or burden; (*h*) actions connected with the office of trierarch or with banks.

---

[1] *emporion . . . epimeletas*.   The *emporion* extended over the greater part of the east shore of the harbour at Peiraeus.

Such are the cases of this class brought up by the five Introducers. But the Receivers-General do the same with cases for and against the tax farmers: those in which the amount at issue is ten drachmas or less they decide summarily, but wherever it exceeds that figure they bring the case into court for decision within a month.

(9) [53] *The Forty*,[1] four from each tribe, who hear cases other than those mentioned above. They are empowered to decide issues involving amounts up to ten drachmas; but if a larger sum is at stake they forward the case to (10) *The Arbitrators*, who endeavour to bring the parties to agreement. If they [2] fail to do so they give a decision, which, if it satisfies and is accepted by both parties, puts an end to the case. But in the event of one or other party lodging an appeal to the courts, the Arbitrators put the plaintiff's evidence, pleadings, and laws quoted into one jar, and those of the defendant into another. Both jars are then sealed, a tablet inscribed with the Arbitrator's decision is attached, and they are handed over to the four members of the Forty who belong to the same tribe as the defendant. These officials take them and bring up the case before a court consisting of 201 jurors if the amount at issue is 1,000 drachmas or below, but 401 jurors if it is in excess of that figure. No laws, pleadings, or evidence may be used that were not submitted to the Arbitrators and enclosed by them in the jars.

The Arbitrators are all men between the ages of fifty-nine and sixty.[3] The Forty take the last of the eponymi of the years of military service, and distribute the arbitrations among the men belonging to that year,[4] drawing lots to decide which arbitrations each one shall take; and every one of them is bound to

---

[1] Originally thirty itinerant justices who went on circuit through the demes; their number was raised to its present level after the oligarchy of the Thirty. —(A.)

[2] In the person of one of their number, as becomes clear in the following account.

[3] This is clear from the lists of archons and eponymi. Besides the ten eponymi of the tribes [see page 263], there are forty-two eponymi of the years of military service [eighteen to sixty]. Originally, when the ephebi were enrolled they had their names registered on whitened tablets, to which were appended those of (a) the Archon in whose year they were enrolled and (b) the eponymus of the citizens who served as arbitrators. To-day, however, these names are inscribed on a bronze pillar erected outside the Council Chamber, near the statues of the tribal eponymi.—(A.)

[4] The eponymi are also used in connection with the army; when the appropriate age groups are to be sent on military service, notice is given that all men of such and such archons and eponymi are to take the field.—(A.)

handle those assigned to him in this way. The law, indeed, provides that anyone who fails to serve as Arbitrator after reaching the age of fifty-nine shall forfeit his civic rights, unless he happens to be holding some other office during that year, or is abroad. These are the only circumstances which will exempt him from the duty.

Anyone who thinks he has been unfairly treated by an individual Arbitrator may appeal to the full board; and if they find their colleague guilty, he loses his civic rights, subject to an appeal to the courts.

(11) [54] Five *Commissioners of Roads*, whose duty it is to employ a gang of public slaves on road repairs.

(12) Ten *Auditors*, with as many assessors, to whom all magistrates retiring from office must hand in their accounts. They are the only officials who audit the accounts of persons subject to this examination, and who bring up those accounts before the law-courts. Any magistrate convicted of embezzlement is sentenced by the court as a thief, i.e. he is condemned to repay ten times the sum he has misappropriated. If the Auditors accuse a magistrate of taking bribes, and the court convicts him, he is fined for corruption and must likewise repay ten times the amount. If found guilty of maladministration, he is fined accordingly; and if he fails to pay up before the ninth prytany the amount is doubled. A tenfold fine is never doubled.

(13) An official usually known as *Clerk of the Prytany* [1] is responsible for all public documents; i.e. he has the general custody of the state archives, and checks the transcripts of all other official papers. He also attends meetings of the Council. At one time he was elected by open vote; and the fact that his name was inscribed on the pillars recording treaties of alliance, as well as grants of (*a*) the title of Proxenus and (*b*) citizenship, proves that the most distinguished men of irreproachable character were chosen to fill this post.

(14) A *Clerk of the Laws*, who attends meetings of the Council and helps to check all transcripts of the laws.[2]

(15) Ten *Commissioners of Sacrifices*, known as *Commissioners of Expiations*, chosen by lot in the Assembly. They offer the sacrifices appointed by oracle, and, jointly with the seers, take the auspices whenever necessary.

---

[1] His full title was 'The Council's Clerk for the Prytany.'
[2] The Assembly also elects *by open vote* a clerk whose sole duty it is to read out documents to it and to the Council.—(A.)

(16) Ten *Annual Commissioners*, as they are called, similarly chosen. They offer certain sacrifices, and supervise all the quadrennial festivals except the Great Panathenaea.[1]

(17) An *Archon for Salamis*, and (18) a *Demarch for the Peiraeus*, officials who celebrate the Dionysia and appoint choregi in those two places. In Salamis, too, the archon's name is publicly recorded.

(C) [55] The officials known collectively as the NINE ARCHONS, the manner of whose appointment in early times has already been described.[2]   At the present day they are chosen by lot (one from each tribe): six Thesmothetae and their clerk, an Archon, a King-Archon, and a Polemarch.   Before taking office, all of them, except the clerk to the Thesmothetae,[3] undergo a pre-liminary examination in the Council of Five Hundred and another in the law-courts.   There was a time when anyone rejected by the Council was there and then disqualified from holding the office; but now there is an appeal to the courts, which have the last word in this examination.

Candidates are asked the following questions:

(1) Who is your father, and to what deme does he belong?
(2) Who is your paternal grandfather?
(3) Who is your mother?
(4) Who is her father, and what is his deme?
(5) Have you an ancestral Apollo and a household Zeus?
(6) Have you a family tomb, and where is it?
(7) Do you treat your parents well?
(8) Do you pay your taxes?
(9) Have you done your military service?

When these questions have been answered the examiner pro-ceeds: 'Call your witnesses!' and when they have been pro-duced he goes on to ask: 'Has anyone anything to say against this man?'   If an accusation is made, he listens to what both parties have to say, and only then invites the Council to decide by show of hands.   In the law-court this decision is made

---

[1] The quadrennial festivals are as follows: (*a*) the Paneguris at Delos (where there is also a sexennial festival); (*b*) the Brauronia; (*c*) the Heracleia; (*d*) the Eleusinia; (*e*) the Great Panathenaea; to which has lately been added (*f*) the Hephaestia, in the archonship of Cephisiphon [329 B.C.]. —(A.)

[2] See page 248.

[3] He is examined only in the law-courts, like other magistrates, whether they are appointed by lot or elected by open vote.—(A.)

by ballot. If no accuser comes forward, the examiner calls
for an immediate vote. Originally, only one member of the
court balloted on behalf of his colleagues; but nowadays all
are obliged to cast their votes, so that if any candidate has
been able by underhand means to get rid of his accuser
there may still be a chance of his disqualification before the
law-court.

When they have passed the examination, the new archons
make their way to the stone on which lie the pieces of the sacrificial victims,[1] and the witnesses swear to the testimony they
have given. Then, standing upon it, the archons take an oath
to carry out their duties in accordance with the laws, and to
accept no present in respect thereof under pain of having to
dedicate a golden statue. After taking this oath they proceed
to the Acropolis, where they repeat it and are thenceforward in
office. [56] The Archon, the King-Archon, and the Polemarch
each choose any two persons they please to act as their assessors.
These officials undergo an examination in the law-courts before
they begin their duties, and hand in a statement of accounts
every time they perform their functions.

1. *The Archon* (1) begins his period of office by issuing a proclamation to the effect that whatsoever anyone possessed before
this date, he shall have and hold the same until the end of his
(the Archon's) term. (2) He appoints three of the wealthiest
Athenian citizens to act as choregi to the tragic poets.[2] Then
he receives the choregi appointed by the tribes for the men's and
boys' choruses at the Thargelia,[3] transacts exchange of properties
for them, and reports any excuses they may offer.[4] The
Archon (3) appoints choregi for the festival at Delos, and a chief
of mission for the thirty-oared ship in which the youths travel
to that island; supervises the sacred procession in honour of
Asclepius (when the initiated sleep in the god's temple) and
that of the Great Dionysia; marshals the procession at the

---

[1] The Arbitrators also take an oath upon the stone before giving their
decisions.—(A.)

[2] At an earlier period he also assigned five choregi to the comic poets, but
this is now done by the tribes.—(A.)

[3] At the City Dionysia there is a chorus representing each tribe, but at the
Thargelia only one for every two tribes, who share the expenses of providing
it.—(A.)

[4] A man may claim exemption, for instance, on the ground that he has
already borne this burden; or that he has fulfilled a similar state service and
the period of his exemption has not yet expired; or that he has not completed
his fortieth year, which is the minimum age for the choregus of a boys'
chorus.—(A.)

Thargelia and that in honour of Zeus the Saviour; and manages the contests at the Dionysia and Thargelia.

(4) Passing now from the festivals superintended by the Archon, we come to the actions and indictments of which he takes cognizance, and which, after preliminary inquiry, he brings up before the courts. They are as follows: (a) For insult or injury to parents; and the prosecutor in these cases is not penalized if he fails to secure one-fifth of the votes. (b) Against guardians, for injury to orphans in their care. (c) Against the guardians or nearest relatives of wards of state, for injury done to them. (d) Against guardians of an orphan for injuries done to his estate. (e) Against a mental defective, for ruining his own property through incapability of managing his own affairs. (f) For the appointment of liquidators, when one party refuses to divide an inheritance in which others have a share. (g) For constituting a wardship. (h) For deciding between rival claims to a wardship. (i) For a grant of inspection of property to which another person lays claim. (j) For the appointment of oneself as guardian. (k) For settling disputes concerning inheritances and wards of state.

The Archon (5) has general supervision of orphans, wards of state, and women who, on the death of their husbands, declare themselves with child; and he has power to fine those who wrong such individuals, or to bring the case before the law-courts. He also leases the houses of orphans and wards of state until they reach the age of fourteen, and takes security from the lessees of such property. Finally, he compels negligent guardians to provide the necessary sustenance for children in their care. [57] So much for the Archon's duties.

2. *The King-Archon* (1) superintends the Mysteries jointly with four *Superintendents of Mysteries* who are elected in the Assembly by open vote, two from the citizen body as a whole, one from the Eumolpidae, and one from the Ceryces. (2) He superintends the Lenaean Dionysia, which consists of a procession and a musical contest. This procession he orders jointly with the Superintendents of the festival, but has sole charge of the contest. He likewise (3) arranges all torch-races, and administers the great majority of ancestral sacrifices.

The King-Archon (4) takes cognizance of all indictments for impiety, as well as (5) determining for the benefit of the old families and the priests all disputes concerning ancient rites.

(6) All actions for homicide come before him in the first instance,[1] and it is he who makes the proclamation warning all polluted persons to keep away from sacred ceremonies.

(7) (a) Cases of wilful homicide, wounding with intent to kill, arson, and the fatal administration of poison are tried by the Council of Areopagus; and they constitute the limit of its jurisdiction as a court of law.

(b) Cases of unintentional homicide, conspiracy against life, and the killing of a slave, a resident alien, or a foreigner, are tried by the court of Palladium.

(c) Cases in which the accused acknowledges the fact of homicide but pleads legal justification [2] are tried in the court of Delphinium.

(d) Cases in which a man returning from exile for involuntary homicide is subject to a further charge of killing or wounding with intent, are tried in the court of Phreatto; and the accused makes his defence from a boat moored offshore.

All cases under (b), (c), and (d) above are tried before the Ephetae,[3] who are chosen by lot.   The King-Archon introduces them, the trial is held within sacred precincts in the open air. Except on the occasion of his trial, when he comes to make his defence, no one facing a charge of homicide may enter a temple, or even appear in the market-place. If the actual offender cannot be identified, the defendant is described merely as 'the doer of the deed.'

(e) Cases in which an inanimate object or a brute beast is accused of homicide are heard jointly by the King-Archon and the tribe-kings.[4]

3. [58] *The Polemarch* (1) performs the sacrifices to Artemis the Huntress and Ares the God of War.   (2) He arranges the ritual games commemorating those who have fallen in battle, and pours the libations in honour of Harmodius and Aristogeiton.

(3) Certain private actions come before the Polemarch—those, namely, which involve resident aliens, both ordinary and privileged.   It is his duty to take these cases, divide them into ten groups, and then assign to each tribe the group falling to it

---

[1] Whenever the King-Archon hears a case he removes his crown.—(A.)

[2] e.g. that he took an adulterer in the act, or killed someone accidentally in battle or in an athletic contest.—(A.)

[3] They most likely sat as a kind of presiding committee, the actual voting being done by jurors.

[4] The hearing (in the court of the Prytaneum) was in the nature of a coroner's inquest. The offending animal was slain; the inanimate object which had caused a person's death was cast beyond the boundaries of Attica.

by lot; after which the officials who introduce cases for the tribes [1] hand them over to the Arbitrators. But the Polemarch himself brings up cases in which a resident alien is charged with acting without the sanction of his patron, or with failing to acquire a patron. Besides these, he brings up all cases of inheritances and wards of state involving resident aliens.[2] Generally speaking, in fact, the Polemarch does for resident aliens all that the Archon does for Athenian citizens.

4. [59] *The Thesmothetae* (1) have the right of giving notice of the days upon which the law-courts are to sit, and also of appointing the magistrates who will be chosen to preside over the various courts,[3] and who must abide by their instructions.

(2) They introduce impeachments before the Assembly, as well as bringing up the following: (*a*) all cases of removal from office by the votes of the people; (*b*) preliminary resolutions of the Assembly directing public prosecutions to be instituted; (*c*) indictments for (i) illegal proposals and (ii) securing the passage of an inexpedient law; (*d*) complaints against the official conduct of the Proedri or their president; (*e*) accounts presented by the generals.

(3) There come before the Thesmothetae the following indictments in which the prosecutor has to pay a fine to the state: (*a*) for usurping the rights of citizenship; (*b*) for employing bribery or any underhand means to secure acquittal on the previous charge; (*c*) for acting as a professional accuser; (*d*) for making a false declaration that someone has been entered on the list of state debtors; (*e*) for falsely appearing as witness to the service of a summons; (*f*) for neglecting to erase, or for re-entering, the name of a state debtor who has paid in full; (*g*) for corrupt erasure of a name from the list of state debtors; and (*h*) for adultery.

(4) The Thesmothetae bring up (*a*) the preliminary examinations of all candidates for office, (*b*) appeals to the court against rejection by the demes of claims to citizenship, as well as (*c*) certain private suits in respect of commerce, mining, and the

---

[1] Since resident aliens were not members of any tribe, lawsuits in which they were concerned were distributed by lot among the groups of four 'jurors' assigned to each of the ten tribes. These groups of 'jurors' normally introduced private actions concerning members of the tribe to whom they were assigned.

[2] A resident alien could not act in a legal capacity except through the agency of a 'patron' who was an Athenian citizen or another resident alien enjoying the special privilege of acting in that capacity.

[3] See pages 303 sqq.

slander of a free man by a slave. (5) They draw the lots which distribute the various courts among the magistrates for both public and private cases; (6) they ratify international contracts; and (7) they bring up (*a*) cases arising out of such contracts, and (*b*) cases of perjury before the Areopagus.

All nine archons, with the clerk to the Thesmothetae as a tenth, draw lots for the assignment of jurors to the heliastic divisions, each performing that duty for his own tribe. [60] So much for the nine archons and their functions.

(D) Ten COMMISSIONERS OF GAMES, chosen *by lot*, one from each tribe, who, after passing an examination, hold office for four years.[1] At the Panathenaic festival (1) they manage the procession, the musical and gymnastic contests, and the horse-race; (2) they provide the *peplos* and, jointly with the Council, the prize vases; and (3) they present the oil to the athletes.

This oil is collected from the sacred olives, the Archon requisitioning it from the farms where the olives grow, at the rate of three-quarters of a pint per tree. At one time the state itself used to sell the fruit; and if anyone dug up or cut down a sacred olive he was tried by the Council of Areopagus and, if convicted, sentenced to death. That law still stands; but since the oil is now paid by the owner of the farm, the procedure has lapsed—the oil has become a state tax on the property instead of being drawn from individual trees.

Well now, the Archon collects the oil for his own year of office and hands it over to the Treasurers for safe keeping in the Acropolis; nor may he take his seat in the Areopagus [2] until he has delivered to them the full amount. And there in the Acropolis it remains until the Panathenaic festival, when the Treasurers measure it out to the Commissioners of Games, and they in turn to the winning competitors. There are prizes of gold and silver for music, shields for manly vigour, oil for gymnastics and the horse-race.

---

[1] [62, lines 1–5] For some of the magistracies chosen by lot (including those of the nine archons) candidates were at one time drawn from the tribe as a whole, whereas those to which appointment is now made in the Theseum were distributed over the demes. But the demes made a habit of selling their votes; so the choice of candidates for these offices is now made from the whole tribe, except only in the cases of membership of the Council and of the Dockyard Guards, when it is still in the hands of the demes.—(A.)

[2] At the end of his term of office.

III. Magistrates Elected by Open Vote:
Military Officers

(CHAPTER 61)

[61] All military commands are filled *by open vote*, as follows:

(A) Ten *Generals*, formerly elected one from each tribe, but now chosen from the entire citizen body. Their respective duties are likewise assigned by open vote: one to command the heavy infantry and lead them on foreign campaigns; one for home defence, who is responsible for patrolling the coast and frontiers, as well as for opposing an invader; two for the defence of Peiraeus, one of whom protects Munychia and the other the peninsula of Acte; and a superintendent of the Symmories,[1] who nominates the trierarchs, transacts exchange of properties for them, and brings up actions to decide rival claims involving them. The other five Generals are detailed for a variety of duties as need arises.

The appointment of these Generals is confirmed in each prytany, provided the Assembly is satisfied with the way they are performing their duties. Any officer rejected on this vote is brought to trial in the law-courts: if he is found guilty the people decide what punishment or fine shall be inflicted; but if he is acquitted he resumes his command.

When on active service, the Generals are empowered to arrest anyone for insubordination, publicly to cashier him, or to impose a fine; but this latter course is very rare indeed.

(B) Ten *Taxiarchs*, one from each tribe. Each has under him a battalion of hoplites belonging to a single tribe,[2] and appoints his company commanders.

(C) Two *Hipparchs*, chosen from the whole citizen body; each commands the cavalry of five tribes. Their disciplinary powers are exactly equivalent to those of the Generals over the infantry, and their appointments are likewise subject to confirmation.

(D) Ten *Phylarchs*, one from each tribe, whose cavalry commands are on the same footing as that of the infantry Taxiarchs.

---

[1] The Symmories were companies into which the richer members of the community were first formed in 377, to defray extraordinary charges in time of war.
[2] To which he himself often belonged.

There is also (E) a *Hipparch for Lemnos*, who commands the cavalry there.

(F) Two *Treasurers*, one each for the two sacred triremes 'Paralus' and 'Ammonis.'

IV. SALARIES

(CHAPTER 62, LINE 6 TO END)

Stipends for service are received as follows: (A) One drachma for attendance at ordinary meetings of the Assembly, but nine obols for the 'sovereign.' (B) Three obols for members of the Judicature. (C) Five obols for members of the Council; but the Prytanes are allowed an extra obol for their maintenance. (D) Nine obols apiece for the maintenance of the nine archons, who also keep a crier and a flute-player. (E) One drachma a day for the Salaminian archon. (F) A free dinner in the Prytaneum for the Commissioners of Games during the month of Hecatombaeon (from the 14th onwards), in which the Great Panathenaea is celebrated. (G) One drachma a day from the treasury of the Delian temple for its Athenian commissioners. (H) An allowance for the maintenance of Athenian officials sent out to Samos, Scyros, Lemnos, or Imbros.

There is no limit to the number of times an army command may be held; but no one is eligible for any other office more than once, excepting membership of the Council, which may be held twice.

V. THE JUDICATURE

(CHAPTERS 63–9)

[63] Juries for the law-courts are chosen by the nine archons and the clerk to the Thesmothetae, each of whom draws lots for that purpose on behalf of his own tribe.

(A) The courthouse has ten doorways (one for each tribe), leading into the twenty balloting chambers (two for each tribe) [1] in which the jurors have their courts assigned to them.

---

[1] One of them was perhaps a waiting-room for the other.

There are (1) a set of one hundred boxes (ten for each tribe),[1] (2) another set of ten boxes in which are placed the tickets of jurors upon whom the lot has fallen, and (3) a couple of urns. Besides these, there is placed near each doorway a number of staves [2] equal to the number of jurors required. Into one of the urns are put as many acorn-shaped ballot-balls as there are staves, marked with as many letters of the alphabet (beginning with the eleventh, *lambda*) as there are courts to be filled.

Men above thirty years of age qualify as jurors, provided they are not state debtors or have not forfeited their civic rights. If any unqualified person sits as a juror, an information is laid against him and he is brought before the court. In the event of his conviction the court decides what penalty to inflict; and if that penalty is a fine the guilty man must go to prison until he has paid not only his debt to the state (if such was the cause of the information laid), but also the fine.

The jurors being divided into ten heliastic divisions *distributed over the tribes*,[3] with an approximately equal number under each letter from *alpha* to *kappa* inclusive, each juror has a boxwood ticket inscribed with his own name, the names of his father and his deme, and one of these letters.

One of the Thesmothetae draws lots assigning letters [4] to the several courts, and an assistant hangs above the entrance to each court the letter thus assigned to it.

[64] Ten of the hundred boxes, marked with the letters *alpha* to *kappa*, are set before the archon who is to draw the lots on behalf of each tribe. Each juror then places his ticket in the box marked with the corresponding letter. The assistant gives the boxes a good shake, in alphabetical order, and the presiding official draws one ticket out of each box. The individual named on each of these tickets is called a 'Ticket-setter.' His duty is

[1] This was because the jurors in each tribe were distributed over all the ten heliastic divisions. In each tribe, all the tickets (see below) bearing the names of the jurors in division *Alpha* were placed in the first box, those of division *Beta* in the second, and so on. According to the number of jurors required, an equal number of tickets was drawn by lot from each of the 100 boxes. Each of the tickets thus drawn had a court assigned to it by lot; and the tickets were then placed in the second set of ten boxes, all tickets of jurors assigned to any given court being placed in the box which bears the letter corresponding to that court. The process is described in great detail below.

[2] Each one marked with the same letter and colour as the courts assigned to the dicast who received it (see page 304).

[3] The ten divisions did not coincide with the ten tribes; each division had an approximately equal number of jurors from all the tribes.

[4] *Lambda, mu, nu*, etc., according to the number of courts to be filled.

to set the tickets from his box in a frame [1] (of which there are ten in each balloting-chamber) bearing the same letter as that written on the box; and he is chosen by lot because, if the same man were repeatedly employed in this duty, he might tamper with the results.

When the presiding official is going to put in the lots,[2] he summons the members of the tribe for whom he acts into the balloting-chamber.   These lots are small wooden dice [3] of two colours, black and white; one in every five is white, the remainder black; and the number of white dice is equal to the number of jurors required.

As the official draws out the lots he calls the names of the persons chosen,[4] the Ticket-setter being included among them.

(B) Each juror, as he is chosen and answers to his name, draws a ballot-ball from the urn.[5]   Holding it out with the letter uppermost, he shows it first to the presiding official, who looks at it and then drops that juror's ticket into the box marked with the letter on the ballot-ball.[6]   The number of these boxes, standing within reach of the official and bearing the letters of the several courts, is equal to the number of courts which have to be filled.

The juror next shows his ballot-ball to the attendant [65] who hands him instead a staff [7] of the same colour as that assigned to the court in which he is to sit [8] and which bears the same letter as his ballot-ball.   This again ensures his going into the right court; if he tried to do otherwise his staff would give him away.

And now, staff in hand, he enters the court marked with the same colour as that staff and bearing a letter corresponding to

---

[1] Sir J. E. Sandys (ad loc.) suggested that this was 'probably a wooden frame fitted with a number of "straight rules" or parallel ledges (κανόνες), stretching horizontally across it.   We may suppose that the upper surface of each of these ledges was grooved and that each ticket, as it was drawn, was inserted with its lower edge in the groove. . . .'

[2] Presumably into the second of the two urns mentioned on page 303.

[3] They differed from ordinary dice by not being marked with pips.

[4] The Archon drew out one lot and one ticket; if the first lot was white the bearer of the name on the first ticket was considered to have been chosen to serve as juror, and so on until the whole number of jurors required had been obtained.

[5] See page 303.   The jurors having now been chosen, it remained to be decided in which court each one should sit.

[6] This is to make sure that the juror takes his seat in the court assigned to him by lot, and to make it impossible for him to choose his court or to arrange to sit in the same court with certain others.—(A.)

[7] See page 303, footnote 2.

[8] Each court has a different colour painted on the lintel of the doorway. —(A.)

that on the ballot-ball which he drew.   As he enters, he hands
over his staff to an officer chosen by lot for this duty, and receives
from him a token.

Ten public servants, one for each tribe, take the boxes (one
for each court) containing the names of the members of the
several tribes,[1] and deliver them to officials chosen by lot, who
will give back to each juror his ticket. . . .

(C) [66] When all the courts have been filled in this way,
there are placed in the first of them [2] two ballot-boxes, together
with a number of bronze dice marked with the colours of the
various courts, and others bearing the names of those magistrates who are to preside over them.   Two of the Thesmothetae,
who have been specially chosen by lot, now come forward: one
of them puts the coloured dice into one box, while his colleague
drops into the other those inscribed with the magistrates' names.
He whose name is drawn first is announced by the crier as
appointed for duty in the court represented by the coloured die
first drawn; the second for duty in the corresponding court; and
so on.   This procedure is intended to make sure that no
magistrate has advance knowledge of the court in which he will
preside, but will take whichever one is assigned to him by lot.

Next, the magistrate who is to preside in each court draws one
ticket from each of the ten tribal boxes [3] and puts them into
another empty box, from which in turn he draws five.   One of
the persons so designated is detailed to look after the water-
clock, and the other four to count the votes at the end of each
case.   The choice of these individuals by lot is a precaution
against their being intimidated beforehand, and a guarantee that
there will be no advance jobbery on their own part.   The other
five men, whose tickets have not been drawn, receive from the
tellers and clock-minder a notice stating (1) the order in which
the jurors are to be paid, and (2) whereabouts in the courthouse
they are to assemble for that purpose when the day's work is done.[4]

[1] The tickets belonging to the jurors in each court had by now been sorted
out into ten boxes.   These boxes were taken by the public officials and
delivered to the proper officials at the ten entrances of the courthouse, to be
returned by them to the jurors to whom they belong.   Those who were not
chosen to serve received back their tickets from the Ticket-setter.
[2] Perhaps the one marked *alpha*.
[3] This was presumably done *after* the tickets had been sorted into the
'tribal boxes' but *before* the latter were carried out to the officials at the
entrances.
[4] The purpose is to divide the jurors into small groups for the receipt of
pay, and not have them tumbling over one another.—(A.)

(D) [67] When the foregoing preliminaries are at an end the cases are called on.   If it is a day for the hearing of private cases, the private litigants have been summoned: four cases are taken in each category recognized by the law; and the parties swear that they will introduce no irrelevant matter into their speeches. If, on the other hand, it is a day for public cases, the public litigants have been summoned, and only one such case is tried.

The length of the proceedings is measured by the water-clock. It is fitted with a short funnel-neck into which the water pours. Seven and a half gallons are allowed for cases where the amount at issue exceeds 5,000 drachmas, and just over two for the second speech on either side.   When the amount involved is between 1,000 and 5,000 drachmas inclusive, five gallons are allowed for the first speeches and 110 pints for the second. When it is below 1,000 drachmas, 8½ gallons and 11½ pints respectively are allowed.   Arbitrations between rival claimants are allotted about 8¼ gallons; here there are no second speeches. The clock-minder places his hand over the neck whenever the clerk is about to read a resolution, law, affidavit, or treaty.   But in criminal cases where the penalty is imprisonment, death, exile, loss of civic rights, or confiscation of goods, the length of the hearing is that of a standard day, i.e. a day in the month Posideon;[1] the flow is never interrupted, and each side is allowed an equal supply of water.[2]

[68] A majority of the courts consist of 500 jurors. . . .[3] Some public cases require a court of 1,000 members, for which purpose two courts combine; while the most important cases of all are tried by 1,500 jurors, i.e. by three courts sitting together.

The ballot-disks are made of bronze, with short stems passing through the centre; in half of them the stems are hollow, in the other half solid.   When the speeches are ended the tellers hand every juror one of each.   This is done in full view of the parties, so that no member of the court may receive two disks of the same kind.   Then, as each juror records his vote, he delivers his token to an official appointed for the purpose, and is given in return a bronze voucher marked with the numeral 3 to indicate that he will get three obols when he hands it in.   This procedure ensures that all the members vote; no one can get a voucher unless he does so.

Two urns, one made of brass and the other of wood, stand in

[1] December to January.   [2] About 83 gallons.   [3] Lacuna in text.

the court. They are placed at some distance from the jurors, so as to prevent anyone surreptitiously inserting a disk. It is in these urns that the votes are recorded. The bronze one is for effective, the wooden one for unused disks; and the former has a lid with an opening so shaped that only one can be put in at a time, thus guarding against the insertion of two together.

Before voting begins the crier asks whether the litigants dispute any of the evidence; for no objection can be received once the voting has started. Then he calls again: 'Hollow stems for the prosecutor (or plaintiff), solid for the defendant!' And now each juror, taking his two disks from the stand [1] and holding the stems in such a way that the litigants cannot distinguish the hollow from the solid, inserts the one he intends to be effective into the bronze urn and the other into the wooden one.

[69] When all have cast their votes, two assistants, directed by the tellers, empty the bronze urn on to a reckoning board which has as many cavities as there are disks, so arranged that the hollow-stemmed may be kept well apart from the solid-stemmed and that both sets may be easily counted. Then the tellers set the disks out on the board—solid stems on one side, hollow on the other. Next, the crier announces how many votes have been cast for the prosecutor (or plaintiff) and how many for the defendant—hollow and solid respectively; and whoever has a majority has won the case. If the votes are equal the verdict goes to the defendant.

If damages are to be awarded, nearly three pints of water are allowed to each party for their discussion of this matter; after which the jurors, having received back their staves in return for their vouchers,[2] proceed to vote once more. Finally, when all the legal requirements have been fulfilled, the jurors are paid in the various balloting-chambers assigned to them by lot.[3]

[1] Probably something like a twin-branched candlestick, on to which the juror placed his disks after receiving them from the teller. It seems that each branch supported a perforated pan into which the stem of the disk was inserted.

[2] The juror has already been given the voucher entitling him to draw his pay; but, as a second vote is necessary, and he may not be paid until this is completed, he temporarily gives up the voucher for the staff, receiving it back again once the final vote has ended.

[3] See page 304.

APPENDIX

(See Introduction, page xiv)

THE constitution of Draco was as follows: (A) The franchise was extended to all who could afford military equipment. (B) The nine archons and the treasurers were to be elected by this body from the owners of unencumbered property valued at not less than ten minae; the other and less important officials from those who could provide themselves with military equipment; the Generals and Hipparchs [1] from those whose unencumbered property was worth at least one hundred minae, and who had legitimate children more than ten years old. It was the duty of these officials to hold to bail the outgoing Prytanes,[2] Generals, and Hipparchs until the audit; for which purpose they were to take four securities of the same property group as that to which the Generals and Hipparchs belonged. (C) A Council of one hundred and four was to be chosen by lot from among those who possessed the franchise. For this Council, as for certain other magistracies, the lot was to be cast among those who were above thirty years of age; and no one might hold office a second time until everyone else had served his turn, after which the lot would cast anew. Any member of the Council who absented himself from a meeting, or from a meeting of the Assembly, was to be fined—three drachmas if he were a Pentacosiomedimnus, two if he were a Knight, and one if he were a Zeugites.

[1] See pages 285, 286.
[2] Probably meaning here the nine archons.

INDEX

INDEX

311

This book designed by
William B. Taylor
is a production of
Heron Books, London

Printed on wood free paper and bound by
Hazell Watson & Viney Ltd,
Aylesbury, Bucks

Printed and bound in England